...nt *Funeral* PROCESSION of His Grace *JOHN* late Duke of
...roper References, *&c.* explaining every Part of that *Pompous Solemnity*

THE
CHURCHILLS

ENDPAPERS The funeral of John Churchill,
first Duke of Marlborough, in 1722 and
the funeral of Sir Winston Churchill, 1965.
FRONTISPIECE Blenheim Palace c. 1750
with the Column of Victory in the
foreground.

THE
CHURCHILLS

KATE FLEMING

Weidenfeld and Nicolson
London

The author and publishers are grateful to His
Grace the Duke of Marlborough for permission
to quote from the *Blenheim Papers* (Vol. 1),
and to Houghton Mifflin Company and William
Heinemann Ltd. for permission to quote from
Winston S. Churchill, Vol. 1 by Randolph S.
Churchill, Copyright ©️ 1966 by
C. & T. Publications Limited, Vol. 11 by
Randolph S. Churchill, Copyright ©️ 1967 by
C. & T. Publications Limited, Vol. 111 by
Randolph S. Churchill and Martin Gilbert,
Copyright ©️ 1973 by C. & T. Publications Limited.

Designed by Margaret Fraser for
George Weidenfeld and Nicolson

Filmset by Keyspools Limited, Golborne, Lancashire
Printed by Morrison & Gibb Limited, Edinburgh and London

ISBN 0 297 76975 8

Contents

Acknowledgments

Photographs and illustrations are supplied by, or reproduced by kind permission of the following: on pages 20, 93, by gracious permission of H.M. The Queen; on pages 8, 18, 19, 25, 28–9, 36–7, 42, 44, 48, 51, 56, 59, 62, 76, 80/2, 81/2, 87, 88, 90, 101, 102, 105, 108, 142–3, 199, 211, by kind permission of His Grace The Duke of Marlborough, Blenheim Collection (photos Jeremy Whitaker); on pages 16–17 by kind permission of His Grace the Duke of St Albans; on page 78/1 by kind permission of Group Captain D. R. Biggs DFC on pages 31, 64, 115, 131, 156–7, 163, 174, 179, 192, 193, 197, by kind permission of Winston Churchill, on page 150 by kind permission of the Churchill Trustees and on page 112 by kind permission of William Gordon Davies. Aerofilms, 212–3; Bodleian Library, 69, 80/1; British Library, 11, 14, 32, 35, 70–71, 72–3, 84, 95, 103, 164, 165; Broadwater Collection, 119, 140–1, 145, 152, 181, 182–3; College of Arms, 81/1; John Frost Historical Newspaper Collection, 159, 167, 200; Heeresgeschichtlichen Museums, Vienna, 54; Mander and Mitchenson Theatre Collection, 146; Mansell Collection, 121; National Maritime Museum, 78/2; National Portrait Gallery, 39; National Trust (Chartwell) 175, 185, 188–9; Popperfoto, 205, 208; Public Record Office, 196; *Punch*, 172; Radio Times Hulton Picture Library, 91, 113, 126–7, 149, 166, 169, 203, 214; Routledge and Kegan Paul, 125; Sir John Soane's Museum, 96–7; Topix, 195; Warden and Fellows of Winchester College, 12–13.

Picture Research by Philippa Lewis
Map designed by Tim Higgins and drawn by Design Practitioners Limited

Introduction

W INSTON is not a common English christian name. That the story of the Churchill family opens, more than 300 years ago, with a Winston Churchill and continues, today, with that man's great-great-great-great-great-great-great-great-great-grandson, another Winston Churchill, implies a conscious sense of family; that a direct descendant of the first Winston has occupied the same house in Oxfordshire since 1627 affirms that sense. Yet another Winston Churchill, the one with whom most people would associate the name, wrote in August 1938 in the preface to the fourth volume of his biography of the first Duke of Marlborough, about his ancestor: 'Happy the State or Sovereign who finds such a servant in years of danger!' Less than two years after writing those words he, also, was to prove such a servant.

And servants is what the two great men were. Supreme power they never had. Their sovereign and their country were their masters and, general and politician alike, they served the State as they saw fit. That they both had an imaginative, broad and courageous understanding of their public duty, as well as an extraordinary aptitude for wartime leadership, was their genius. That their contribution helped determine the successful outcome of wars, which, if lost, might have brought foreign domination of the British Isles, was their achievement.

This is the story of where the Duke of Marlborough came from, how he achieved what he did, and how, in so doing, he accumulated great riches, built a palace, and assured the prosperity of his descendants and their position among the aristocracy of England; and how in those days, when government and the aristocracy were in closer cahoots, a tradition of political service smouldered on within the walls of Blenheim Palace, through the eighteenth and nineteenth centuries, down from Dukes two to seven, until in Queen Victoria's reign it flared up brilliantly, if ephemerally, in Lord Randolph Churchill, and then more powerfully and steadfastly in his son, Winston.

1
The First
Sir Winston

Winston Churchill married Elizabeth Drake during the Civil War in England. He was a young cavalier and she, or at least her mother, Lady Drake, was a parliamentarian. It was thus a fortunate marriage for Churchill because, after the war he, as a discredited officer of the King, was able to shelter in his mother-in-law's house in Devon, and enjoy the protection of her 'good affection' to Parliament. In marrying Miss Drake he had also made a good match socially, for the Drakes were an old and well-connected Devon family, (though no relation to Sir Francis Drake, whom Elizabeth's father, Sir John, considered an upstart). And through her mother Miss Drake was related to George Villiers, first Duke of Buckingham – that handsome, powerful and unprincipled favourite of both James I and Charles I. The Churchills were by comparison a humbler lot. Winston Churchill had no illustrious relations; his ancestors, minor country gentry or yeomen, had tilled the land in Dorset for many years and fade into the distance in parish registers. There were no titles in his family, merely some evidence that his great-great-grandfather was a blacksmith. The brilliant, if flashy, Villiers blood was to improve the stolid, duller Churchill stock.

It was possible for Winston to marry the more respectable Miss Drake because his father, John Churchill, had done well for himself and had risen in the world. John Churchill had left Dorset to take up a career in law in London. He had joined the Middle Temple, made a success in his profession, and became Deputy Registrar of Chancery. He resigned the post in 1639 and returned to Dorset where he had bought, presumably with his earnings from the law, the estate of Newton Montacute in the parish of Wootton Glanville, and leased

OPPOSITE The first Sir Winston Churchill (*c.* 1620–88), painted by Sir Peter Lely.

9

another, Minterne, from Winchester College. As his son was to do later, he had married above himself. His wife, Sarah, was the daughter of a knight, Sir Henry Winston of Standish in the Cotswolds, who was a gentleman of good connections and considerable means. John Churchill's good marriage, the lands he had acquired, his status as a lawyer, all meant that he too was now a gentleman and that his sons would be the sons of a gentleman.

Of these there were two: the elder, John, died as a child; the younger, who survived, they called Winston – presumably to perpetuate the better name of Sarah's family. If that were the reason they would not have been disappointed had they been able to gaze into the future, for perpetuity is what they achieved.

No sooner had John Churchill retired to his land in Dorset than civil war broke out. Most of the gentry in the western counties were for Church and King, and John Churchill, a newcomer to those ranks, was no exception. He acted as a King's Commissioner in Dorset, gathering funds for the royalist cause, an activity for which he later had to pay a penalty of £300.

His son, Winston, was also to be fined – £450 – for his more energetic allegiance to the King. He was only 21 when the war began in 1642 but he joined up with alacrity and fought hard throughout as a captain in the King's Horse. When the expected quick conclusion to the war did not come, the ardour of many of the amateur young royalist officers dimmed and they returned to their estates to prevent their sequestration by parliamentary commissioners. Not so, Captain Churchill. He fought on – to the end. He was, both then and after the war, as loyal an adherent to the crown as any man of his time. But with the defeat of the King in 1646, his military duties over, he quit his horse and retired to Lady Drake's house, Ashe, in Devon. There, in straitened circumstances, he awaited the return of the monarchy he supported and a better turn of fortune.

Despite the fact that Lady Drake's family had much to thank the King for in the way of riches and titles, she herself was a vehement parliamentarian. She was a lady of spirit – the sort who thrives on danger and upheavals. In 1644, Lord Poulett, the commander-in-chief of the royalist forces at Axminster, ordered his troops to burn down her house, Ashe; it was at the time being fortified by Roundheads. The soldiers set fire to the house and 'stripped the good lady, who, almost naked, and without shoe to her foot but what she afterwards begged, fled to Lyme for safety'. There she endured further humiliations. Incensed by the treatment she had received, she demanded compensation from their commander-in-chief and obtained it. She must have needed every penny, for her fine Elizabethan house was ruined.

One wing, however, was still habitable, and after the war she lived in it with her daughter Elizabeth and her son-in-law, Colonel Churchill, overlooking, presumably, their political differences. Their lives were punctuated by the birth of Churchill children. Winston and Elizabeth had twelve, but only five survived into adulthood, and only four into middle age. The success of those four was striking. Arabella, the eldest, became the mistress of a royal duke and the mother of a great French general; John became a greater – indeed the greatest – English general, and a duke to boot; George was Admiral of the Fleet; and Charles, the youngest, also became a distinguished general. But who in those hard years would have predicted such glittering futures for the children, born as they were to impoverished parents, brought up in a charred house, dependent on their grandmother's charity? The outlook, from their father's royalist point of view, was dismal.

He, Winston Churchill, had been educated at St John's College, Oxford, where he had been noted for his sedateness and his application to his studies, and afterwards he had gone to London to study

A 1645 edition of Saxton's map of Dorset, the county in which the Churchill family had its roots, and in which, a few years before this map appeared, they became landowners.

11

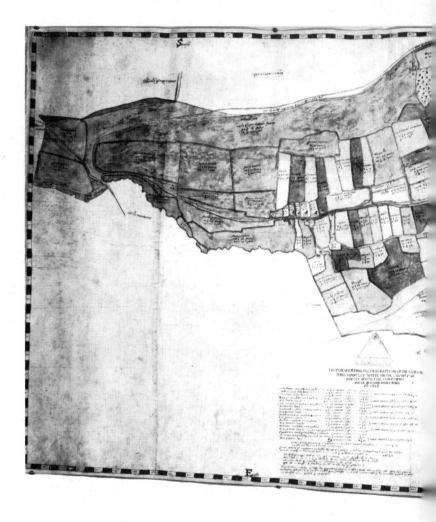

the law. The civil war had intervened. After the war, in 1652, he went back to London to be called to the Bar and set a seal on his earlier training. Seal it was, for he did not go on to practise law but returned to Devon to study history. He investigated his own ancestry and managed, rather dubiously, to trace his forebears back to some Lords of Courcelle who came to England with William the Conqueror. Families then liked to be able to boast Norman ancestry, and so Colonel Churchill must have been pleased with his researches, for they made his family more respectable than his Dorset origins implied.

He went on to write his version of the history of England. It was entitled *Divi Britannici: Being a Remark upon the Lives of all the Kings of*

A map of the estate of Minterne in Dorset, drawn by John More in 1616. The estate was leased by John Churchill from Winchester College in 1642. The house, which was built there by his son, Winston, still stands.

this Isle, and was dedicated 'To his most Sacred Majesty Charles 11'. In the introduction he addressed the King persuasively and elegantly: 'Great Sir,' he wrote 'If the Reading of History in General, be not only a Recreation, but a Restorative, and such as by which some Princes have recover'd the Health of their Bodies, others the Distemper of their Mind, many have learn'd to settle, and most to preserve the Weal of their estates; meeting therein with divers occurrences . . . cannot but be a subject worthy your Royal Regard'. The book was an apologia for the monarchy in the form of a comprehensive and erudite history of England set out ruler by ruler. (The stylish illustrations of all their coats of arms were said to have made it popular among students.) He began with his view of the

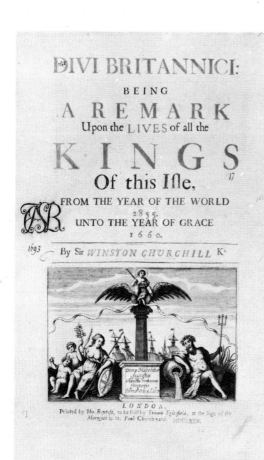

The title page (left) of the first Sir Winston Churchill's history of the Kings of Britain, and (right) his dedication of the book to King Charles II.

King's duty to his Parliament: 'The restraint by his Coronation oath being like a Silken Cord, that may be stretched without breaking upon the discovery and for the prevention of any publick mischief or inconvenience'; and ended with a vigorous attack on recent events: 'But this last Age of ours, I confess, hath brought forth an unnatural Race of Men, who inspired with the discipline of Daring beyond any of their Ancestors, put out the laws first . . . and after committed a Horrid Rape on the Body Politick, begetting such a Brood of Monsters as made all the World (and themselves at last) afraid'. Was his Puritan mother-in-law, Lady Drake, his protector and chatelaine, one of the 'Brood of Monsters'? The book was not published until 1675; so scholarly was it that its authorship was attributed to Clarendon, but although it was noticed it was not widely read.

With the Restoration, when 'the abused populace (like water which heated contrary to its nature returns to its first condition, and becomes so much the colder) submitted themselves to their lawful sovereign, with like Zeal as they fell off from him in the first place', Colonel Churchill's fortunes improved. He was returned to Westminster as member for Weymouth in 1661 on the wave of royalist 'Zeal' and retained his seat until the end of that Parliament in 1679. A rigid Tory, he showed in his parliamentary work that sedateness and application for which he had been noted at Oxford. Because of his solid qualities he was sent to Ireland with six other commissioners to try to execute the impossible 1662 Act of Settlement (which thirty-six commissioners had already failed to do). Clarendon described these seven as 'gentlemen of very good extractions, excellent understandings and above all suspicion for their integrity, and generally reputed to be superior to any base temptation'. But it was an arduous assignment – there were too many claims for too little land – and Churchill, fed up, returned to England in 1664. He was knighted at Whitehall for his loyalty and services to the King, and later that year was appointed Junior Clerk Comptroller to the Board of Green Cloth. This was a permanent official post in the royal household, and, although it involved the rather mundane duties of housekeeping below the royal stairs, it was a position to be reckoned with for it meant close contact with the court and therefore, probably, a favour or two. But his knighthood and an augmentation to his coat of arms, on which he put the apt motto *fiel pero desdichado* (faithful but unfortunate), were the only rewards that Churchill received for his unswervingly loyal service to the crown. He toiled on uncomplaining, while colleagues of lesser integrity were given money, lands and better titles. In his subsequent twenty-two years of dogged service at court, he rose only two small steps in the hierarchy of the royal household. But although his status there was lowly it is improbable that the careers of his children would have been quite as sparkling as they were, had their father not held that post.

One other small honour that did come his way was to be elected to the newly formed Royal Society; he later became a Fellow. But while his colleagues were plotting the course of a new comet or calculating the spring of a cheese maggot, Sir Winston, despite his observations on the properties of water, showed no interest and seldom attended the meetings.

The Act of Settlement in Ireland proved so difficult to execute that an Act of Explanation (consisting of 234 clauses in 136 folio pages) was introduced to clarify its content. Back went Sir Winston to Ireland in 1665 to explain the intricacies anew. When, four years later, the commissioners' work was wound up they could be com-

The coronation procession of Charles II on 22 April 1661, painted by Derek Stoop. Samuel Pepys wrote of the scene: 'So glorious was the show with gold and silver that we were not able to look at it.'

mended for it; it was to their credit that a modicum of stability was maintained in Ireland for the next 100 years or more.

Sir Winston resumed his work as courtier and Member of Parliament, and gradually assumed the role in Parliament of spokesman for the King. As Charles's unpopularity grew, so Sir Winston's job became more difficult, and his position more precarious. Towards the end of the Parliament he was the object of much hostility from other members, and with the overwhelming Whig victory in the election of 1679 lost both his seat in the House of Commons and his position at court. He remained out of things for the rest of Charles's reign and spent his time in the country, patiently biding, as he had done before, a better time.

That time came when James II came to the throne in 1685. James managed to obtain, through a reorganization of the borough corporations, the return of a predominantly Tory Parliament, and

16

among the members that were duly elected was Sir Winston Churchill – this time as member for Lyme. He took up his former duties where he had left off. But shortly before the reign came to its ignominious end when James fled the shores of England never to return, Sir Winston Churchill, that faithful servant and most staunch supporter of both James and Charles, died. Perhaps it was as well that he was spared the revolution of 1688, for where would his allegiance have lain then?

2
Royal Favourites

THE COURT OF CHARLES II, described as an 'entire scene of gallantry and amusements', was a limited affair. It gathered its courtiers and bestowed favours on their families. If companions or playmates were needed for the royal children, the courtiers' children, who were known and trusted, could be called upon. It was therefore quite natural that before Sir Winston had been at the Board of Green Cloth a year his eldest child, Arabella, a lanky girl of sixteen, should be offered an appointment as maid-of-honour to the Duchess of York (formerly Ann Hyde, the daughter of the Earl of Clarendon), and that a little later his next child, John, should become page to James, Duke of York, Charles's brother and heir. Sydney Godolphin, who was five years older than John Churchill, was also a page, and the two boys became close friends. This friendship and others that were struck among the privileged court children, both at this time and rather later when little Princess Anne, the Duke and Duchess of

RIGHT Arabella Churchill painted by Mary Beale. She was described in the *Memoirs of the Comte de Grammont* as 'a tall creature, pale-faced, and nothing but skin and bone'.
LEFT Her brother John, aged twenty-two, painted by Kneller.

DVKE AND DVTCHES OF
YORK WITH PRINCES
MARCY AND ANN

James, Duke of York, with
his first wife Anne Hyde
and their two daughters,
Mary (carrying wreath) and
Anne. After James, first
Mary (together with her
husband William of
Orange) then Anne became
sovereigns of England.
Arabella Churchill bore
James four children, and
John Churchill became first
his page and later Gentle-
man of the Bedchamber.

York's daughter, formed her coterie, were to have repercussions
far beyond the royal nursery walls.

Arabella, by all accounts, was a modest, gentle, plain girl. So
when the Duke of York, no less a lecher than his brother Charles II,
took a fancy to her, 'the court was not able to comprehend how, after
being in love with Lady Chesterfield, Mrs Hamilton and Miss
Jennings, he could have any inclination for such a creature' – 'that
ugly skeleton', as Miss Hobart had called her. But the Duke had his
reasons for his choice. One day when he was showing her how to
improve her seat on a horse, 'Miss Churchill lost her seat, screamed
out and fell from her horse', it was reported in the *Memoirs of the
Comte de Grammont*: 'She was so greatly stunned that her thoughts
were otherwise employed than about her decency on the present
occasion; and those who first crowded round her found her rather
in a negligent posture: they could hardly believe that limbs of such

exquisite beauty could belong to such a face'. For the next twelve years those legs and doubtless her other charms continued to attract James, and she bore him four children. He gave her a large house in St James's Square – a smart new area of London developed by Harry Jermyn. There she brought up her family, and there, while his fancy persisted, he paid her many a visit.

When his wife died in 1671, James scouted around for a new and more suitable duchess (his marriage to the commoner Ann Hyde had never been thought quite befitting). He wanted a Catholic and a princess; he found both in Mary of Modena. But his second marriage (which took place by proxy) caused only a momentary pause in his relations with Arabella. These continued for several years until, in the end, she was supplanted by another maid-of-honour, Catherine Sedley. Miss Sedley was no beauty either, but she had a sharp mind and an acid turn of phrase which entranced the foolish James. It is she who is credited with the remark about his mistresses: 'What he saw in any of us, I cannot tell. We were all plain, and if any of us had wit, he would not have understood it'.

Arabella accepted the change in her position with equanimity and expressed no bitterness at the loss of royal favour. She sold her house for £8,000, sent her children to be educated in France (where, ten years later, they were received by their father's court in exile at St Germain), married Charles Godfrey, a fellow officer of her brother, and set about a new family life; before long she had given birth to another four children. She outlived most of her family and died in 1730 at the age of 82.

It is a moot point how much John Churchill profited from his sister's very special position; as was his wont he kept very quiet on the matter. In his will he left 'an annuity of £400 in trust for [his] sister Godfrey for life' – an indication perhaps of long affection. But although his wife, Sarah, was always disparaging about Arabella 'and her train of Bastards', for young John Churchill his sister's liaison cannot have been to his disadvantage.

He became a page after a scanty education, first in Dublin while Sir Winston was sorting out the Act of Settlement, and then at St Paul's in London. Books and learning were not to his taste. 'He was eminently illiterate, wrote bad English, and spelled it still worse', wrote Lord Chesterfield. When asked by the Duke of York one day during a parade of the Guards in Hyde Park what profession he would choose, he is reputed to have wished for 'a pair of colours in these fine regiments'. No sooner asked than granted: in 1667, at the age of seventeen, he obtained a commission in the King's Own Company of Foot Guards, and the following year was under enemy

A painting by Samuel Cooper of Barbara Villiers, later Duchess of Cleveland, described as 'a woman of great beauty, but most enormously vicious and ravenous'. Her daughter by John Churchill, Barbara (born in 1672), became a nun and subsequently prioress of a convent in France, which did not prevent her having an illegitimate child by the Earl of Arran.

fire in Tangier. He spent three years in that English dominion fighting the Moors and gained the rudiments of his military knowledge in the field rather than on the parade-ground.

As a young ensign he returned to England from northern Africa, and cut a striking figure at court. There 'the beauties were desirous of charming, and the men endeavoured to please' and 'all studied to set themselves off to the best advantage'. He was handsome and already possessed the charm for which he was famed throughout his life; he had travelled and seen action; he had left a mere boy and returned a seasoned officer. With such qualifications, he fell straight into the sensual clutches of the King's tricky mistress, Barbara Villiers, Duchess of Cleveland. She was his cousin, his senior by nine years. Said to be the fairest and the lewdest of the royal concubines, she had been a most unfaithful and temperamental mistress to

Charles II for ten years or so, and had borne an assortment of children. 'She was a woman of great beauty, but most enormously vicious and ravenous'. Fortunately for John Churchill the King's attention was now turning towards Louise de Keroualle, so that, although annoyed, he suffered Barbara's new lover with comparatively good humour. John was almost certainly the father of her last child, Barbara, born in July 1672. 'All agreed that a man who was the favourite of the king's mistress, and brother to the duke's favourite was in a fair way of preferment, and could not fail to make a fortune.'

He had none yet. Barbara however had acquired a lot of money. It was said that 'she was as liberal of her purse as of her person', and she is thought to have given John, who was poor by court standards, £5,000. With this he prudently purchased an annuity of £500 in a new life insurance scheme concocted by Lord Halifax, and thereby obtained for himself a measure of financial security. To receive lavish gifts from your mistress was fine, but to spend it in such an eminently sensible way was shocking; such money was to be frittered away or furtively hidden – that was the etiquette of the day. From that moment John Churchill's 'carefulness' was always noticed and ever resented. Indeed he never became a generous man even at the end of his life when he was one of the richest in the country.

The next few years saw the playing out of his affair with Barbara, and his remarkable rise from ensign by way of marine captaincy to colonel, a rank he reached at the age of twenty-four. His first double promotion to marine captaincy came after the naval battle of Sole Bay, in which the Dutch took the combined fleets of the French and English by surprise.

The next year, 1673, he served on land under the French King Louis XIV and, after displaying great courage at the siege of Maastricht, was thanked publicly by Louis (who had been present, as at a picnic, with a retinue of women, painters, poets, courtiers). Louis would have little reason to thank him again. However, although it was clear after the Anglo-Dutch Treaty of 1674 that the Anglo-French pact was outmoded, some English troops remained in French pay, and among them a regiment now commanded by John Churchill. Under the Vicomte de Turenne, the greatest commander of the day, that regiment took part in the battle of Enzheim, and Colonel Churchill, though resentful at having to fight a foreign war, none the less acquitted himself admirably and was mentioned in Turenne's dispatches. To serve under the master Turenne was an invaluable experience, and it is from him that Churchill must have learnt, in those days of orthodox, stereotyped warfare, the value of the unorthodox. When he returned to England in 1675, a successful twenty-four-year-old colonel, a brilliant future seemed assured;

no one would have guessed that it would be nearly thirty years before he was given command of an army, that his meteoric rise would slow down to a crawling pace.

On his return to court he set about another 'campaign', or so it has always been described. As his affair with the Duchess of Cleveland was coming to an end the young colonel met, danced with and fell for fifteen-year-old Sarah Jennings, maid-of-honour to the new Duchess of York. She was not as beautiful as her elder sister, Frances – 'la belle Jennings', whom the Duke of York courted – but she was vivacious and attractive, and for John Churchill it was love at first acquaintance if not at first sight; he determined she should be his. His suit took nearly three years.

Saint-Evremond in the *Memoirs of the Comte de Grammont* compared the European customs of courtship: 'In Holland, unmarried ladies are of easy access, and of tender dispositions; but as soon as ever they are married, they become like so many Lucretias: in France, the ladies are great coquettes before marriage, and still more so afterwards; but here it is a miracle if a young lady yields to any proposal but that of matrimony'. Sarah Jennings was true to the English tradition. John swamped her with protestations of love and every endearment: she remained cool almost to the point of cruelty, expressing distrust in all his overtures – 'I find all you will say is only to amuse me and make me think you have a passion for me, when in reality there is no such thing'. The intensity of his letters in which he beseeches her to love him, to submit to him, and assures her over and over again of his utter devotion, shows this to be one of the few occasions on which he was not master of himself. In the end she did yield – not with the best grace – and some time in the winter of 1678–9 they were secretly married.

It was not a match that was approved of by his family or by hers. He had no means, no house, no property, no prospects of a fat inheritance, and by the rules of the game should have sought a richer hand. She, although an heiress in a small way (her father, Richard Jennings, owned property worth about £4,000 a year), should have found a husband who, if not wealthy, at least could boast a decent title. But it was a love match – a rare bird then – and nobody trusted or applauded a love match. Yet it remained one until the end of their lives when they were as deeply involved with each other as they had been at the beginning; their marriage never developed into one of habit. In his fifties John wrote from the wars: 'I am only sure that I can never be happy till I am with my dearest Soul' (The Hague, April 1705); 'You may be assured that you are dearer to me than all the world besides' (Elst, June 1705). And she in her way adored her 'ever dear Lord Marlborough'. The year before she died, an old lady of 83,

Sarah Churchill (right)
playing cards with Lady
Fitzharding, painted by
Sir Godfrey Kneller. She
had 'a fiery temper and a
fairy face' and a 'prodigious
abundance of fine fair hair'.
It took John Churchill
nearly three years to
persuade her to marry him.

she wrote on her bundle of his letters: 'Read over in 1743 desiring to
burn them but I could not doe it'.

Sarah never possessed the wifely attributes of submission, humility and obedience; she was proud, imperious and forthright. She
had an incisive mind, but bad judgment – made worse by her unshakeable faith in it – and although her no-nonsense attitude to many
things was admirable, her lack of sensitivity frequently rendered it
foolish. This rather masculine side of her personality complemented
a gentle feminine trait in him, and her spontaneity contrasted with
his reserve. They were extraordinarily happy together.

It was five years before they had a home of their own. Until that
time they either lodged uneasily with old Sir Winston in Dorset, or
trapesed after the court of the Duke of York, which, because of the
prickly situation in London after the Popish Plot of 1678 and the
Duke's well-known Catholic sympathies, was forced to reside first in
Brussels and then in Edinburgh. The young Churchills danced
attendance wherever.

John and Sarah Churchill built Holywell House in Hertfordshire c. 1684. Sarah had spent her childhood on its estate, and this, her first home, was always one of her favourites. The house was pulled down in 1827 and the estate has long since been covered by the town of St Albans.

Sarah, who later said that she thought that 'anyone that has commonsense or honesty must needs be very weary of everything that one meets with in courts', had entered the English court at the age of twelve or thirteen when it had been a nest of little future queens: there were the Duke of York's new wife, Mary of Modena (aged fifteen), the Duke's daughters, Mary (eleven), who was to marry Prince William of Orange, and Anne (eight), later Queen of England. Anne and Sarah became friends; Anne conceived a passion, a sort of schoolgirl crush, for the dominating and confident Sarah. Anne, whose mother, the Duchess of York, was dead, was a neglected and timid child and was naturally attracted to Sarah's strong personality. She wrote her many letters that, until their momentous breach more than twenty-five years later, were as full of devotion as were those of John Churchill.

When Charles II felt safe enough on the throne to allow his

Catholic brother to return from Edinburgh to London, the Churchills came too and began a more settled married life. They built a small house at Holywell in Hertfordshire, where Sarah had been brought up, and their family life flourished. Their first child, Harriet, had died as a baby, but Henrietta, who was born in 1681, survived, and so did Anne, born in 1684. Anne was named after Princess Anne who, after her marriage in 1683 to the eligible but dull Prince George of Denmark, had taken on Sarah as Lady of her Bedchamber. Prince George was known as '*Est-il possible?*' because it was all he ever said. Although Princess Anne liked her husband and grew to love him deeply, her marriage was no check on her intense, emotional relationship with Sarah. In this she insisted on frankness and equality, on breaking down the royal barriers. 'She grew uneasy to be treated by me with the form and ceremony due to her rank', wrote Sarah later, 'nor could she bear from me the sound of words which implied in them distance and superiority'. She demanded that in their letters they should use ordinary names: 'Morley and Freeman were the names her fancy hit upon, and she left me to choose by which of them I should be called. My frank open temper naturally led me to pitch upon Freeman'. Apart from their husbands, Mr Morley and Mr Freeman, the only other person to whom they accorded this honour of equality was Sydney Godolphin, otherwise 'Mr Montgomery'.

So began an extraordinary correspondence that continued until the latter part of Queen Anne's reign. In it Mrs Morley perpetually begged for the presence of Mrs Freeman, declared how she could not bear to be parted from her, reiterated her love and 'kindness' for her. They are immature letters and ones which, later, Anne cannot have been pleased to reread. That is just what, in an attempt to heal their broken friendship, Sarah tactlessly made her do. Sarah's was not a sentimental nature and although, as a friend, she was loyal and open (to a fault), she did not fully reciprocate Anne's feelings. As for Anne's letters, Sarah thought they were 'very indifferent both in sense and spelling, unless that they were generally enlivened with a few passionate expressions, sometimes pretty enough but repeated over and over again without the mixture of anything either of diversion or instruction'.

When James II came to the throne in 1685 his subjects ignored his religion and gave him a tremendous welcome, his Parliament granted him a generous allowance and everything promised well – especially for the favoured Churchills. They were promptly made Lord and Lady Churchill of Sandridge. But things looked less auspicious when, on the second Sunday of his reign, James went to Mass in state, and worse when he commissioned Sir Christopher Wren to build a rich Catholic chapel for his palace at Whitehall.

The last and first pages of a letter from Queen Anne to 'my dear Mrs Freeman' alluding to their different opinions of the Whigs, and, because it was written after the death of her last child, signed 'your poor unfortunate faithful Morley'. Anne wrote over three hundred letters to the Marlboroughs.

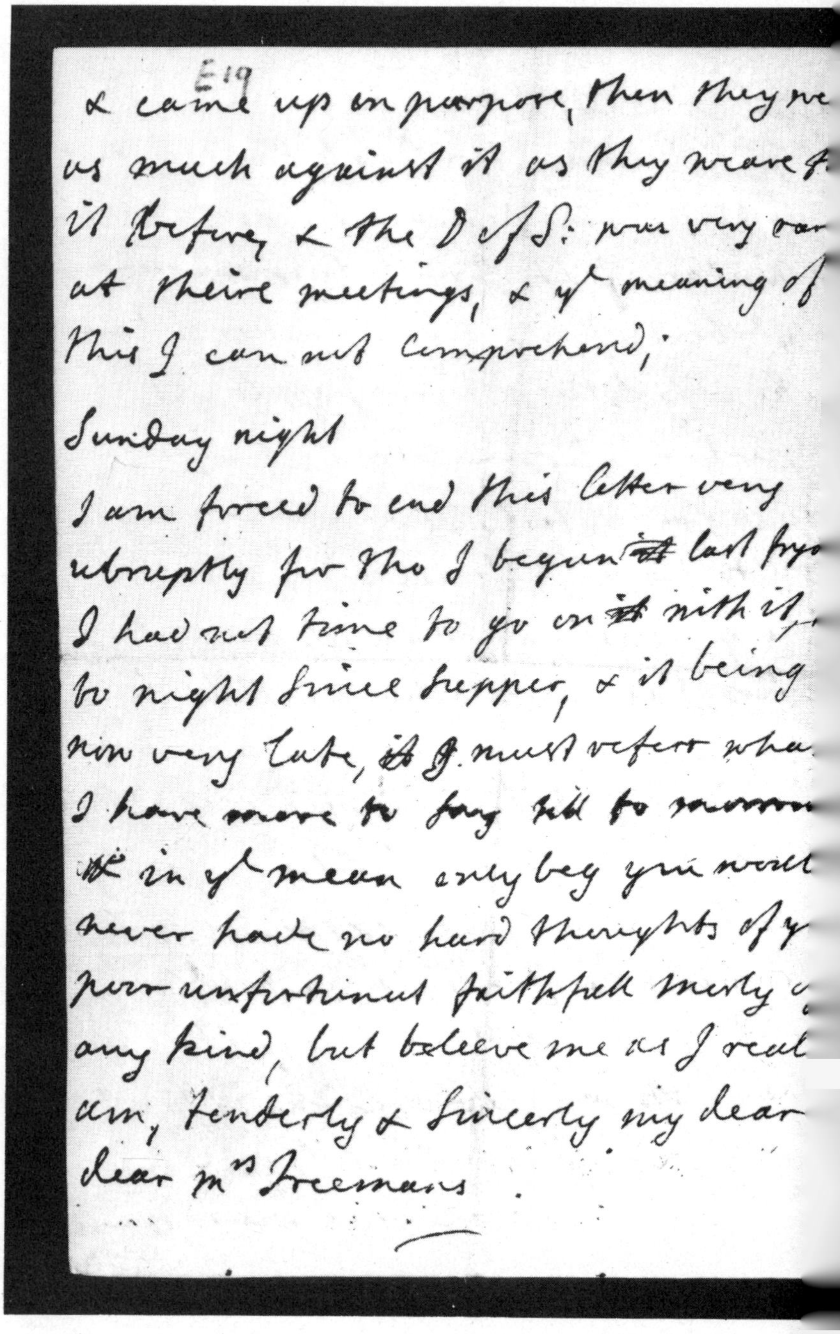

E 19

& came up on purpose, then they were
as much against it as they weare of
it before, & the D of S: was very ear
at theire meetings, & ye meaning of
this I can not comprehend;

Sunday night

I am forced to end this letter very
abruptly for tho I begun it last fryd
I had not time to go on it with it,
to night since supper, & it being
now very late, it I must refer wha
I have more to say till to morrow
it in ye mean only beg you would
never have no hard thoughts of y
poor unfortinat faithfull morly of
any kind, but beleeve me as I real
am, tenderly & sincerly my dear
dear mrs Freemans

Windsor fryday June ye 11th
must begin this letter with thanks
r ye two I received to day from my
ear mrs Freeman, for tho we differ, it
a very great satisfaction to me to
now your mind freely upon all subjects,
therfore I again beg you to continue yt
nue kindnes; I am very sory you
ink I can treat any thing you say
if it came from mr James, sure I should
an unheard of monster if I could be
nable of yt, I own I can not have yt
od opinion of some sort of people
you have, nor yt ill one of others,
lett the whigs brag never soe much
theire great services to their Country
of their numbers, I beleeve
e revolution had never bin, nor the
ccion seteled as it is now, if the

The Duke of Monmouth, the eldest and most handsome of Charles 11's bastards, was then living in Holland. He made a guess – a bad one as it turned out – at the political temper in England, and, egged on by the Earl of Argyll, decided to sail for England and raise a rebellion while the Earl of Argyll was to launch a simultaneous invasion of Scotland.

On 11 June 1685 Monmouth landed at Lyme in Dorset, where within twenty-four hours he was joined by 1,500 men. Messengers from Lyme galloped to London and relayed the news to their MP, the old cavalier colonel, Sir Winston Churchill. He in turn told the King. In no time Sir Winston's son, Lord Churchill (now Brigadier-General), was marching down the Great West Road at the head of troops of the Blues and his own Dragoons. To his chagrin he was not appointed commander-in-chief – that post went to the senior but less experienced Frenchman, the Earl of Feversham (who, although a nephew of Turenne, was no great soldier); 'I see plainly that I am to have the trouble,' Churchill lamented, 'and that the honour will be another's'.

Monmouth reached Bristol to find that Feversham and the royal troops had beaten him to it. Disheartened by this setback he became still gloomier when he heard that Argyll's uprising had been suppressed and that the Earl had already been put to death. It was a despondent rebel troop that, marching north from Bridgewater, suddenly came upon the royal forces camped somewhat shambolically at Sedgemoor. Monmouth saw his chance and decided to make a surprise attack on them at night. It has been said that when he did so Feversham was asleep, but that Churchill was awake and equipped and that he alerted the troops. As dawn rose after several hours of bloody fighting Monmouth was seen to be defeated. He was captured and soon executed. The rebels were dealt with by the notorious Judge Jeffreys at the Bloody Assize in a particularly vicious and sadistic way: some 400 were hanged and 1,200 were sold as slaves for the Barbados plantations. Feversham got the Garter and command of the 1st Troop of Life Guards, and Churchill, now Major-General, command of the 3rd Troop. The unofficial credit for the Battle of Sedgemoor (the last among Englishmen on English soil) went to Churchill; his prompt reaction was thought to have saved the day. The *London Gazette* announced that he had 'performed his part with all the courage and gallantry imaginable'.

James felt that the victory gave him a mandate to pursue ever more vigorously his popish policies. He 'had now two things in view, to make himself absolute and to establish popery'; that was how Sarah put it in the history of England that she began to write and never completed. Such a course he followed until the leading men in the

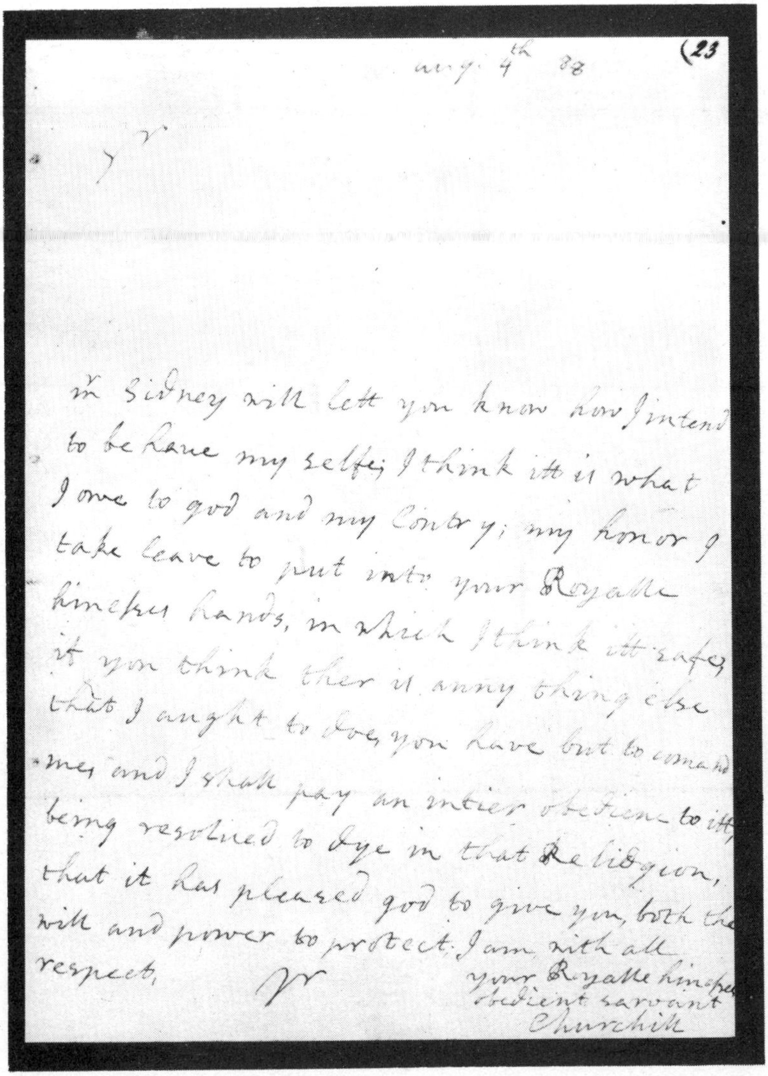

aug. 4th 88
(23)

yr

in Sidney will lett you know how I intend to behave my selfe; I think itt is what I owe to god and my Contry; my honor I take leave to put into your Royalle hineses hands, in which I think itt safe; if you think ther is anny thing else that I ought to doe, you have but to comand mes and I shall pay an intier obedience to itt; being resolved to dye in that Religion, that it has pleased god to give you, both the will and power to protect. I am with all respect,

yr

your Royalle hineses obedient servant Churchill

A letter from John Churchill to William of Orange, dated 4 August 1688, offering the Prince his 'entire obedience'. William, as King, never wholly trusted that pledge, for he knew that Churchill continued to correspond with his former master, James II, in exile at St Germain.

country could bear it no longer. In the spring of 1688 they sent a letter to Prince William of Orange asking him to invade England. William was both James's son-in-law (having married his daughter Mary in 1677) and his nephew (being the son of his sister Mary) and had therefore a reasonable claim to the throne.

Throughout the summer and autumn of 1688 the corridors of power were filled with whisperings as the views of peers and politicians about a possible invasion were sounded. In June James clapped seven Protestant bishops in the Tower for refusing to read

Naissance du prince de Galles, fils de Jacques II.

A drawing by Vantiès in 1688 of the birth of a son to Queen Mary, second wife of James II. In spite of the fact that there were said to be sixty-seven people present at the birth, a rumour soon spread that the child, James (the Old Pretender), was not the Queen's but had been smuggled into the room in a warming pan

his Edict of Toleration from their pulpits; it was an unpopular action and there was cheering when they were acquitted at the end of the month. Then the Queen – most unpopularly – gave birth to a son; so unexpected was this baby that it was widely believed to be another's smuggled into the Queen's bedchamber in a warming pan. Genuine or not, James Edward Francis, Prince of Wales, opened vistas in Protestant minds of further Catholic Kings up with which they would not put.

By October James was aware that a 'great and sudden invasion, with an armed force of foreigners, will speedily be made in a hostile manner upon this our kingdom'. He mustered his army to meet it. On 5 November William with 3,600 cavalry, 10,600 infantry and 20,000 spare muskets for sympathizers, landed at Torbay. He marched to Exeter and remained there while James dithered at Salisbury suffering from indecision, insomnia and nosebleeds. Feversham was his commander-in-chief and Churchill second-in-command of an army of more than 20,000, which should have been sufficient for the purpose of forestalling William. Trouble began when some cavalry colonels left James and went over to William. Then on the night of the 22nd, Churchill, with the Duke of Grafton and 400 cavalrymen, also slipped away to join the invaders, followed the next day by the Prince of Denmark and the Duke of Ormonde.

James was shattered. Irresolute, nervous, galled by these defections – particularly that of his supposedly faithful servant, Churchill – he returned to London, only to find that his daughter, Anne, had also quit him; she had left Whitehall with Lady Churchill on the 23rd and fled to Nottingham. By Christmas James and his family had crept away from the shores of England never to return and William had perpetrated a bloodless coup. Was Churchill right to desert his benefactor at his hour of need? Or was it an act of the utmost ingratitude? In his parting letter to James he stated that his desertion 'could proceed from nothing but the inviolable dictates of my conscience and a necessary concern for my religion'. He was never a very religious man.

William and Mary became joint sovereigns of England. James went to France, where a French courtier is supposed to have remarked: 'When you listen to him, you realize why he is here'. William was glad of the throne because it gave him the power to align England with his United Provinces of Holland against France. This gave him a real prospect of curbing Louis XIV's extravagant ambitions in the Low Countries and the rest of Europe. To eliminate Louis's threat to the independence of the United Provinces by limiting his empire and maintaining a balance of power in Europe was William's lifelong ambition. He did not care very much for the English and the English did not care very much for him, but in 1688 they suited each other's needs: England had secured a truly Protestant monarch and William had secured England's hand in his designs on the continent. To get this hand into working order he immediately employed John Churchill to reorganize the armed forces, and at his coronation in April 1689 gave Churchill an earldom. Churchill took the name of Marlborough after a cousin on his mother's side, a distinguished sailor who had been killed at sea fighting the Dutch in 1665.

Not surprisingly, William soon declared war against France. The new Earl of Marlborough was given command of 8,000 men under Prince Waldeck in Flanders. He trained these men superbly, attended to their comforts and needs, and under his care they showed themselves to be the finest in the Dutch army against the French Marshal d'Humières at the battle of Walcourt in 1689. The old Dutch soldier, the Prince of Waldeck, wrote to William: 'Colonel Hodges and the English did marvels and the Earl of Marlborough is assuredly one of the most gallant men I know'. Accordingly, he was made Colonel of the Royal Fusiliers, a post which brought with it a salary most welcome for supporting his new title.

By the end of that year James had gone to Ireland and swiftly established control over much of it. William hurried over to deal with this threat, and at the bloody battle of the Boyne in July 1690 sent James scurrying back to France. Marlborough suggested to William that he might lead a seaborne expedition to capture the southern Irish ports of Cork and Kinsale and so prevent any further French arms or soldiers landing in Ireland. It was an imaginative plan; William saw the point of it and gave his consent. Marlborough reached Cork on 22 September 1690 and within a week had taken it. He then moved on and captured the more stubbornly defended Kinsale. It proved a smooth, efficient and highly effective operation; at a stroke it had erased the threat of a French invasion from Ireland and had isolated the remaining French troops in Ulster. Marlborough's brother, Brigadier Charles Churchill, after a leading part in the action, was made Governor of Kinsale. Marlborough himself had ambitions for the lucrative post of Master-General of the Ordnance and also hoped for the Garter: neither came his way.

The fact was that neither William nor Mary liked Marlborough. William, who was only six months younger than him was probably to some degree jealous of him, for Marlborough was the soldier of genius that William would have liked more than anything to have been. To some degree he was also distrustful of him, for he had after all been James's closest servant and indeed did, in 1692, open a correspondence with James in exile. Queen Mary said: 'I neither trust or esteem him'. But perhaps the greatest obstacle to a good relationship between the King and his would-be commander was Sarah's intimate friendship with Anne. Sarah did not endear herself to the new King and Queen. She disapproved of William being given the crown for life: 'At first I did not see any necessity for such a measure; and I thought it so unreasonable that I took a great deal of pains (which I believe the King and Queen never forgot) to promote my Mistress' pretensions'. When she then urged Anne to elicit a grant from Parliament (it gave her £50,000) rather than accept the allowance that William and Mary wished to give her as a royal favour, the King and Queen were offended. Gradually a nasty quarrel blew up between the royal sisters. Mary ordered Anne to dismiss Sarah from her service. Anne refused. Mary insisted. Anne was adamant. Then suddenly, in January 1692, the King dismissed Marlborough from all his offices. The incident caused great excite-

Aankomst van zyn
KONINGLYKE HOOGHEST
in Engeland, den 15 Novemb. 1688

C. Allard Excudit.

William of Orange (fig. 1), after an invitation
from the 'disgruntled noblemen' of England,
arrives in Torbay with his army on 5 November
1688. Eighteen days later Churchill left James
and joined William.

The Marlborough family painted by Closterman *c.* 1696.
The children from left to right are Elizabeth, Mary, Henrietta, Anne and John.

ment and although no reason was given the diarist John Evelyn noted that it was for 'excessive taking of bribes, covetousness and extortion on all occasions from his inferior officers'. Sarah, who later said with truth that 'the Duke of Marlborough never took a bribe', claimed that she was the reason, but it seems likely that Marlborough's business with the Jacobite court at St Germain and his loud voicing of anti-Dutch feeling in London were also strong factors. And indeed in May that year Marlborough was implicated in a Jacobite plot and, like so many other important figures in British history, sent to the Tower.

While Marlborough was locked up in the Tower, his younger son, Charles, died. (The Marlboroughs, apart from Henrietta and Anne already mentioned, had four other children: John, Charles, Elizabeth and Mary.) Both he and Sarah were deeply upset by the death of their small son. Sarah wrote her husband a letter at this time (one of the few that he did not burn on her instructions) in which she said: 'Wherever you are, whilst I have life, my soul shall follow you, my ever dear Lord Marlborough, and wherever I am I should only kill the time wishing for night that I might sleep and hope the next day to hear from you'.

Lords Halifax and Shrewsbury stood Marlborough bail and he left the Tower after six weeks to remain out of favour and out of work for six years. Sarah, despite repeated demands from the Queen for her removal, held on to her job as Anne's Lady of the Bedchamber; Anne refused to let her go. Attitudes hardened between the two royal households. Anne moved hers from Whitehall to Syon House just outside London, and there they grumbled about William, calling him the Monster or Mr Caliban or the Dutch Abortion. Mary paid a visit to Anne after she had given birth to a child and, after a cool interview in which Mary talked about Sarah not the baby, the sisters never saw each other again. Mary never had any children and although none of Anne's survived beyond boyhood (it is thought that she buried sixteen children in all) Mary was not to know that and it is likely that jealousy played some part in the sisters' sour relationship.

Mary died suddenly of smallpox in 1694. After that there was a thaw between William and Anne; Anne moved into St James's Palace and began to be treated as heiress to the throne. And Marlborough, although still corresponding with St Germain, slowly inched his way back into royal favour. By 1698 he was restored to his rank in the army, to his position on the Privy Council and, with the establishment of a household for Anne's nine-year-old son, the Duke of Gloucester, was made the Duke's governor. William sanctioned the appointment thus: 'My Lord, teach him but to know what you

OPPOSITE A portrait by Kneller of Anne with her son William, Duke of Gloucester. He was the only one of her children to survive any length of time, but even he died just after his eleventh birthday. His broad head may be evidence of hydrocephalus.

are, and my nephew cannot want for accomplishments'. Twelve-year-old Jack Churchill, Marlborough's surviving son, became Master of the Horse to the little Duke. But hardly had his household begun to function than the boy fell ill and died. What Anne must have suffered through her miscarriages, her births, her babies, is impossible to imagine, but from this moment she always signed herself in her letters to Sarah 'your poor unfortunate faithful Morley'.

The problem that troubled Europe in general and William in particular at the end of the seventeenth century was that of the Spanish succession. The facts were, in essence, that the enormous Spanish Empire that comprised parts of the old and the new world was ruled over by the failing Charles II. He had no children and no obvious heir. His increasingly diseased body and demented mind presaged an approaching death, and the other European monarchs hovered like vultures over his throne. Louis XIV had a valid Bourbon candidate for it in his grandson, the Duke of Anjou; the Holy Roman Emperor, Leopold, had two valid Habsburg candidates, his son the Archduke Charles and his grandson the Electoral Prince Joseph Ferdinand of Bavaria. After the Peace of Ryswick, which wound up the war of the League of Augsburg in 1697, secret diplomatic efforts were made to arrange a fair partitioning of the Spanish inheritance. These resulted in the 1st Partition Treaty, which, however, was soon rendered irrelevant by the death of one of the candidates, the Electoral Prince of Bavaria. So then there were two contenders for the Spanish throne, and another Partition Treaty was drawn up and signed by Louis and William, but not by the Emperor Leopold, for although it made his son heir-in-chief it did not grant him Italy, which he coveted. William's overriding concern was to prevent the whole inheritance, which included the Spanish Netherlands, that sensitive barrier between France and Holland, as well as valuable overseas trading posts, going to Louis's grandson. He saw plainly that such an event would be a calamity for Europe, for it would make Louis's supremacy unassailable. Before the war of the League of Augsburg, 'the French sphere of influence . . . had blanketed all Europe save the Palace in which the Prince of Orange happened to be spending the night'. Now, thanks entirely to William's tenacity in chipping away at the French block, it had 'withered away almost to nothing'. William was desperate to preserve and improve such a position. The Spaniards themselves, barely consulted, were keen to keep their Empire intact. But would Louis keep his word over the Second Partition Treaty? He had shown no qualms before in breaking honourable agreements.

In the event Charles II with a decrepit hand signed a will that left absolutely everything to Louis's grandson, Philip of Anjou. Soon after, on 1 November 1700, he died. Louis was faced with the choice of accepting the will and repudiating the treaty, or repudiating the will and abiding by the treaty. The will, of course, proved irresistible, and, 'despising the restraints of treaties', on 16 November Louis told the Spanish Ambassador in France to acknowledge the eighteen-year-old Duke of Anjou (described as hypochondriac, unreliable and over-sexed) as King Philip v of Spain. William, when he heard the news, trembled. He appreciated the consequences of Louis's action, and knew that he was powerless to combat them, for his English Parliament was in an obstinately pacific and insular frame of mind: it had already forced him to disarm after the Peace of Ryswick. Fortunately for William, both England and Holland were provoked into a more aggressive temper by two outrageous and ill-considered actions by Louis. First, he swooped down on the Dutch barrier fortresses along the frontier of the Spanish Netherlands, thus scotching William's achievements in the previous war and thereby roused Dutch fury. William commented sadly: 'It is now more than twenty-eight years that I have worked without interruption to save that barrier for the republic, and you can easily imagine how angry I am to see it lost in a single day, without firing a shot'. Second, when James II died at St Germain in September Louis recognised James III – that 'supposititious child' of the warming pan past – as King of England, and the English were enraged. Now William had the material with which to forge a workable alliance to confront Louis and obstruct his total domination of Europe. But just as William's plans were reaching fruition and support from Parliament was forthcoming, so his constitution, which had always been frail, collapsed, and in March 1702, after a fall from a horse, he suffered complications from which he died.

William was smoothly succeeded by Anne. Two months later, war, his war, was declared on France by the Grand Alliance of England, Holland and the Holy Roman Empire, and the armies, his armies, were mustered. Marlborough, with his friend and benefactress Mrs Morley on the throne, was primed and ready to command. A glorious age was dawning. Poor William got little thanks from his subjects.

> He had their Rights and Liberties restor'd
> In Battle purchas'd, and by Peace secur'd:
> And they with English Gratitude began,
> To feel the Favour and despise the Man.

3
Captain General

AT THE ACCESSION of Queen Anne, the Earl of Marlborough was fifty-two, and although he was often tormented by migraine he was fit and possessed phenomenal physical energy. He was keen to command. Fortune now smiled with full radiance on him and his family: he became Captain-General of Anne's armies at home and abroad, and Master-General of the Ordnance; the Order of the Garter, that plum he had long coveted, was conferred on him on the fifth day of the new reign. Sarah became Groom of the Stole, Mistress of the Robes and Comptroller of the Privy Purse (which duty she performed most conscientiously and economically). Anne wanted to give her the attractive perk of the Great Lodge in Windsor Park and so made her Ranger of Windsor Great Park. The Marlboroughs were now very rich – he would shortly be earning £60,000 a year and she, about £7,000. Their family at this moment consisted of two married daughters, two unmarried daughters and their surviving son. Their two married daughters, Henrietta Godolphin (she was married to Mr Montgomery's son) and Anne Spencer (married to the Earl of Sunderland's heir) both became Ladies of the Bedchamber. Marlborough's two brothers had their share of the bounty too. George, having waited for ten years, became Admiral first of the Red and then, a week later, of the Blue, and virtual head of the Admiralty under the uninspired Prince George, whom Anne insisted on making Generalissimo and Lord High Admiral; George Churchill was also made Deputy Ranger of Windsor Little Park. Charles rose immediately to the rank of Lieutenant-General and was given the posts of Lieutenant of the Tower and Deputy-Lieutenant for Tower Hamlets; he also became the Master of the Queen's Buck-

OPPOSITE Marlborough is shown a plan of the siege of Bouchain in 1711 by his chief engineer, Colonel Armstrong. Sarah declared that this portrait by Seeman was 'as like him as ever I saw.'

The diamond-studded sword which was presented to Marlborough by the Emperor Charles of Austria. Sarah later refused to give it to her grandson, the third Duke, for she was afraid that he would sell it to pay his debts. 'That sword my Lord would have carried to the gates of Paris,' she said. 'Am I to live to see the diamonds picked off one by one and lodged at the pawnbroker's?'

hounds. Mr Montgomery was made Lord Treasurer, the nearest equivalent to a modern Prime Minister. Favouritism was rampant.

There were political alignments within the tightly-knit group of friends, Mr and Mrs Morley, Mr and Mrs Freeman and Mr Montgomery. Anne loathed the Whigs with a passion; Sarah held strong Whig convictions which she rammed down Anne's throat, as only she could, certain that she would in this way convert her to her way of thinking. Marlborough and Godolphin, although classed as Tories, were non-party men, both deeply committed to the prosecution of the war. Broadly speaking, the Whigs were in favour of the war and would vote the necessary supplies whereas the Tories disliked it and considered that, if action had to be taken, the English should limit themselves to the naval sphere, in which they were now supreme. Military action in the 'Cockpit' of Flanders the Tories reckoned both costly and pointless and, in line with their naval leanings, they preferred any land action to be as close to the sea as possible; in this way the capture of, say, Antwerp was applauded but action in deepest Europe (Blenheim, for instance) was beyond the pale. When out of power the group of friends had remained intact despite differing views, which were then mere matters of opinion, subjects for discussion. But once in positions of power, when opinions became policy and national decisions depended on them, the group could not withstand the strains of disagreement, and it was slowly and tragically to break up.

Anne minded desperately about her Church, the Church of England, and considered the Tories to be the party of the Church. She soon gathered Tory men about her, giving them nine places in her first Cabinet and moderate Whigs only three. Before the end of the summer a general election had returned her a Tory Parliament. The moderate Tory, Robert Harley, was elected Speaker of the House of Commons. The Whigs, although dominant in the Lords, saw themselves as public enemies – yet only they could fully support the war.

In the early summer of 1702 Marlborough set off with everybody's good wishes to conduct the first of his ten campaigns in the War of the Spanish Succession. Campaigns in the eighteenth century, like pheasants in the twentieth, had their seasons. They lasted from April to October, or later if the weather was good and the matter in hand unfinished. After that the troops packed up and made for winter quarters, while their commanders set off on diplomatic rounds to concert plans for the following year's campaign and to try and extract the necessary money and supplies from their leaders at home.

It is to be remembered that Marlborough was never in supreme command. In July 1702 he was made Deputy Captain-General of the Republic and, as such, was the foremost general in the European armies massed against France, but every action had to be taken after consultation with the two Dutch deputies assigned to his expedition. On the whole these were cautious men who adhered to the conventions of eighteenth-century warfare – manoeuvres and sieges – and who anyway had themselves to refer back to higher authority at The Hague. Marlborough was above all things imaginative and daring; the Dutch deputies were not. They fought according to the text book and throughout the war their hindrance caused him enormous frustration and baulked many of his bold schemes. But had he had a freer rein perhaps the boast that he had never entered a battle he did not win could not have been made.

Daniel Defoe said: 'Now it is frequent to have armies of fifty thousand men of a side standing at bay within sight of one another, and spend a whole campaign in dodging – or, as it is genteely termed – observing one another, and then march off into winter quarters'. Sieges also were sanctioned. There were many reasons for this: since there was a formalised method of siege warfare and prescribed rules for the showing of a white flag they were easy to conduct; at the end of the year towns taken could be notched up on the scoreboard and then used in peace negotiations; and furthermore Flanders was so heavily punctuated with fortresses that they could not be ignored. The eighteenth century had a conscience about bloodshed, and sieges were thought to be less costly in human life than battles. But Marlborough preferred battles. He would like to have followed Turenne's dictum: 'Make few sieges and fight plenty of battles; when you are master of the countryside the villages will give us the town'.

The French in 1702 were poised to swoop down on to Holland and gobble it up. They held every fortress along the Rhine and the Meuse with the exception of the tough and important Maastricht. Marlborough declared to the Dutch that he would 'rid them of their troublesome neighbours' and spent that first campaign manoeuvring along the Meuse. His tactics irked the French and they were obliged to abandon their positions along it. Marlborough mooted battle no less than four times when he considered the conditions favourable, but the Dutch exercised their veto each time. Marlborough even sent an apology to the French commanders, Boufflers and his nephew, Arabella's son, the Duke of Berwick, for the lack of sport. But by the end of the season Kaiserwerth, Venloo, Ruremonde, Stevensweert, Liège and later Rheinberg had capitulated and given the Allies command of the navigation of the Rhine and the Meuse. They dispersed into winter quarters well pleased with the results.

Louis was peeved, having found the Allied army a more cohesive and formidable force than he had anticipated. Queen Anne was, of course, delighted. 'It is very uneasy to your poor, unfortunate,

45

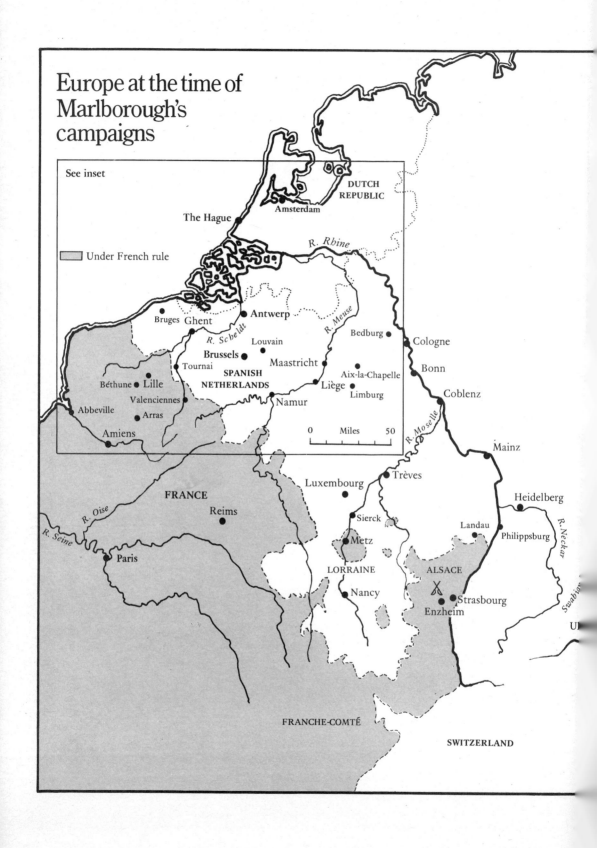

Europe at the time of Marlborough's campaigns

See inset

DUTCH REPUBLIC

Amsterdam

The Hague

Under French rule

R. Rhine

Bruges Ghent Antwerp

Bedburg Cologne

R. Scheldt Louvain

R. Meuse

Brussels Maastricht Bonn

Tournai

Béthune Lille SPANISH NETHERLANDS Aix-la-Chapelle Coblenz

Valenciennes Liège Limburg

Abbeville Arras Namur

Amiens

0 Miles 50

R. Moselle

Mainz

Luxembourg Trèves

FRANCE

R. Oise Reims Heidelberg

R. Seine Sierck Landau

Metz Philippsburg

R. Neckar

Paris LORRAINE ALSACE

Nancy Strasbourg

Enzheim

Swabia

FRANCHE-COMTÉ

SWITZERLAND

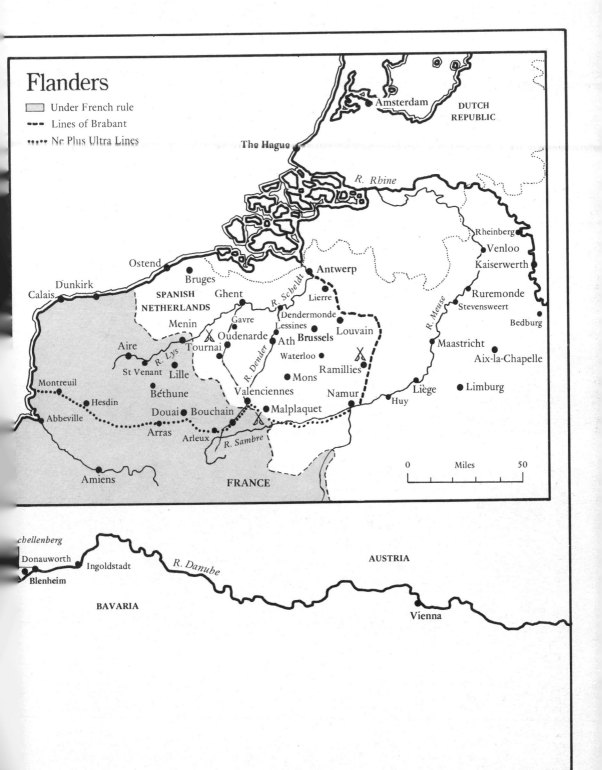

Flanders

- Under French rule
- --- Lines of Brabant
- ••••• Ne Plus Ultra Lines

Amsterdam

DUTCH
REPUBLIC

The Hague

R. Rhine

Rheinberg

Venloo

Kaiserwerth

Ostend

Bruges

Antwerp

Ruremonde

Calais
Dunkirk

SPANISH
NETHERLANDS

Ghent

R. Scheldt

Lierre

Stevensweert

Bedburg

Menin

Gavre

Dendermonde

Lessines

Louvain

Maastricht

Aire

Tournai

Oudenarde

Ath

Brussels

Aix-la-Chapelle

St Venant

R. Lys

Lille

Waterloo

Ramillies

Montreuil

R. Dender

Mons

Namur

Liège

Limburg

Hesdin

Béthune

Valenciennes

Huy

Abbeville

Douai

Bouchain

Malplaquet

Arras

Arleux

R. Sambre

Amiens

FRANCE

0   Miles   50

chellenberg

Donauworth

Ingoldstadt

R. Danube

AUSTRIA

Blenheim

BAVARIA

Vienna

John, Marquis of Blandford, painted by Kneller. To the great sorrow of his parents, he died of smallpox at the age of seventeen in 1703. His godfather, Godolphin, said that he was 'not only the best-natured and the most agreeable but the most free-thinking and reasonable creature that one can imagine for his age.'

faithful Morley', she wrote to Sarah, 'to think she has so very little in her power to show how truly sensible I am of all my Lord Marlborough's kindness, especially at a time when he deserves all that a rich Crown could give. But since there is nothing else at this time, I hope you will give me leave, as soon as he comes, to make him a duke. I know my dear Mrs Freeman does not care for anything of that kind, nor I am not satisfied with it, because it does not express the value I have for Mr Freeman, nor nothing can ever express how passionately I am yours, my dear Mrs Freeman'. Sarah was, indeed, opposed to the title, having, she said, 'no taste for grandeur'. But Marlborough accepted the dukedom; it gave him a firmer diplomatic standing in Europe – and he liked the honour. Anne was also keen to give him £5,000 a year, but this he declined because of the political storm such a gift would cause. So she offered him £2,000 a year from her privy purse instead; this also was refused, although eight years later Sarah, out of favour, reminded Anne of the offer and Anne most generously paid up, arrears and all.

48

That winter, while Parliament squabbled over the Occasional Conformity Bill, Marlborough was back with his family. In February 1703 his third daughter, Elizabeth, married the Earl of Bridgwater – a happy occasion. But later that month his seventeen-year-old son and heir, the Marquis of Blandford, died of smallpox in Cambridge. He had been a fine and promising boy and it was a terrible blow to the Marlboroughs both as parents and potential dynasts. Marlborough confided to Lord Ailesbury: 'I have lost what is so dear to me, it is fit for me to retire and not toil and labour for I know not who'. A few weeks later, after altering his will, he sailed sadly for The Hague. It is interesting to note that, but for a reversion to it by the fifth Duke of Marlborough, the name Churchill would have died in the family with that young Marquis.

It was a depressing start to what was to be a disappointing campaign. Marlborough intended in 1703 to capture Bonn, the sole obstacle to the control of the Rhine for the 300 miles from its mouth to Philippsburg. He then wanted to take Lierre and Antwerp on the coast, thus destroying the French lines that guarded Brabant. Bonn fell in May, but the Dutch blocked part two of the 'Grand Design'. Marlborough remained tactful, courteous, calm, but in his letters home he expressed his exasperation. The Queen urged him to continue and wrote: 'I never will forsake your dear self Mr Freeman nor Mr Montgomery, but always be your constant faithful servant, and we four must never part'. So he polished off the season by personally directing the siege of Limburg, an activity that proved most therapeutic. When the time came to disband, the Allies were able to notch up Bonn, Huy and Limburg, but it was the French who left the field with the higher morale and the more advantageous position for 1704. In fact, because of the setbacks on the Upper Rhine to the Imperial commander, the Margrave of Baden, and because of the defection to the French of the Elector of Bavaria, the fall of Vienna looked certain. France was poised to plunge at the Empire and strike a deadly blow to the Habsburgs.

Marlborough was acutely aware of the gravity of the situation and formulated for the coming year his boldest scheme so far. So bold was it that he realised that the faint-hearted Dutch deputies would never give their approval – so he decided not to tell them about it. Not only would he dupe the French, but he would dupe his colleagues as well. Failure of the plan would bring the most dire recriminations, but such a consideration did not trouble him. He planned to march to the Danube.

Leaving a token defence force in Flanders he intended to lead the main body of the army along the Rhine, across the Neckar and then east through the Swabian Jura to the Danube – in all 250 miles.

There he would join forces with the Imperial army, confront and defeat the French and the Bavarians, and thereby save Vienna and also the all-important Grand Alliance. 'Should I act otherwise,' he declared, 'the Empire would be undone, and consequently the Confederacy.' Not only were the logistics of such a march formidable, but the chances of the troops being in a fit state to fight after trudging such a distance were also slim. He hoped that the French would keep pace with him on the south bank of the Rhine, expecting him to turn south and attack at any time; with any luck they would not detect his true strategy until he was well away into the hills of the Swabian Jura. The Dutch he hoped to cajole along with him; once certain places were reached they would have no choice but to support the next move. Marlborough told Godolphin: 'My intentions are to march to Coblenz and to declare that I intend to campaign on the Moselle. But when I come there, to write to the Dutch states that I think it absolutely necessary for the saving of the Empire to march with the troops under my command to join with those that are in Germany that are in Her Majesty's and the Dutch pay, in order to take measures with Prince Lewis of Baden for the speedy reduction of the Elector of Bavaria.' In terms of eighteenth century warfare it was breathtaking.

On 19 May 1704 twenty-one thousand Allied troops set off due east from Bedburg, murmuring loudly about campaigning on the Moselle. Like a 'scarlet caterpillar' they wound their way along the Rhine. The Moselle joins the Rhine at Coblenz, and when at Coblenz the caterpillar failed to wheel south down the Moselle, but crossed over it and pressed on east along the Rhine, the French, 'observing' under Marshal Villeroi, were puzzled. At this stage the Allies were joined by five thousand Prussians and Hanoverians. Were the thin Allied force left behind in the Netherlands to be attacked by the French, it could always be speedily reinforced by Marlborough's troops whipping back down the Rhine on barges. But that danger did not seem very great as the main body of the French, thirty thousand men, was with Villeroi shadowing Marlborough along the Rhine. The Dutch sized up the security of the situation in the west and voted him further troops. When the 'scarlet caterpillar' reached Mainz it seemed likely that Strasbourg was its objective, particularly as bridges were being built at Philippsburg on Marlborough's orders, and a frisson ran through the French army – Louis was especially sensitive about Strasbourg. Only to Marshal Tallard, now approaching from the south, did it occur that Marlborough might have designs on the Danube. Not until after 3 June, when the cavalry, followed by the infantry under General Charles Churchill, Marlborough's brother, had crossed the Neckar

Prince Eugene of Savoy
(1663–1736) was an
eccentric bachelor whose
'only passion was warfare'.
He was, for Marlborough,
the one Allied general on
whom he felt he could rely,
his most dependable
colleague in battle.

and headed away from the Rhine into the hills, did the French fully
realise what was happening. The news, when it reached Versailles,
caused a sensation. For Marlborough there was now no going back –
he had declared his hand; action was assured. He met the two other
Allied generals, Prince Lewis, Margrave of Baden, and Prince
Eugene of Savoy at Gros Heppach on 12 June. With a vast Allied
force of one hundred and ten thousand in close contact and good
order the trumps were now in their hands. The enemy was separated
(Villeroi and Tallard near Landau and Marsin and the Elector near
Ulm) disorganised and unsure what to do next. Tallard and the
Elector of Bavaria did not manage to concert their forces until
5 August, Tallard having taken five weeks to complete a march only
half as long as that made by the 'scarlet caterpillar'. The caterpillar,
averaging ten miles a day (marching in the early morning and resting
in the heat of the day), had taken less than six weeks to cover 250
miles, and at the end of it was, to Marlborough's credit, in excellent
shape. His trusted aides, William Cadogan, Adam Cardonnel and

Henry Davenant, had taken the greatest care of the details: ample gold and bread had been carried with them, the larger, heavier guns had been left behind (it was hoped, vainly as it turned out, that the Imperialists would have some to spare), a new pair of shoes for everyone had been waiting at Heidelberg. 'We generally began our march about three in the morning,' wrote Captain Parker, 'proceeded about four leagues or four and a half by day, and reached our camping ground by nine. As we marched through the country of our Allies commissars were appointed to furnish us with all manner of necessaries for man and horse; these were brought to the ground before we arrived, and the soldiers had nothing to do but pitch their tents, boil their kettles and lie down to rest.' Such efficient organisation had paid off. Prince Eugene of Savoy complimented Marlborough on his troops and added: 'Money, which you don't want in England, will buy fine horses, but it can't buy that lively air I see in every one of those troopers' faces'.

It was the first time that Marlborough and Eugene had met and their mutual liking and understanding was immediate. Prince Eugene was a hot-tempered and unprepossessing forty-year-old bachelor. He was a soldier of genius, which is what the other Imperial commander, the tetchy and unreliable Margrave of Baden, was not. The Margrave was, however, the senior of the three in rank and experience (having fought against the Turks for many years). From this moment Prince Eugene always acted in complete accord with Marlborough, never seeking to exert his own authority or question a decision for which he could not at first see a reason, and Marlborough in turn trusted him implicitly. Their high opinion of each other never wavered, and several campaigns later Marlborough remarked: 'I not only esteem, but really love that Prince'.

So Eugene, whom Marlborough could trust, was left with 28,000 men to defend the Lines of Stollhofen on the Upper Rhine, while he and the Margrave, whom Marlborough wanted to keep in his sight, moved on east to seek out the Elector of Bavaria. Their first success was the storming of the Schellenburg Heights, which they accomplished straight after a fifteen-mile march. It was difficult and bloody but it precipitated the capitulation of Donauworth on the Danube, and thus gave the Allies a valuable bridgehead and communications point on the river. It was an expensive prize – both sides suffered about 5,000 casualties – and reactions at home were mixed. Addison wrote:

> How many generous Britons meet their doom,
> New to the field, and heroes in the bloom!
> Th'illustrious youths, that left their native shore

> To march where Britons never marched before,
> (O fatal love of fame! O glorious heat,
> Only destructive to the brave and great!)
> After such toils o'ercome, such dangers past,
> Stretched on Bavarian ramparts breathe their last.

The Allies then spent July shamefully ransacking the Bavarian countryside. Marlborough hoped thus to bully the Elector into submission, but the Elector remained defiant as support, in the shape of Marshal Tallard and his army, was slowly drawing nearer. (Tallard was a lavish entertainer – unlike Marlborough, who was always criticized for his stinginess and meagre table – and his procession included two mule trains of good food and the best wine, which perhaps in part accounted for his tardy arrival.)

On 7 August the Margrave went off with fifteen thousand men to besiege Ingoldstadt on the Danube; his personal absence may have been of greater benefit to Marlborough than the numerical presence of his men. On the 8th Tallard finally reached the Bavarians. On the 11th Marlborough and Eugene came together near Donauwörth. The following day Tallard camped at Blenheim, and early on the 13th the Allies advanced on their sleeping camp. There were 56,000 French and Bavarians with 90 cannon to 52,000 Allies and 66 cannon, so when the French saw the movement in the Allied camp they instantly assumed that they were up and off for, according to the rules of the game, the inferior force in such a position would gently retreat. But to their surprise they soon realised that they were under attack. The battle proper began at half past twelve. Marlborough, as Addison put it:

> In peaceful Thought the Field of Death surveyed,
> To fainting Squadrons sent the timely aid,
> Inspir'd repuls'd Battalions to engage,
> And taught the doubtful Battel where to rage.

The 'Battel' was decided by six when Marlborough scribbled a note to Sarah on the back of a bill of tavern: 'I have not time to say more but to beg you will give my duty to the Queen, and let her know her army has had a glorious victory. Monsieur Tallard and two other Generals are in my coach and I am following the rest . . .'

As night fell the Regiment of Navarre ceremoniously burnt their colours to prevent them falling into enemy hands (which already held 200 other colours and standards) and the remnant of the Franco-Bavarian force limped off towards Strasbourg.

> Till the dark Cope of Night with kind Embrace
> Befriends the Rout and covers their Disgrace.

A French illustration of the Battle of Blenheim. In
the foreground the battle still rages but in the
distance (fig. 7) French soldiers flee across the
Danube (fig. 6). On the left is the village of Blenheim
(fig. 2) under attack by the Allies.

For the first time in centuries England had assumed the military leadership in Europe and Louis was forced to forget his plans of expansion and think of safeguarding what he already had. With 'the dissipation of that alarm which the French arms had long inspired', the Allies could even contemplate Paris as a goal.

The broad tactics used by Marlborough at the battle of Blenheim (and again at Ramillies and Malplaquet) were to attack both enemy flanks vigorously, thereby hoping to make the enemy call on its forces in the centre to reinforce the flanks; then, at the crucial moment, he would lunge into the weakened centre with his cavalry and split the enemy line in two. By the time of Malplaquet the French were wise to this ruse, and consequently the slaughter there was enormous.

The Margrave, of course, was extremely cross at having been left out of the victorious action, and the resentment that he harboured for a long time rebounded on the Grand Alliance.

When Marlborough, tired and plagued with headaches, reached London in December he was greeted with exultation and triumphal parades. The Queen could not wait to shower him with more good things; she determined that he should have £5,000 a year for life – no refusing this time – and that he should become Colonel of the 1st Guards. She also gave him the Royal Manor and Park of Woodstock near Oxford where she would build at her expense a magnificent castle of Blenheim for him and Sarah. Marlborough liked Castle Howard in Yorkshire and so he asked its architect, John Vanbrugh, to draw up plans for his new house at Woodstock. He already had the title for his posterity, now he would have the house and land to complement it (fifteen thousand acres bringing in £6,000 a year was most fitting).

Bolstered by the victory of 1704, Marlborough set his sights on Paris for 1705. He proposed to leave most of the allied force on the defensive in Flanders and, together with the Margrave, to thrust forward up the Moselle through Lorraine towards Paris. The Margrave, suffering from a bad toe, was in a thoroughly bad temper and altogether at his most uncooperative. Marlborough was obliged to wait for him without rations near Sterk, some way up the Moselle – in vain; the Margrave never came with his reinforcements, and Marlborough was forced to retire and abandon the plan, much to the relief of the Dutch who did not care for his, indeed, precarious position up the Moselle.

He found consolation in piercing the lines of Brabant, which he succeeded in doing by wily outmanoeuvring of the enemy. In so doing he broke the deadlock in that theatre of the war. But he was then denied a battle at Waterloo, chiefly by General Slangenburg, the most restrictive Dutch general. Had Marlborough won his Waterloo he would have destroyed French power in the Netherlands. As it was Villeroi heaved a sigh of relief. He saw Marlborough as 'a furious wild beast. True it was caged by the Dutch veto, but it was tearing at the bars, and at any moment might break out in frightful strength and rage'.

If Paris had been the goal of 1705, Italy was the objective of 1706. Marlborough devised a scheme of marching to Italy where things had not been going at all the Allies' way. But vigorous French action against the Margrave on the Upper Rhine and total lack of enthusiasm from his colleagues put paid to that idea, and as usual he found himself firmly planted in Flanders. Louis, partly to mask the economic exhaustion in his country and partly as a bid for a reasonable peace, had ordered his generals to be more aggressive, and

OPPOSITE Marlborough's note to Sarah hastily written on the back of a tavern bill on the evening of the battle of Blenheim informing her of the victory. Colonel Parkes carried the note across Europe and delivered it to Sarah, who told him to take it to the Queen. 'It was the custom to give the messenger of victory five hundred guineas, but Colonel Parkes, invited to name his reward, asked instead a miniature of the Queen. His request was granted, and in addition Anne gave him a thousand guineas in her relief and joy.'

57

Marlborough was suddenly confronted by a French army which had crossed the Dyle and was seeking battle. Never one to shirk such a challenge, he entered the field of Ramillies on 23 May in good spirits and with confidence. Because of dense fog the two armies did not know they were so close and, when it lifted on the morning of the 23rd, they were surprised to see each other ranged out in full splendour.

By using roughly the same tactics as at Blenheim – ferocious attacks on the enemy's wings followed by a deep plunge into the centre of the line – the Allies won the day; a victory made all the more glorious by an effective pursuit afterwards. The French army was shattered and poor Villeroi, routed by the 'wild beast', was to answer for the disaster. The citizens of Belgium declared themselves for Charles III (the Allied candidate for the Spanish throne) and, as Marlborough entered Brussels, other towns in the Spanish Nether-lands (Ghent, Bruges etc) fell like ninepins. When Vendome arrived from Italy to replace the discredited Villeroi he remarked: 'Every-body here is only too ready to raise their hats at the mention of Marlborough's name'. With Dendermonde, Menin and Ath in the bag at the end of the campaign and Prince Eugene successful in Northern Italy, it had been a wonderful year for the Allies. Never would Marlborough's star shine as brilliantly again. Never could the Grand Alliance be so united. Never again would that gang of friends, Mrs Morley, Mr Montgomery, Mr and Mrs Freeman, be as true to each other and as inseparable as they had been. The days of England's undivided commitment to the war were numbered.

The snag at home was that Anne, since becoming Queen, had grown more and more disaffected with Sarah. Sarah had not noticed the change and continued to harangue Anne with her Whig views, completely failing to take into account Anne's loathing of anything Whig. She failed even to notice that she had been supplanted as Anne's closest friend. The new favourite was a young cousin and, ironically, a protegée of Sarah, Abigail Hill. The truth dawned early in 1707 with the secret marriage of Miss Hill and Colonel Masham. When Sarah chided Abigail for not informing her of the event it emerged that the Queen had not only connived at it but had actually been present at the ceremony. Sarah had been excluded and was furious.

Abigail had another influential cousin, Robert Harley, the moder-ate Tory who was Speaker of the House of Commons. As the Queen turned more and more towards Abigail so too did Harley, seeking to influence the Queen through her new confidante. And as the Queen began to listen to Harley so she began to listen less to her wise old friend and trusted Treasurer, Godolphin. The trouble was that the

OPPOSITE This picture by Sir Godfrey Kneller shows the Queen presenting, as he described it, 'a Model of Blenheim drawn on paper' to 'a warlike Vigorous figure representing Millitarry Meritt'. Architecture and Posterity look on, while an Eagle holds 'an Imperiall Laurell Crown' over 'Millitary Meritt's' head. Victory is on the far left, and beside him is Hercules. Below the Queen is 'the Golden Cornucopia Shead by her Majesty's Affections.' History is sitting on the right writing on a 'winged Hour Glass (Signifying Perpetuall Record)', and behind History are some 'figures of Plenty'. Apollo is overhead. It was commissioned by Anne in 1708, but this, a sketch for a larger picture, was all that Kneller did, because of a 'State Difference happening between the Queen and the Duke of Marlborough'.

Whig junto now sat very firmly in the seat of government and so Godolphin as Lord Treasurer was, willy-nilly, chained to them. When they demanded and obtained the appointment of the Earl of Sunderland (Marlborough's Whig son-in-law) as Secretary of State, Anne was not only infuriated but also felt threatened, her power checked. Since she now associated Godolphin with the dreadful (as she considered) Whigs, she was happy to heed Harley's Tory counsel at Godolphin's expense. Marlborough also lost his special position with the Queen and had to bow before the Whig wind. The French, more cowed than ever before, might have been prepared for peace after the 1706 campaign, but the Allies, bucked by their success, were now committed to 'no peace without Spain' (i.e. they wanted the entire Spanish inheritance for their candidate, Charles III); this had not been their demand at the outset of the war and was certainly too heady for Louis. Peace was not, therefore, close.

So Marlborough's fertile mind formulated another grandiose strategy. He was always capable of seeing the situation as a whole, of seeing the war in its continental perspective. His sight was never restricted to the river valleys of Flanders. This time he intended to attack the South of France. A combined naval and military action at Toulon on the Mediterranean would, he hoped, draw French forces away from Flanders and out of Spain and so leave room for the Allies to surge forward in Flanders and also relieve the severe pressure on them in Spain. Only Vienna did not appreciate the plan and the trusty Prince Eugene, who was to lead the expedition, did not like the sea or anything to do with it. He was not keen, but he complied.

However before Prince Eugene had even started marching along the coast from Italy towards Toulon, the Duke of Berwick, the formidable young French commander of Churchill blood, won a decisive victory over General Galway at Almanza in Spain (it was a victory of an English general in command of French troops over a French general in command of English troops). This was an enormous setback to any Allied prospects in Spain. Then Marshal Villars caught the Imperialists napping on the Rhine, and swiftly and silently took the lines of Stollhofen from the Margrave of Bayreuth (the successor to the Margrave of Baden, who had perished in January from his festering toe). Dismayed by the strength of its defences, Prince Eugene retired from Toulon after a few feeble assaults, and so nothing was achieved there either. Marlborough had pinned his hopes on that operation, and its failure, together with the earlier disasters in the other theatres of the war made him 'much out of humour and peevish'. France had almost effortlessly kicked off the terriers snapping at her heels.

Nor was there much solace for Marlborough back in England: his wife was quarrelling with everybody; the Queen was turning sour on Godolphin; his brother, Admiral George Churchill, was accused of maladministration and corruption at the Admiralty; the Whigs were supreme. Despite these developments the Duke was still highly influential and as great a celebrity as ever. But the commotion caused by the post mortem on the fiasco at Almanza obliged both Marlborough and Godolphin to tender their resignations. It was a moment of triumph for Harley. But the country was not yet ready to dispose of its Captain-General and its Treasurer, and in the event it was Harley who had to back down – albeit temporarily. The Whigs were again victorious and the Queen was not pleased. Any chance of a reconciliation between Anne and Sarah was now dim and the Queen's relationships with Marlborough and Godolphin, who were now obliged to execute Whig policy, were bleak. The abortive Jacobite invasion in March only served to strengthen the Whig hand (as it was the Tories who were tainted with Jacobitism) and to return them with a large majority after the election in May.

Back went Marlborough to Flanders where the French, under Vendome and Burgundy (Louis's nephew), held the initiative and were inching forward. By the beginning of July 1708 they were masters of the middle Scheldt and so formed a barrier between Marlborough and the coast. Marlborough, bent as always on confrontation, hurtled towards them and forestalled them at the River Dender at Lessines. The French, having no idea that it was the main body of the Allied army that had reached Lessines, withdrew to the River Scheldt without undue haste. On the night of 10 July they camped at Gavre on the east side of the Scheldt, intending to cross to the west the following day. Their general plan was to hold the Scheldt. Marlborough meanwhile dashed the fifteen miles from Lessines to a point on the Scheldt a little way south of the French, and then hurried as many troops as possible across the river. Vendome was staggered when he was told that the Allied army was so close; only the dust rising from their marching columns convinced him they were there. From that moment, early on 11 July, it was a race to see which army could rally itself into reasonable battle formation quickest. Since the two huge forces were essentially on the move, rather than formally lined up as was usual, generalship would be crucial. In the end the 80,000 Allied troops benefited from Marlborough's brilliant masterminding of the action – again he had 'taught the doubtful Battel where to rage' – and from the division and confusion among the French commanders, and emerged the victors from the field of the battle of Oudenarde. After darkness had fallen the French troops, of which there had been 85,000 at the out-

set, retreated in disorder to Ghent. Some Huguenot officers in the Allied army called out the names of French regiments in the darkness – 'A moi, Picardie', 'A moi Roussillon', – and many unwitting French soldiers were taken prisoner in this way.

The initiative in Flanders was thus wrested from the French and the shattered state of their army enabled the Allies to notch up further successes in August and September. Lille, with defences brilliantly designed by Vauban, was thought to be unassailable, but after four months dogged bombardment by the Allies it capitulated on 10 December. At the very end of the year Marlborough determined to recapture Bruges and Ghent, which had surrendered to Burgundy back in June. No sooner had he achieved this than early in 1709 a powerful frost gripped Flanders and brought the season of warfare sharply to an end. The frost tightened its grip and did not let go until March. Coming after a poor harvest, it caused frightful famine throughout France. Livestock perished, seedcorn shrivelled in its bed, soldiers on the march literally froze to death. The bitter cold, lack of food and shrunken economy all but forced France to accept the Allied peace terms. Not only were there secret negotiations between Grand Pensionary Heinsius and Versailles, but Marlborough was also corresponding on the same subject with his nephew Berwick, reminding him of a previous offer from Versailles of two million gold livres for his part in arranging an acceptable peace. But as the Whigs clung to 'No peace without Spain', so the French held out.

In England the rifts in the old partnership were widening and becoming harder to seal. Sarah's behaviour was more tactless and her reproaches to Anne more vehement, and Anne was sick of her. In the coach on the way to a thanksgiving service for the victory of Oudenarde at St Paul's they had a row about Anne's jewels, which were the responsibility of Sarah as Mistress of the Robes, and Sarah told the Queen to shut up. Sarah was present at the deathbed of the pathetic Prince George in October 1708 and behaved with indelicacy. Eventually she began to keep away from court. Anne, smitten with grief by the death of her husband and riddled with gout, leant heavily on Abigail. Sarah had healthy children and grandchildren, not to speak of a victorious husband. Anne, by contrast, had no children and her husband, poor 'Est-il possible', considered by many a buffoon, was now dead. To make matters worse the new power of the Whigs made Anne feel her royal authority curbed. Marlborough, sensible of the precariousness of his position in the changed atmosphere, hoped to be given the Captain-Generalcy for life, and he searched the offices of the Privy Seal for a precedent.

Marlborough's victory at Oudernarde depicted in a tapestry at Blenheim Palace. Three rooms at Blenheim are hung with tapestries of Marlborough's campaigns, commissioned by the Duke from the designer de Hondt and the Brussels weaver Judocus de Vos.

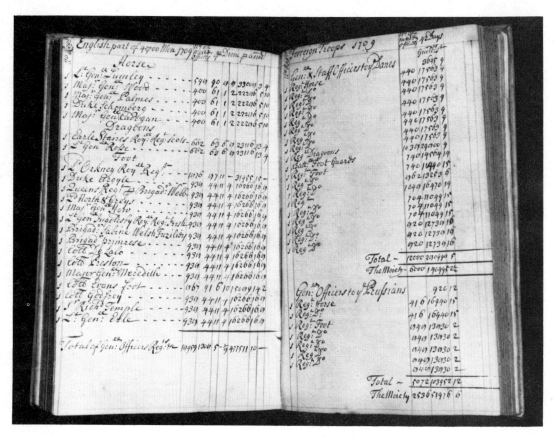

Marlborough's battle order book for the year 1709.

The outrageousness of the Allied peace terms, in particular Article 37, which stipulated 'that the whole monarchy of Spain is delivered up and yielded to King Charles III', goaded the battered French into further action. Gold and silver plate was melted down to finance another campaign. The famished army struggled into order under the loud-mouthed, ostentatious but effective Marshal Villars to fight for a better peace. By mid-June 1709 the two armies, each affected by the problem of forage and supply, were mustered once again in Flanders. The Allies set about Tournai, lost a lot of men in taking it and went on to invest Mons. It was in the neighbourhood of Mons that on 11 September Marlborough fought his last and his bloodiest battle. Villars, bent on intervening in the siege of Mons, confronted the Allied army at the village of Malplaquet. Unlike the mobile and unorthodox battle of Oudenarde, this was a battle of classic formation, on which Marlborough tried to impose his well-tried tactics of flank attacks followed by a thurst in the centre. He was only just successful; it was judged an Allied victory, but on points rather than a knock-out. The result was that Mons fell and that two war-weary armies were pulverised. About 25,000 Allied soldiers were killed or wounded out of an army of 110,000. The Dutch in particular suffered very heavy casualties and the French lost perhaps 12,000 of a smaller army of 80,000. The French resistance had been stalwart and France had again deflected the blow that the Allies might have struck at her heart. Villars, with one leg smashed by a cannon ball, was applauded for his effort.

Marlborough asked the Queen outright for the Captain-Generalcy for life. She refused, adding: 'You seem to be dissatisfied with my behaviour to the Duchess of Marlborough. I do not love complaining, but it is impossible to help saying on this occasion I believe nobody was ever so used by a friend as I have been by her ever since my coming to the crown. I desire nothing but that she would leave off teasing and tormenting me and behave herself with the decency she ought both to her friend and Queen'. The next day she wrote to Sarah: 'It is impossible for you to recover my former kindness, but I shall behave myself to you as the Duke of Marlborough's wife and as my Groom of the Stole'. Marlborough had written to Sarah in August, just before the battle of Malplaquet, when his mind might well have been on other matters: 'It has always been my observation in disputes, especially in that of kindness and friendship, that all reproaches, though ever so just, serve to no end but to make the breach wider'. Unfortunately it was not in Sarah's nature to listen to such judicious advice, and she wrote a tirade to Anne, reminding her of her former 'kindness' and piling reproach on reproach. Anne did not reply.

Marlborough had added in this letter to Sarah in August: 'If anybody had told me eight years ago that after such great Success, and after you had been a faithful servant twenty-seven years that even in the Queen's Life-time we should be obliged to seek Happiness in a retired Life, I could not have believed that possible.'

But although favour was fast diminishing, a retired life was still some while away. It was Abigail's family who began to receive plum appointments, and concern about the power of Abigail 'the chambermaid' grew in Marlborough's and Godolphin's minds. After the foolish impeachment by the Whigs of Dr Sacheverell, the high-flyer accused of preaching a seditious sermon on that emotional topic 'the Church in Danger', it was but a matter of time before the Whigs toppled and crashed. Marlborough thought it wise to leave early for The Hague that spring. In April, Sarah was granted her last audience with the Queen, who repeated coldly to her: 'Whatever you have to say, you may put it in writing'. Sarah felt that Anne was so unreasonable 'that I could not conquer myself, but said the most disrespectful thing I ever spoke to the Queen in my life'. But any remorse was short-lived. She felt that her insubordination was 'what such an occasion and such circumstances might well excuse if not justify'. Such was her inability ever to conceive of being in the wrong.

With Sarah out of favour, Godolphin almost powerless and the Whigs' fall inevitable, Marlborough's position was weak. The reins he held in Flanders might snap or be taken from him at any moment. The dismissal of Sunderland, the Whig Secretary of State and Marlborough's son-in-law, was also imminent. Anne loathed him. Marlborough beseeched her not to sack him until the end of the year for the sake of the campaign. Sarah could not resist butting in: 'I was overcome,' she wrote later, 'by the consideration of Lord Marlborough, Lord Sunderland and the publick interest and wrote ... to the Queen ... begging, for Lord Marlborough's sake, that she would not give him such a blow, of which I dreaded the consequence, putting her in mind of her letter about the Duke upon the victory of Blenheim ...'. After a harsh reply from the Queen, Sarah wrote: 'I could not forbear, for my own vindication, to write a second letter ...'. The result was 'whether my interfering in this matter hastened the execution of the design, I cannot say. Certain it is that I did not retard it, for Lord Sunderland was presently after dismissed from his office'.

While Marlborough was conducting a comparatively gentle campaign in Europe (both armies were wary of bloodshed after the carnage of Malplaquet) the situation at home deteriorated rapidly from his point of view; the Queen curtly and callously dismissed her old friend Godolphin in late August 1710. That, followed by a Tory landslide in the election in October, had deprived Marlborough of all political support at home. He was on his own, his power severely docked. One historian has written that Malplaquet 'was less important to the peoples of Europe than the bloodless change of ministry in England'. When the Duke returned in January 1711 with the fortresses of Douai, Béthune, St Venant and Aire under his belt, he found he was not at all popular with the new Tory ministry of Harley, St John, Buckingham and Rochester, for it was bent on peace. He saw no future in staying in England and within six weeks had returned to Europe, having first delivered up his wife's gold key of the Wardrobe to the Queen. It had been a humiliating occasion. Anne had demanded the key in three days and Marlborough, on bended knee, had pleaded with her for ten, whereupon Anne had insisted on two. As Marlborough hatched the plans for what was to be his last campaign against France, Louis was delighted to hear of the turn of events in England.

The previous year, on his birthday in May 1710, Marlborough had said: 'I am this day three score, but I thank God I find myself in good health that I hope to end this campaign without being sensible of the inconvenience of old age'. Yet at the end of it he was tired and drawn; his exhausted condition had been much remarked upon during his short spell in England that winter, and his migraines were as bad as ever and accompanied by 'giddiness and swimmings in my head, which also gave me often sickness in my stomach'. But nothing impaired the brilliance of his generalship in this, his last campaign. With an army of 90,000, he intended to pierce the Ne Plus Ultra lines. These constituted a strong ninety-mile front from the Flemish coast to Namur and were defended by a French army of 120,000 under that stalwart showman, the general that France looked on as her last hope, Marshal Villars, who had rigged up his shattered leg in an iron contraption. Marlborough began by taking Arleux and, after strengthening its defences, moved westwards along the lines. One French detachment immediately recaptured Arleux and demolished its defences – an action that suited Marlborough – while Villars and the rest of the army shadowed the Allied force. Near Arras the Allied army formed up as if to strike at the lines, but even as the columns moved into position the artillery surreptitiously crept away eastwards. Then more detachments followed the artillery until, when night had fallen, Marlborough ordered all the troops, to their amazement, to march at top speed back the way they had come to Arleux. It was a tall order – forty miles in eighteen hours – and some infantry fell by the wayside. Five hours later the French realised what had happened and raced after them on their side of the lines. They had a shorter and better road, but it was the allies who reached the defenceless Arleux first and, with the greatest of ease and the minimum of bloodshed, were able to cross over the enemy lines. As the troops poured through, Villars saw that he had been superbly outgeneralled. It had been a neat, courageous and highly risky operation. The French could not face a battle and Marlborough with his inferior numbers for once did not seek one, but turned his attention to the fortress of Bouchain.

Bouchain was a formidable proposition. Captain Parker, who was there, said:

I must confess I did not like the aspect of the thing. We plainly saw that their entrenchment was a perfect bulwark, strong and lofty, and crowded with men and cannon pointed directly at us . . . But while I was musing, the Duke of Marlborough rode up quite unattended and alone . . . It is quite impossible for me express the joy, which the sight of this man gave me at this very critical moment. I was now well satisfied, that he would not push the thing unless he saw a strong probability of success.

And indeed he ordered the army to retire. But before the middle of

September, by very complicated and ingenious tactics, he had forced Bouchain to 'beat a parley'. It was a triumph. He was now able to look down the River Oise to Paris, which was separated from him by only two small fortresses. But the peace negotiations on which the new Tory ministry had embarked were too far advanced for the government to be able to countenance such a direction for the war.

To all but Marlborough's detractors in England, the campaign had been impressive; it seems no less so now. 'The pure military artistry with which he deceived Villars', a recent historian has written of the early part of the campaign, 'has few equals in the annals of military history'. Perhaps the fact that three tapestries at Blenheim commemorate 1711 shows that Marlborough, who never uttered a word about his battles and sieges once they were done, was proud of that year's achievement.

Three weeks after the capitulation of Bouchain, as Marlborough was on his way home, preliminaries for a separate peace between Great Britain and France were signed. The Tories did not feel they had to stand by the commitments of the Whigs and so the other partners in the Grand Alliance were left somewhat in the lurch. Sir Winston Churchill pointed an accusing finger back through time at those Tories:

Just as they had obtained power, not by free debate in Parliament, but by a backstairs intrigue with the Queen, so they sought a peace by a greedy and treacherous desertion of their allies. In the first case, they infringed every principle of Parliamentary government as accepted in Great Britain today. In the second, they violated the whole structure of personal and international good faith of which British governments have so often prided themselves on being the architects and defenders.

Marlborough disliked and distrusted these peace moves and had a supporter in the heir-apparent to the British throne, the old Electress Sophia of Hanover. She is alleged to have said: 'If the Queen had made an ape her general, and this ape had won so many victories I should be on the side of the ape'. But this ape now had to face a charge of financial malpractice involving some £350,000. Marlborough repudiated the allegation and had adequate answers for the various accusations. But on 31 December 1711 the Cabinet Council recorded: 'Being informed that an information against the Duke of Marlborough was laid before the House of Commons, by the Commissioners of public accounts, her Majesty thought fit to dismiss him from all his employments, that the matter might undergo an impartial investigation'. The Queen's letter of dismissal has not survived since Marlborough, in a rare show of temper, tossed it into the fire on receiving it. But from his sad and hurt reply it seems that the letter was

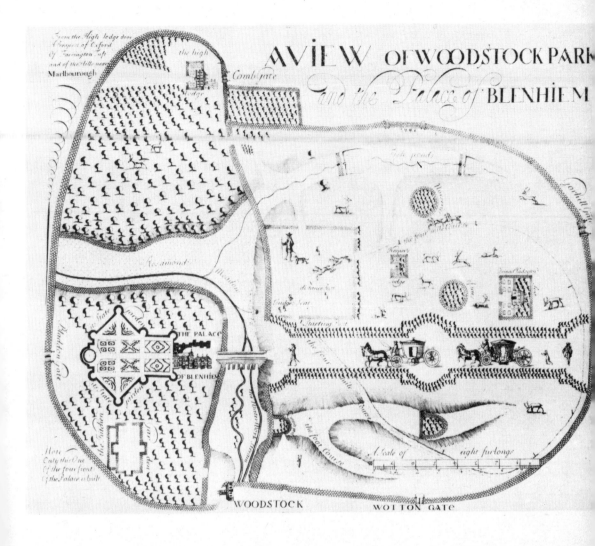

A VIEW OF WOODSTOCK PARK and the Palace of BLENHIEM

inadequate and unjust – an unbefitting end to a glorious association of more than thirty years. Louis XIV commented wrily: 'The affair of displacing the Duke of Marlborough will do for us all we desire'.

Marlborough was replaced as Captain-General by the Duke of Ormonde. Restraining orders imposed on the new Captain-General obliged him to conduct a spineless and uncooperative campaign in Flanders, while Marlborough, having vindicated himself from the charges against him, could only urge action from the House of Lords. For the rest, he was happy to lead the family life that he had longed for throughout the war, and to devote himself to the completion of Blenheim. He was impatient to move in to his splendid house. Five years

A sketch plan *c.* 1710 of Woodstock Park. Anne gave Marlborough the park which had been 'a seat royal ever since the days of King Alfred' in 1704. The foundation stone of Blenheim Palace was laid there on 18 June 1705.

69

The north face of Blenheim Palace in an engraving, *c.* 1745, for Tyndal's 'Continuation of Rapin's *History of England*'. The palace was, as the title of the engraving declares, 'Built at the Expense of the Publick and settled on the Duke of Marlborough and His Posterity.'

earlier he had written to Sarah: 'When it is half built it may be enough for you and me; and I do assure you that I should be much better pleased to live with you in a cottage than in all the palaces this world has without you'. Now, neither was it finished, nor were they yet living in it. Work had been stopped once in 1710, and was to stop again in 1712 when funds were not forthcoming from Parliament. While abroad, Marlborough had often asked Sarah to report on the progress. 'By your saying nothing to me of going to Woodstock', he wrote on one occasion, 'I find your heart is not set on that place as I could wish'. He was right. Sarah liked nothing about the enterprise. To his dismay, she began to build a house of her own in London. Its foundation stone bore the inscription: *1709 Anno Pacifico*. 'Neither truth nor good Latin' said someone and she had it altered.

The situation in England was prickly for the Marlboroughs and after the death in September 1712 of their old friend and colleague, Sydney Godolphin, whom Sarah thought 'the best man that ever lived', they decided to pack up and go abroad. Marlborough transferred £50,000 to The Hague and made the necessary arrangements. Addison bade him farewell:

> Go, mighty prince, and those great nations see,
> Which thy victorious arms before made free; . . .
> O censure undeserved! Unequal fate!
> Which strove to lessen *Him* who made *Her* great;
> Which, pampered with success and rich in fame,
> Extolled his conquest but condemned his name.

The old couple – they had now been married some thirty-five years – spent the end of Queen Anne's reign touring Europe. They were welcomed and fêted wherever they went. Sarah at first enjoyed the new experience, but then grew very homesick. ''Tis much better to be dead than to live out of England' was her plaintive verdict. 'I should be very well content with the worst of my country houses.' Marlborough, better adapted to living abroad – after all in the previous ten years he had spent more time in Flanders than in England – was more content. He worked at maintaining good relations, not only with London but also with Hanover and with the Jacobites at St Germain, presumably keeping his options open for a future time. But with the death from smallpox of a favourite daughter, Elizabeth, Countess of Bridgwater, they decided to return home.

The 'solemn and magnificent funeral procession' of the Duke of Marlborough on 9 August 1722. Horseguards and footguards lead the procession, then come six mourning horses, covered with black cloth, each followed by 'forty persons in mourning cloaks, and gloves, on horseback, two and two'. The Duke's body in armour (fig. 56), is borne on a chariot with a canopy of black velvet, adorned with badges and trophies of war. The chief mourner (fig. 60) is the Duke of Montagu, followed by Marlborough's other sons-in-law, the Earls of Godolphin and Sunderland, as well as eight more dukes and six more earls. The coaches in figs 70 & 71 were sent by George I and the Prince of Wales; they are followed by 'the coaches of the nobility according to their several precedencies and degrees'. As was the custom, Sarah and her daughters did not attend. Vanbrugh said 'I don't know whether it won't cost her ten thousand pounds. What a Noble monument wou'd that have made, whereas this Idle Show will be gone in half an hour and forgot in two days.' In fact the bill came to £5265.

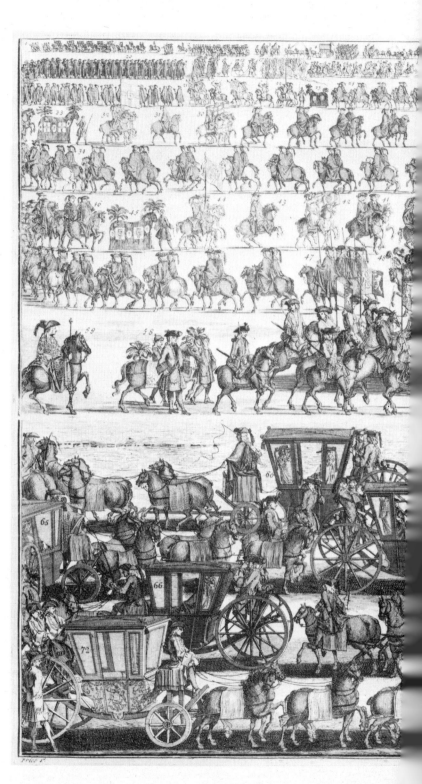

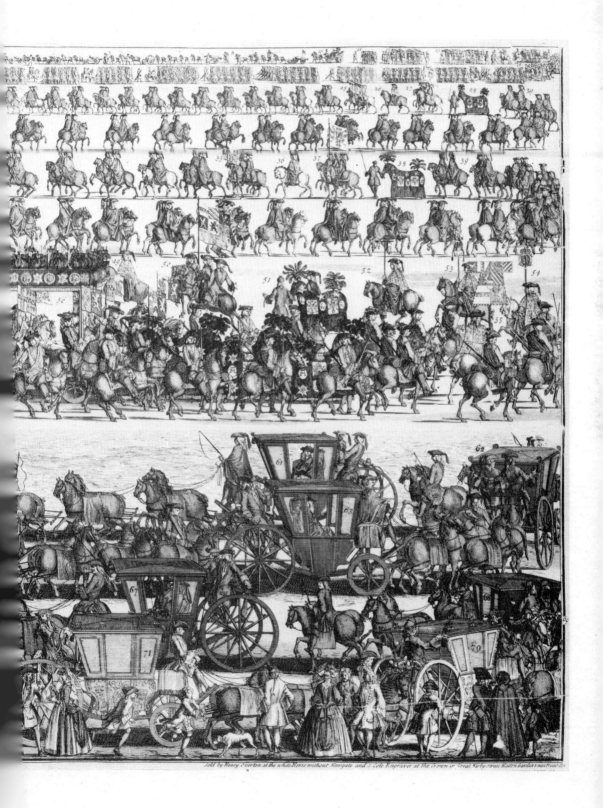

Sold by Henry Overton at the white Horse without Newgate and I. Cole Engraves at the Crown in Great Kirby street Hatton Garden, where Prints &c.

By the time the Treaty of Utrecht was signed and all Europe was able to heave a sigh of relief and put away its armies, Anne had become sick. She had been too ill to attend the peace celebrations for the signing of the Treaty and was scarcely able to walk. The gout from which she had suffered throughout her life became increasingly nasty. When on 1 August 1719, after weeks of pain, made no lighter by the constant presence of her quarrelsome ministers, she died, her physician said: 'I believe sleep was never more welcome to a weary traveller than death to her'.

The following day those two other weary travellers, the Marlboroughs, landed at Dover. And when George 1 arrived from Hanover a month or so later to accept the crown, Marlborough was reinstated in all his former offices – and his daughters and sons-in-law received profitable appointments too. On that wheel of royal favour the Marlboroughs were back at the top and the Duke, although old and tired, was once again in the centre of affairs. He was active in the House of Lords. From there he directed the operation against the Jacobite uprising in 1715; the Royal Artillery, which dates from then, was to some extent his creation. But in 1716 the death from pleuritic fever of the daughter he probably loved best, Anne Sunderland, triggered off a paralytic stroke that deprived him of speech. Although it seems unlikely that Sarah's tonic of boiling vipers (French ones from Montpelier were said to be the most efficacious) in broth helped, he partly regained his speech. But words remained difficult for him and rather than show his disability, he kept silent.

One consolation was that in 1720 his palace was at last fit to be lived in. He and Sarah moved in. He was delighted with the magnificent building and happy to be with Sarah, although their contentment was somewhat marred by the quarrels she would pick with everyone: with the Duke's faithful aide Cadogan; with her son-in-law, Sunderland; with the architect, Vanbrugh, who quit the site long before the building was finished; and not least with her two remaining daughters, Henrietta Godolphin and Mary, Duchess of Montagu, who replied in kind. The even-tempered old Duke, ever diplomatic, wrote to Mary with a shaky hand: 'I am not well enough to write so long a letter with my own hand; and I believe I am the worse to see my children live so ill with a mother for whom I must have the greatest tenderness and regard'. Even at his deathbed mother and daughters were not on speaking terms. His daughters went in to see him. 'They stayed a great while, and not being able to be out of the room longer from him', wrote Sarah later, 'I went in though they were there and kneeled down by him. They rose up when I came in and made curtseys, but did not speak to me, and after some time I called for prayers. When they were over I asked the Duke of Marlborough if he heard them well, and he answered, "Yes and he had joined in them."' Shortly after, on 16 June 1722, he died.

Sarah arranged a funeral of 'solemn splendour and martial pomp' and tried, characteristically, to scotch the rumours that soon spread of unseemly deathbed scenes. He wanted to be buried in the chapel at Blenheim, but it was not finished so his body lodged in Westminster Abbey for a few years. Swift wrote meanly:

> His grace! Impossible! what dead!
> Of old age too, and in his bed!

Marlborough's reserved nature had made him seem a cold man and his miserly habits added to that impression. Nor was his cool ambition, his ruthless eye for the main chance, endearing. But his broad vision, his calm control in action, his courage made him a superb general. His troops held him in the greatest respect, but not perhaps in affection. But his courtly charm concealed deeper feelings, which, in an English way, he preferred not to show. Burnet described him as:

A man of noble, graceful appearance, bred up in court, with no literature; but he had a solid and clear understanding, with a constant Presence of Mind. He knew the Art of living in a Court beyond any man in it. He caressed all people with a soft obliging deportment, and was always ready to do good offices. He had no fortune to set upon; this put him on all the methods of acquiring one; and that went so far into him, that he did not shake it off, when he was on a much higher elevation. Nor was his expense suited enough to his posts; but when allowances are made for that, it must be acknowledged that he is one of the greatest men the Age has produced.

Lord Chesterfield concurred and attributed his rise in the world to 'the graces', which he possessed 'in the highest degree, not to say engrossed them'. He added:

His figure was beautiful; but his manner was irresistible by either man or woman . . . He was always cool; . . . and nobody ever observed the least variation in his countenance. He could refuse more gracefully than most people could grant; and those who went away from him the most dissatisfied, as to the substance of their business, were yet personally charmed with him, and in some degree, comforted by his manner. With all his gracefulness, no man living was more conscious of his situation, or maintained his dignity better.

Sarah made a comment, which, typically, sheds more light on her than on him: 'He was naturally genteel without the least affectation, and handsome as an angel tho' ever so carelessly dressed'.

ah DAUGHTER AND HEIRESS
RICHARD IENNINGS OF SANDRIDGE
THE COUNTY OF HERTFORD ESQ.
E OF IOHN CHURCHILL
DUKE OF MARLBOROUGH

4

The Richest Dame

ARABELLA, MARLBOROUGH'S SISTER, outlived the Duke. Her husband, Charles Godfrey, held a respectable position at court, and a steady way of life led her to a ripe old age. Horace Walpole, who was impressed by her famous past as a royal mistress, remembered meeting her when she was very old and retained 'a perfect idea of her face which was pale, round and sleek'. When she died in 1730 at the age of eighty-two there was no mention in her will of her famous son, James, Duke of Berwick, the victor of Almanza and a Marshal of France. She was buried in Westminster Abbey in her brother Admiral George Churchill's grave.

The Admiral had been buried there twenty years earlier. His portrait at Greenwich shows a stolid face and a hefty figure – more of a Churchill than a Villiers. He had been a competent sailor and, like his father, Sir Winston, a pedestrian politician of narrow Tory views. His fortunes followed the vagaries of those of his brother, the Duke, and soared like those of his other relations with the accession of Queen Anne. He never went to sea again after she came to the throne, but took over the administrative side of the Admiralty under her husband, Prince George. There he dealt with recalcitrant admirals and was egged on by the Duke to promote novel plans of combined attacks by land and sea. Much of the resentment that was felt about the favouritism shown to the Churchills was directed at the Admiral. At home and at his desk, lacking in charm though not in responsibility, he was an easy target. Held accountable for the lack of protection of merchant shipping from French raids, he was too stubborn to resign.

But when the Pretender succeeded in sailing to Scotland and back

OPPOSITE Sarah, Duchess of Marlborough, painted by Kneller when she was in mourning for the death of her son Charles.

The two brothers of the Duke of Marlborough, both painted by Kneller: General Charles Churchill (right), and Admiral George Churchill (left) whose epitaph in Westminster Abbey contains these words: 'Invictissimi ducis Marlburghii frater non idignus'.

without being apprehended Churchill was blamed again and it was plain that he must go. The difficulty was that he was the confidant and right hand man of Prince George and, as Anne would brook no criticism of anything that was in any way connected with her unremarkable husband, it was a delicate matter. Marlborough, to whom it fell to drop the hint, could not face doing so for several months. However, he was saved embarrassment by the death of Prince George when Admiral Churchill's appointment conveniently lapsed. George retired to his house at Windsor – a perquisite that had come with the Deputy Rangership of Windsor Little Park – and occupied himself with his aviary. There he too soon died with no title or estate to his name – despite the taunts of 'royal favourite' – merely a sum of £20,000, which he left in part to his one illegitimate son, George, and in part to one of Arabella's children, Francis Godfrey.

The other brother, Charles, the soldier, was also dead. Like both George and John, he began his career as a page. He then became an ensign in a Company of Foot and thereafter made regular progress up the steps of the military ladder, assisted now and again no doubt by his brother's influence. In the war, as General in command of the English Infantry, he served the Duke superbly, showing the utmost loyalty and reliability. In 1708 his career – he was by then Governor of Guernsey – was cut short by a stroke which incapacitated him

78

He inherited old Sir Winston's estate in Dorset, and there at Minterne he spent the final years of his life with a rich wife whom he had married in middle age. When he died in 1714 Minterne passed to his wife, then to her relations, the Goulds. They sold it in the eighteenth century to the Digby family. Two centuries later, in 1939, Randolph Churchill married the Honourable Pamela Digby of Minterne, and so brought about a brief reunion between the family and that old house in Dorset.

Of Marlborough's immediate family three crotchety duchesses remained – Sarah, Henrietta Godolphin (now Duchess of Marlborough) and Mary, Duchess of Montagu – and a host of grandchildren. Henrietta had succeeded to the title through a special dispensation granted to her father in 1706, which enabled the dukedom to pass through the female line.

Sarah still had twenty years in which to campaign, to litigate, to build, to recriminate, to justify, to accuse – on and on she went with redoubtable energy. Her overriding concerns were her houses and estates, her children, whose poor behaviour she recorded in a green book entitled *An Account of the Cruell Usage of my Children*, her grandchildren, to one or two of whom she showed blatant favouritism, and Sir Robert Walpole (Lord Treasurer for most of those twenty years), whom she detested. It was enough for someone openly to oppose Walpole for him to meet with Sarah's approval. She did not care much for the Hanoverian court either, having an especial dislike for George II's wife, Caroline of Anspach, a clever, attractive and powerful woman, and a friend to Walpole. When Caroline died in 1737 of a ruptured womb Sarah declared: 'As it is no treason, I freely own that I am glad that she is dead'.

So she kept her distance from the court, moving between her houses at Holywell in Hertfordshire, the Lodge at Windsor, Marlborough House in London and Blenheim. In 1723, the year after the Duke's death, she bought the Wimbledon estate of Sir Theodore Jansen, a former director of the South Sea Company, who had lost his money with the bursting of that bubble. There she began to build another house. She considered land an excellent and trustworthy asset and bought an estate or two every year so that at her death she owned some thirty in all. So shrewd was her business acumen that, thinking the South Sea Company an unsound investment, she had sold her shares at the top of the market – and added a neat £100,000 to her fortune.

Holywell House and Marlborough House were her favourite residences. Although she never liked or appreciated Blenheim – 'I mortally hate all Grandeur and Architecture' she said – but she was

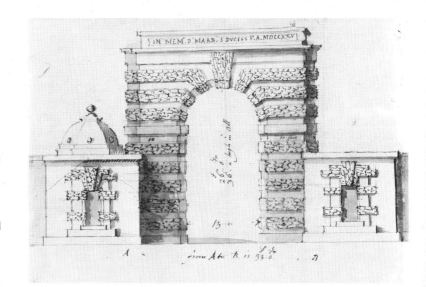

RIGHT Nicholas
Hawksmoor's proposal for
the north gate of
Blenheim Park.

BELOW In the saloon at
Blenheim Laguerre painted
a fresco with his own
self-portrait (left) and that
of Dean Jones,
Marlborough's chaplain.

Sir John Vanbrugh, holding his plans for Blenheim, painted by Kneller. Sarah and he quarrelled violently over the extravagance of his ideas and he left Blenheim in 1716 before the building was completed, complaining of her 'intolerable treatment'. 'She resolved I shou'd never have a farthing,' he said later when they went to law. 'My carrying this point enrages her much and the more because it is of considerable weight in my Small Fortune, which she has heartily endeavour'd so to destroy as to throw me into an English Bastile to finish my days as I began them in a French one.' For Marlborough, however, he always had the greatest veneration.

A saloon doorcase in Blenheim Palace decorated with the arms of a Prince of the Holy Roman Empire. Marlborough was presented with this title by the Emperor in 1705 and it remains in the family today.

bent on finishing it as her 'dear Lord Marlborough' would have wished, for it had been 'very close to his heart'. In fact the two additions which she made to it – the triumphal arch and the column of victory – are the two features which make it so very much his house, his monument. The construction of the whole building lasted from 1704 to 1732. The very best craftsmen – Nicholas Hawksmoor, Grinling Gibbons, Sir James Thornhill, Laguerre – came to work at Blenheim after finishing St Paul's Cathedral. Everybody squabbled and there was nothing but trouble. Parliament, which had to foot many of the bills, often objected and indeed work came to a halt several times. While Marlborough had written longingly from Flanders of his magnificent palace Sarah had fallen out with everyone concerned. She strongly disapproved of Vanbrugh and his fancy plans and in 1716 she sacked him, whereupon he accused her of: 'Far-fetch'd, Labour'd Accusations, Mistaken Facts, Wrong Inferences, Groundless jealousies and Strain'd Constructions'. She took over the direction of the work herself, a responsibility that she later regretted. He referred to her as 'that BBBB old B, the Duchess of Marlborough' – which was hardly surprising for when he went to Woodstock to see the result of his handiwork, he found the gate barred; Sarah had given instructions that he was on no account to be admitted. All he could do was look over the wall. In the end, when all the problems of its construction were over, Sarah was moved by the splendour of the building. She thought it would be 'a wonderful fine place', and added: 'I believe it will be liked by everybody, and I am glad it will be so, because it was the dear Duke of Marlborough's passion to have it done'.

Her passion had been Marlborough House in London, started in 1709 and finished three years later at a cost of nearly £50,000. She wanted it 'strong, plain and convenient', and, designed by Sir Christopher Wren, the house was much more to Sarah's taste, which was 'to have things plain and clean from a piece of wainscot to a lady's face'. Today it is the Commonwealth Secretariat and, although, much altered, it is obviously not a house for which 'plain' can ever have been the right epithet. The Duke disapproved of the project and before the battle of Malplaquet tried to dissuade her from it – without success. The land was leased from the Crown and reverted to it in 1817 with the death of the fourth Duke.

At first Sarah thought that her other house that she had built at Wimbledon would be delightful and also convenient, being 'within an hour's driving to London upon a good road'. But in the end she decided it was 'an ill sod, very damp and I believe an unhealthy place, which I shall very seldom live in; and consequently I have thrown away a vast sum of money upon it to little purpose'.

OPPOSITE A contemporary broadsheet of Rysbrack's statue of Queen Anne, commissioned by Sarah for Blenheim. 'It will be a very fine thing,' Sarah wrote to her granddaughter, Di, '& though but one figure will cost me £300, I have a satisfaction in showing this respect for her, because her kindness to me was real, and what happened afterwards was compassed by the contrivance of such as are in power now.'

The house at Windsor she handed over, despite their differences, to her daughter, Henrietta, Duchess of Marlborough.

Sarah was now middle-aged and fearsome, irascible and difficult, but she was still handsome. 'She had still at a great age considerable remains of beauty, most expressive eyes and the finest hair imaginable, the colour of which she said she had preserved unchanged by the constant use of honey-water', wrote Lady Mary Wortley-Montagu. And she was also very rich. She received two proposals of marriage in her widowhood. The first, from Earl Coningsby, came too soon after the Duke's death for her to consider it. To the second,

An early-eighteenth-century engraving of Marlborough House, designed by Sir Christopher Wren for Sarah, who demanded that it must be 'strong, plain and convenient'. It took two years to build and cost £50,000.

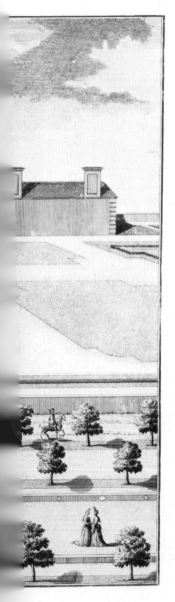

from the Duke of Somerset, an arrogant man of whom she had had, until then, a poor opinion, she replied: 'If I were young and handsome as I was, instead of old and faded as I am, and you could lay the empire of the world at my feet, you should never share the heart and hand that once belonged to John, Duke of Marlborough'.

Not only was Sarah intent on preserving and honouring the memory of her 'ever dear Lord Marlborough', she was also keen to vindicate her own reputation. She believed that there were many misconceptions and lies about her behaviour towards Queen Anne. *An Account of the Conduct of the Dowager Duchess of Marlborough, from her first coming to Court to the year 1710* was an attempt to clear the matter up. It is a strong and readable book, clearly honest in a subjective way. When it was published in 1742 it was attacked by Dr Johnson and praised by Henry Fielding. She asked Voltaire to help her write it, but he declined. She remarked: 'I thought the man had sense but I find him at bottom either a fool or a philosopher'. She also made many attempts to find a biographer for the Duke. In her will she left £500 each to Richard Glover and David Mallett to do the job. She stipulated that there were to be 'no flourishes', just 'short, plain facts', and that 'no part of the said history may be in verse'. Nothing came of the project.

Sarah hated poetry, and poets she considered beneath contempt. It was this prejudice that blighted her relationship with her eldest daughter, Henrietta. As a child, Henrietta had adored her mother and her letters reveal an affectionate and dutiful daughter. She married, to general approbation, Mr Montgomery's somewhat dull son, Francis Godolphin, by whom she had two children, Henrietta and William, or Willigo, who was now heir to the dukedom and, alas, a rascal. Like Sarah, Henrietta was haughty and obstinate, but she also had a strong romantic side to her nature. Writers, artists and poets were, to her, romantic. This attitude led her to become a literary snob and she began to cultivate the company of Congreve, Gay and their friends. Indeed Congreve became 'as regular . . . as the wine' at her table – a development her mother abhorred. She frequently chided her for keeping such 'low company'. On one letter from Henrietta to her mother, Sarah wrote: 'This letter was from Lady Godolphin before she was ruined by the very bad company she keeps'. Congreve was twelve years older than Henrietta and towards the end of his life, when he was an invalid, they were inseparable. His contemporaries seem to have considered Henrietta rather a joke. Pope probably had her in mind when, in his *Of the Characters of Women*, he wrote of a proud peeress who 'sins with poets through pure love of wit'.

It was widely believed that Mary, the daughter Henrietta gave birth to in 1723, was Congreve's. There seems no reason to doubt this and it would explain why, in his will, he left £10,000 to Henrietta, although she can hardly have needed it. He died in 1729 and was buried in Westminster Abbey. Henrietta installed a bronze tablet over his tomb 'as a mark how deeply she remembers the happiness and honour she enjoyed in the sincere friendship of so worthy and honest a man'. 'I know not what "pleasure" she might have had in his company, but I am sure it was no "honour"' was Sarah's tart comment on the 'silly epitaph'.

Francis Godolphin was a most complaisant husband. He was executor of Congreve's will and pall-bearer at his funeral. He adored his daughter, Henrietta, while his wife doted on Mary. No one had much time for Willigo, Marquis of Blandford. His sister, Henrietta, a kind girl, called him 'Lord Worthless'. Sarah, as dynast, worried about the future of the family with this unsatisfactory young man as head of it. She was horrified when he unexpectedly married the daughter of a Dutch burgomaster, who was not, she thought, a suitable wife for the future Duke of Marlborough. There she was wrong; not only was the girl rich, but she also had much more sense than her husband, the Duke-to-be. However they had only been married two years and were still childless when Willigo died – of drink.

Henrietta was unmoved by the death of her son. 'She very truly says that his behaviour towards her must justify her being at least indifferent to his death; and that anybody who had any regard to Papa's memory must be glad that the Duke of Marlborough was now not in danger of being represented in the next generation by one who must have brought any name he bore into contempt.' Henrietta herself died two years later in 1733. She refused to be buried at Blenheim and was put in the tomb of her father-in-law, Mr Montgomery; it was not far from Congreve's. Sarah owned up to feeling 'much more than I imagined formerly I could ever do. By which I am convinced there is such a thing as natural affection'.

And so the Marlborough heritage shifted from the Godolphins to the Spencers – to the children of John and Sarah's adored daughter, Anne, Countess of Sunderland. She had died in 1716. A presentiment of an early death had prompted her to write a note to her husband about the future of their children: 'Pray get my mother, the Duchess of Marlborough, to take care of the girls and if I leave my boys too little to go to school; for to be left to servants is very bad for children and a man can't take care of little children that a woman can'. So Sarah had taken charge of three of the five children. She doted on the youngest, Diana, and her letters to this grandchild reveal the kind and affectionate side of her nature that did exist, but was so seldom

86

Henrietta, second Duchess of Marlborough (1681–1733), painted by Kneller. Her father, the Duke, because he had no male heir, obtained an act of Parliament to enable his title to pass through the female line.

evident. As Anne's eldest son, Robert, had died in 1729 it was her second son, Charles, who became the third Duke of Marlborough on the death of Henrietta. Sarah did not like him. She much preferred the third son, John, and it was to him that she left most of her enormous fortune, considering Blenheim and the dukedom quite enough for Charles.

She suspected that Charles gambled – the worst vice in her book. She had a horror of the Marlborough riches being dissipated by spoilt grandchildren, and so she paid the most scrupulous attention to their affairs. 'I am labouring like a packhorse every day to save him from cheats', Sarah wrote to Di of Charles; and indeed he was extravagant and did on occasion gamble. Nor was she pleased when he married Elizabeth Trevor, for Elizabeth was the daughter of a former political enemy of Marlborough's. And although when, on becoming Duke in 1733 Charles and Elizabeth dutifully visited Sarah at Windsor, she did revise her low opinion of the couple, she never really came to like Charles, nor was she ever reconciled to his marriage.

Sarah liked his sister, Anne, Viscountess Bateman, a favourite at Queen Caroline's court, even less; indeed, she hated her. She is said to have blackened Anne's portrait, remarking: 'She is much blacker within'. History has failed to put Anne's case.

Lady Diana Spencer, who was largely brought up by her grandmother, Sarah, became the old Duchess's favourite grandchild. After a plan to marry her to the Prince of Wales was foiled, she married the fourth Duke of Bedford, but died of tuberculosis at the age of twenty-six in 1735.

When Charles became Duke he also became the owner of Blenheim. It was therefore thought fair that John should take on Althorp, the Sunderland property. John married Lady Georgina Carteret on Sarah's instructions and they initiated a cadet line of Spencers. John's son became the first Earl Spencer, the ancestor of the seventh Earl who lives at Althorp today. The fact that Sarah left so much more money to John than to Charles accounts for the fact that Althorp can still boast better pictures than Blenheim.

Five duchesses, one countess and a viscountess accounted for Sarah's seven grand-daughters, and as such they sweep graciously out of the story – all except Diana, Duchess of Bedford, Sarah's favourite. Diana's tact and kind nature enabled her to circumvent any impending quarrels with her grandmother; it was no mean achievement. Sarah at one time tried to marry her to the Prince of Wales. He had quarrelled with his parents and Walpole and was therefore a desirable match in Sarah's eyes. But Walpole heard of the scheme and put an end to it. When instead Di married Lord John Russell, later Duke of Bedford, Sarah provided her with a dowry of

UNIDENTIFIED PORTRAIT

(513)

43

of a portrait of the above (head and shoulders), illustrate.—THOS. T. GESSON.

Similar to SARA MALBOROUGH or Family —

c

to Nature had been largely adopted by rich and poor alike, the former making them the basis of a fashionable cult as exemplified by Marie Antoinette in her shepherdess *rôle*.

At Wembley: A little-known Portrait of Rodney

In the Jamaica Court, in the West Indian Pavilion at the British Empire Exhibition, is an

rassed, and a strong Tory with an autocratic hostility to the American rebels; while the Navy was rent by party politics.

Delayed by contrary winds, the fleet sailed at last in December, 1779, Sandwich having told Rodney that the fate of the Empire was in his hands; and that spirit was in every British sailor's heart on the glorious 12th of April. He

SILVER POWDER-BOX AND SOAP-BOX   PARIS, 1787   IN SIR GEORGE MURRAY'S COLLECTION

44

£30,000 and a promise of £100,000 in her will. She wrote to her two or three times a week advising about this, complaining about that.

When Di became unwell – it was thought that an uncomfortable pregnancy was the trouble – Sarah was full of good advice, and in particular recommended her to take a lot of fresh air. For this purpose she despatched the Turkish tent that Marlborough had used on campaign to enable Di to sit out of doors. The carters were uncooperative and the tent took a long time to reach the invalid. Meanwhile neither did she feel any better nor did her pregnancy advance. In Sarah's letters a refusal to admit to herself that there was something seriously wrong can be detected. The tents and fresh air were of no use. In September 1725, aged twenty-six, Diana died of galloping consumption.

Sarah, old Tartar as she was, was profoundly distressed. With the death of her last love her will to live died too. She was thoroughly tired of her life and not at all well. Gout made her incapable of walking. 'I would desire no more pleasure than to walk about my gardens and parks', she wrote the year after Di's death; 'But, alas! That is not permitted; for I am generally wrapped up in flannel, and wheeled up and down my rooms in a chair. I cannot be very solicitous for life upon such terms, when I can only live to have more fits of gout.' And the following year, 1737, she stated: 'I am a perfect cripple, and cannot possibly hold out long: and as I have little enjoyment of my life, I am very indifferent about it'. But she did hold out. A year later she declared: 'I am so weary of life that I don't care how soon the stroke is given me'. But still the stroke did not come. It seemed near in 1742 when her doctor said, 'She must be blistered or she must die' – to which she sharply and characteristically retorted, 'I won't be blistered and I won't die'. And she didn't – not for two more years. Then, in 1744, she was buried together with the Duke in the chapel designed by Rysbrack at Blenheim.

> Beneath this monumental Bust,
> Here lies entombed Dame Sarah's Dust . . .
> Who can lament a full ripe death
> When eighty-five resigns its breath . . .
> Let House and Tomb preserve in Fame
> The Bravest Man, the Richest Dame.

5
Dukes
at Blenheim

S ARAH HAD SAID at a family gathering: 'What a glorious sight it is
to see such a number of branches flourishing from the same root!'
and John Spencer mumbled under his breath: 'Alas the branches
would flourish far better if the root were underground!' His brother
Charles had written to his wife about rebuilding at Blenheim: 'If she
will be so good as to die soon that I may be able to clear my debts,
I believe I shall build; but if she is spiteful enough to live much
longer, I fear I shall not build'. Ungrateful grandchildren.

She had now obliged them. The enormous inheritance was theirs.
Links with its origin, with the time before Blenheim had been built,
with their poorer Dorset ancestors, were broken. The grandchildren,
born into the premier aristocracy in the country, took their position
for granted and never cast their eyes back. As so often, the sinew and
the guts which had forged that fortune slackened with the achievement of it. Ambition evaporated. Marlborough's lean energy and

LEFT Charles Spencer,
third Duke of Marlborough
(1706–58). He 'had virtues
and sense enough to deserve
esteem, but always lost it by
forfeiting respect,' said
Horace Walpole.

RIGHT John Spencer-
Churchill, seventh Duke
(1822–83), grandfather of
Winston Churchill. 'The
Duke was extremely kind,'
wrote Jennie, his
daughter-in-law, 'and had
the most courteous and
grand seigneur appearance
and manner.'

91

Sarah's strength and capability had engendered weaker, wavering grandchildren. No lack of talent was passed on, but the necessary drive for its full exploitation was lacking.

For the next hundred years the Dukes of Marlborough sat back at Blenheim dabbling in this, dabbling in that, marrying Lady this or the Honourable Miss that. Changes provoked by the prevailing fashion were made to the house, pictures were bought, hangings were shifted, rooms were refurnished, flower-beds scrapped. Fads affected the gardens and the interior of the house while Vanbrugh's elaborate facade remained unchanged.

Eton and Oxford or Eton and the Guards were the norm for the education of the Spencer boys, a tradition that continues today with the Spencer-Churchills. Good marriages for the girls: scratch any established English peerage and you will find a Spencer or a Spencer-Churchill wedding somewhere. The fortune fluctuated – downwards mostly – but a lucrative sale of some treasure or restrictive guardianship by trustees kept it afloat. So colossal was John and Sarah's bequest that the eleventh Duke benefits today. The younger sons, the hard-luck cases of the primogeniture system, were less fortunate. Mostly they fell away from the ranks of the aristocracy to settle down as country gentlemen or pillars of the church or officers in the army. Until the seventh Duke, that is. His younger son showed that combination of ambition and ability not seen in the family for two hundred years. But that was not until Queen Victoria's reign. First the Georgians.

Charles was nearly forty when his grandmother died. Since taking his seat in the House of Lords ten years earlier he had played an active part in public affairs, bound up as they were in those days with the social life of the court and the aristocracy. A certain oscillation of allegiance had marked that part – an inconstancy often to be observed in the Marlborough family. To start with Charles did what Sarah told him. On her guidance he took sides against Sir Robert Walpole and the earthy court of George II and Queen Caroline generally opposing Walpole's measures in the House of Lords. As the robust Walpole had the wholehearted support of the King and Queen, those who opposed him sought their own royal patron. This they found in Frederick, the ineffectual Prince of Wales, around whom they clustered – Charles among them. There was a year between Charles and Frederick in age and as both were disliked by King George and Queen Caroline they were likely colleagues in the politico-aristocratic factions of the time. At Frederick's marriage Marlborough looked magnificent in 'a white velvet and gold brocade, upon which was an exceeding rich Point d'Espagne'. He supported Frederick in the extraordinary rows that he had with his parents, the

John Wootton's painting 'Death of a Stag' portrays a royal hunt in Windsor Great Park *c.* 1737. The Prince of Wales is ordering John Spencer, a ranger of the Park, to kill the stag that has been brought to bay. Behind John are Lord Baltimore, John's brother the third Duke of Marlborough, the Earl of Jersey and the Marquis of Powis.

King and Queen, and was thought to be solidly behind the Prince. So it was a great surprise when, in 1738, Charles kissed King George's hand and made it up with him and his court. Sarah was furious; she suspected the machinations of Elizabeth, his Duchess. The King's hand, once kissed, was as generous as ever. A regiment, a position at court (Lord of the Bedchamber) and a prestigious county appointment (Lord Lieutenant of the Counties of Oxfordshire and Buckinghamshire) were Marlborough's within the year. The following year he became Colonel of the 1st Royal Dragoons, and then Colonel of the 2nd Horse Guards; two years later came the Garter. Three-quarters of a century after Sir Winston Churchill had received the first royal favour for the family from Charles II the practice of liberally rewarding loyal support was just as healthy.

The favours were short-lived. At the battle of Dettingen in 1743 the third Duke commanded a brigade – creditably. The battle had been a muddle. Disenchantment with the high command for its bungling of the situation and irritation with Hanoverian officers provoked the Duke's resignation. On his return to England, he flounced off in indignation to Langley, his house in Buckinghamshire, failing to pay his respects at court on the way. The slight lost him his jobs. Sarah was delighted. Horace Walpole explained cynically that Marlborough had rejoined the opposition in order 'to reinstate himself in the old Duchess's will'. A little unjust perhaps, as six months before she died rumours of a Jacobite invasion prompted the Duke once more to pledge his support for the King, for which he received the concomitant promotions.

After Sarah's death, and then Sir Robert Walpole's, Charles's political course steadied. With his brother-in-law, the Duke of Bedford (Di's husband), he remained a supporter and friend of Henry Fox. In 1744 he gave away the bride at Fox's secret wedding, an event succinctly dealt with by Horace Walpole: 'Mr Fox fell in love with Lady Caroline Lennox; he asked her, was refused, and stole her. His father was a footman, her great-grandfather a King: *hinc lachrymae!* all the blood royal have been up in arms'. It was much talked about.

'The constant topic of conversation of almost all our coffee houses in town' in 1754 was the election in Oxfordshire. For years Oxfordshire, a county of convivial Jacobitism, had returned two Tory members to Parliament. Nobody objected. But Charles decided that it was time for Whig representation. In the ducal league of pocket boroughs Marlborough could boast but two tame Members of Parliament – those for Woodstock and St Albans – whereas the Duke of Newcastle or the Duke of Bedford would return several. Two members for a shire would enhance his standing considerably. This

An engraving dated 1777 of Woodstock. Many members of the Churchill family have represented the constituency in parliament, for it remained a family perquisite until the beginning of the century.

may have been the reason he decided that Oxfordshire should be
contested in 1754. Elections were vastly expensive and his decision
was seen as an example of his extravagance. Together with the Earl
of Macclesfield, the Harcourts and the Norths he put forward Lord
Parker and Sir Edward Turner as Whig candidates. Their Tory
opponents were Sir James Dashwood and Lord Wenman. After
much work, extensive propaganda and great expenditure on the
part of the aristocratic Whigs, and the Tories too, all four candidates
were declared returned. But the Whig House of Commons took little
time to reverse this decision and declare Parker and Turner duly
elected. At the next election on the accession of George III in 1761
the two parties agreed to share the representation, one member each.

'Canvassing for Votes' by
William Hogarth was based
on the Oxfordshire election
of 1754, in which the third
Duke spent a great deal of
money promoting his
Whig candidates.

Lord Charles Spencer, the Duke's second son was returned for the Whigs, and a Blenheim candidate represented the shire for the next fifty years. The bill for the 1754 campaign was about £20,000. Parliament contributed £3,000. It is unlikely that the impecunious Duke could have paid the balance and it probably fell to the Maccles-fields to settle up.

Charles did try to economise; he went through the household accounts and decided to cut back on many items. For instance, the £1,790 a year spent on wine was to be cut by £50, and the £178 on candles by £20. Such carefulness was not in his nature and he never succeeded in curbing his extravagance. Fortunately for his heirs he had 'forfeited by his follies the management of his own estate' and his affairs were well tied up in trusts.

His family was the first to use Blenheim as a home. The Duke himself preferred his house, Langley, in Buckinghamshire. He had bought the property in 1738 when, because he had aligned himself with Walpole and the court, Sarah had turned him out of Windsor Lodge. Langley had belonged to Abigail Masham and was sold to Charles by her widower – an ironical fact and not one that can have appealed to Sarah. But for Charles it was 'a charming little place' and there he built a fine Georgian house that he filled with pictures. Collecting was the passion of the rich and the Sunderlands had a flair for it: they were connoisseurs and Blenheim, after Langley, profited from their expertise. Charles inherited from his father the keenness and the eye that had been responsible for the famous Sunderland library. The first Duke of Marlborough had also pur-chased many excellent pictures and tapestries, but there had been an ostentation in his acquisitions, a desire for the very best that money could buy rather than an innate appreciation of the work of art. He had written to Sarah in 1706 about the equestrian portrait of Charles I: 'It is certain there are not in England so fine pictures as some of these, particularly King Charles on horseback done by Vandyke. It was the Elector of Bavaria's, and given to the Emperor, and I hope it is by this time in Holland'. It was the provenance that impressed the first Duke as much as, if not more than, the picture. But the Spencer sensibility had tempered the Churchill rawness in his grand-children.

When Charles and Elizabeth moved to Blenheim after Sarah's death they did not have the wherewithal to make any drastic altera-tions and the house remained as she left it. They were not equal to its magnificence; their personalities were overshadowed, not set off by its splendour. The Duchess in particular had a very timid nature and relied on her husband for support and reassurance. Unlike the first Duchess she had neither the courage of her convictions nor the strength of the extrovert. But she was an excellent mother and she created a happy family life for her children, which is more than can be said for Sarah. The Duke, like his grandfather, was utterly uxorious, and his marriage to Elizabeth was successful. He was honest and had the bluff courage that comes with pride, but like his wife lacked confidence. He also suffered from self-consciousness and was a little cowed by the weight of the name of Marlborough. People, Sarah in particular, complained that he mumbled. 'The greatest bashfulness and indistinction in his articulation' was how Horace Walpole put it. It was a sign of the diffidence that he longed to overcome.

He was delighted to be made Lord Privy Seal in 1755, but quite content to step down at the end of the year to the more lowly position of Master-General of the Ordnance. Keen as he was for influence and prestige, he jibbed at responsibility. Only up to a point did he want to prove himself worthy of his name.

At the outbreak of the Seven Years' War Charles was given an opportunity to bring new honour to that name. Championed by Pitt, he was given command of an expedition that was to cross the Channel and attack St Malo. Through no fault of Marlborough's the plan failed. The Duke was not blamed for the fiasco, far from it. With Pitt's full support he was made commander-in-chief of the British forces and sent to Germany. In those foreign fields he had a chance to prove himself and to enjoy the life of a soldier away from the cocoon of Blenheim. But before his generalship was put to the test he contracted a 'camp fever and bloody flux', from which he died. He was only 48. It is most unlikely that Charles would have matched his grandfather in martial skill had he been put to the test, for although proud and tough he lacked the inspiration and necessary tautness of will for effective command. As Louis xv said: 'His grandfather indeed used to frighten our subjects, but this is quite another sort of man'.

The only bequest he was able to make, so entrammelled were his affairs, was £2,000 to his 'dear wife, Elizabeth'. She was lost without him and survived him by only three years. At his death in 1758 their three sons were still under age, although their two daughters had married. Diana, the elder, had become the wife of Viscount Bolingbroke, but it was a marriage sufficiently disastrous to warrant a divorce – a rare development. Her second husband was Topham Beauclerk, a great-grandson of Nell Gwynn and Charles II. He was a dashing fellow, a brilliant conversationalist – Dr Johnson envied his wit – and a cad. Lady Diana Beauclerk moved out of court circles into the artistic and literary world that her new husband frequented. She was an accomplished artist herself. Her lively drawings and watercolours of Arcadian scenes and cherubic children were enjoyed by her friends then and have lost none of their charm today. She also made designs for the new Wedgwood china, decorated her friends' houses and painted some of the rooms at Strawberry Hill for Horace Walpole.

Diana's sister, Betty, was very beautiful. She became an elegant lady-in-waiting to Queen Charlotte and married the Earl of Pembroke, who however spent very little time with her. At court she was much admired by George III, who, in his mad moments, rambled on about her. 'While playing at picquet he distinguishes her by the Queen of Hearts, kissing it whenever he saw it. This evening he had the King of Hearts himself and said, "Oh, if the Queen of Hearts would fall to the King"'.

As George III came to the throne in England a reign of Georges began at Blenheim. The fourth, fifth and sixth Dukes were all called George – and a thoroughly undistinguished lot they were. George, the fourth Duke, was not yet of age when his father died of the 'bloody flux' and he succeeded to the title. He was still in the hands of tutors appointed by his mother, who stipulated that George should 'apply himself to the Modern History of Europe and laws of his own country in which he is born to be a principal actor, and I make no doubt a very shining and exemplary one'. Alas, a rather dim supporting role was all he rose to in the event. Not that the start of his career did not promise well. Before he was twenty-two he had taken his seat in the House of Lords, was Lord Lieutenant of Oxfordshire, and a popular figure at court; his handsome appearance was widely remarked upon.

His looks, his title, his heritage, all meant that he was, after the King, the best catch in the country in the eyes of ambitious mothers with unmarried daughters. The winning campaign for his hand was conducted by Gertrude, Duchess of Bedford, and 'after long hopes and trials on their [the Bedfords'] side, and a vast repugnance on his, the Duke of Marlborough has at last married their daughter'. 'The Duke of Bedford was always known to be a man of business, but he never despatched a matter quicker than this', wrote Mrs Scott of the *fiançailles*. Lady Caroline Russell, the bride, was tough and not very attractive, but she proved a good wife and the couple were as devoted to each other as his parents and great-grandparents had been. Not a breath of scandal, not a murmur of adultery.

At the age of twenty-two the Duke of Marlborough was made Lord Chamberlain, and at the age of twenty-three he was Lord Privy Seal under the Earl of Bute in George III's first, short-lived administration. The King changed his ministry in 1765 and Marlborough resigned without regret. But he lodged a request for the

OPPOSITE The family of the fourth Duke of Marlborough and his wife Caroline, painted by Sir Joshua Reynolds in 1777. The children, from left to right are George, Marquis of Blandford, Charlotte, Henry, Anne, Elizabeth and Caroline. The Duke was a great collector, and, as was the fashion, particularly interested in the classical world. Blandford is holding a crimson morocco case containing some of the Marlborough gems, and the Duke has a cameo in his hand.

Net Cash arising from the Duke of
Marlborough's Landed Estates
since he became of Age

From Feby 8. 1760 to Feby 8. 1761.
Bedford }
Hertford } ..... £ 2340 . 1 . 4
Bucks ..... 3090 ..
Oxon ..... 5670 . 3 . 11
Wilts ..... 729 .. 1
£ 11829 . 5 . 4

From Feby 8. 1761 to Feby 8. 1762.
Bedford }
Hertford } ..... 2842 . 19 . 5
Northampton ..... 1213 . 19 . 2
Lincoln ..... 1190 . 3 . 2
Oxon ..... 6809 . 9 .
Bucks ..... 3115 . 19 . 9
Wilts ..... 2895 . 13 . 3
£ 18068 . 3 . 9

From Feby 8. 1762 to Feby 8. 1763.
Bedford ..... 284 . 13 . 1
Hertford ..... 520 . 11 . 9
Northampton ..... 885 . 17 . 6
Lincoln ..... 982 . 9 .
Bucks ..... 3120 . 10 .
Oxon ..... 7250 . 16 . 2
Devon ..... 443 . 1 . 1
Wilts 2195
Sussex ..... 66 . 10 .
£ 15749 . 8 . 7

Feby 8. 63 to Aug 8. 1763.
Bedford ..... 497 . 1 . 8
Hertford ..... 50 ..
Northampton ..... 522 . 8 . 6
Bucks 1879
Oxon ..... 3076 . 14 .
Wilts 1223
Devon 220
Sussex 20
£ 7488 . 4 . 2

The account book of the Marlborough estates giving the fourth Duke's income from his lands between 1760 and 1763.

Garter. He badgered the Duke of Bedford, who was his uncle and his father-in-law, to procure it for him. The King wished to spite the Bedfords, and dallied. Not until 1767 was Marlborough's wish granted. Thereafter he retired to Blenheim and resisted employment. He had neither the inclination nor the confidence to play anything but the most perfunctory part in public affairs.

He had unfortunately inherited all the weakest strains of his father's character; diffidence, taciturnity, extravagance and that sensibility which prevented him from doing anything much for fear of rebuff. He and his wife led a very sheltered life at Blenheim – 'ennui itself' was how William Coxe, one of the tutors, described it. Only their eight children and the occasional amateur theatricals that were performed in the house enlivened the quiet tenor of their years there. Almost their only contact with affairs of state was through John Moore, George's former tutor, who had become Archbishop of Canterbury. The Duke and Duchess turned to him for advice on every occasion. His sane and helpful replies were peppered with words of encouragement and phrases to bolster their weak morale. 'The truth is the Duke of Marlborough need never want employment', Moore wrote to the Duchess, 'nor either of your graces society. But both will be wanted till the Duke resolves not to be afraid of a little employment and both your graces resolve not to be afraid of society.'

There was, for instance, great consternation at Blenheim in 1786 when King George and Queen Charlotte announced they were to pay a visit. The Marlboroughs, full of doubt and apprehension, hastily wrote to Archbishop Moore for advice. Soothingly, he assured them that they had nothing to be ashamed of and much to be proud of. And indeed, after all the fuss, 'it all went off very well', the Duchess was glad to report. 'We have nothing to equal this' was the King's gracious comment.

George, the fourth Duke, was the first to live at Blenheim and like it. He lived there for more than fifty years and altered much in that time. His most radical change was to the garden. He brought in Capability Brown, who abolished Henry Wise's elegant formal gardens in favour of undulating lawns and strategic clumps of trees. Only Vanbrugh's kitchen garden with its fourteen-foot walls escaped Brown's rampant grass. Vanbrugh's bridge below the house

An engraving by Bartolozzi from the book written by the fourth Duke on his famous gem collection, *Gemmarum Antiquarum Delectus*, published *c.* 1790. In all he had 739 stones, including chalcedony and onyx, sardonyx and sard, amethyst, garnet, sapphire, agate and lapis lazuli. They were sold at Christie's in 1875 by the seventh Duke for 35,000 guineas.

had spanned the stream of the Glyme – a wretched trickle for such a splendid bridge. So Brown flooded the dip and created the curvaceous lake, which gave a worthy setting to the bridge and at the same time proportion to the house in relation to the bridge and to the surrounding land. It was masterly.

George, another collector, purchased the Zanetti gems, a rich collection of cameos and carved precious stones. He added further jewels and built up the Marlborough gem stone collection, which became famous. Further pictures and furniture filled the halls and the galleries. The Duchess, Caroline, one day inquired exactly how many rooms there were in her house; 187 furnished and many more in the towers unfurnished was the answer. Few were wasted, for the household was enormous. On the occasional expeditions that the Duke and Duchess made to Bath their company numbered more than sixty; that included a watchman, baker, confectioner, laundrymaid, usher, postilions, nurserymaids and others.

After the death of his wife in 1811 the Duke seldom ventured out from the Blenheim community. Astronomy was his passion and he spent long hours in solitude gazing at the stars. He was a hypochondriac and dreaded anything that might in any way ruffle the tranquil monotony of his existence. It is said that he remained for three years without uttering a single word. Not long before the wretched George III died after many years of incoherency in a straitjacket, George, the fourth Duke, was found dead in his bed.

He had maintained a courteous relationship with the King throughout his life. His children were of the Prince of Wales's generation, and George, Marquis of Blandford, like the Prince of Wales, was the despair of his parents. He was guilty of the same kind of misdemeanours – expensive foppery, exotic tastes, a rakish style of life. He was the epitome of a Regency buck. Lord Henry, the more intelligent second son, was the hope of the family. He joined the diplomatic service and was said to be bright. An early death was pronounced a terrible waste. But the fact that Henry's rudeness when Minister in Sweden had prompted an indecent picture from the Swedish King as a gift on his departure from the Swedish court suggests that his future as a diplomat might have been less than glittering.

After Henry's death, as Blandford was considered irredeemable, it fell to the third son, Lord Francis Spencer, to pursue a respectable career. Lord Francis obliged and for his solid efforts in both politics and the army was rewarded with a barony. He became the first Baron Churchill of Wychwood and his father settled the very acceptable property of Cornbury in Oxfordshire on him.

All but one of his sisters dutifully married fellow aristocrats. Lady

A miniature by Richard Cosway of George, fifth Duke of Marlborough (1766–1840), who, on succeeding to the title in 1817, revived the name of Churchill. A member of the Fox family said that, in appearance, he was 'pleasant, but looks like a West India property overseer'.

Charlotte, however, took a fancy to a young Oxford don, Mr Nares, who sometimes took part in the amateur theatricals at Blenheim. Stuck at home in that atmosphere of '*ennui* itself' it was quite natural that she should fall in love with one of the few visitors to the house. But though she was twenty-seven her parents refused to countenance the match, so the couple eloped to Henley and married without their consent. The Duke then gave his daughter an allowance of £400 a year and the Duchess barred her the door at Blenheim. For five years the couple lived happily and Charlotte gave birth to a daughter. Then she died; perhaps the unkind ostracism of her parents had broken her spirit. After the Duchess's death the Duke was reunited with his son-in-law, Nares, then Regius Professor of Modern History at Oxford, and with his granddaughter: in his will he provided well for the little girl. He also insisted that Charlotte's body be returned to Blenheim. It was the Duchess who had

taken the cruel line and the weaker Duke had not had the strength to
overrule her. Their granddaughter, Miss Nares, grew up and
married her first cousin, the son of the Marquis of Blandford.

Blandford was a keen gardener and during his father's lifetime
lived at White Knights near Reading. There he employed 23 men to
keep his remarkable gardens in order. He thought nothing of paying
£500 for an unusual plant or shrub – the more exotic it was the better
he liked it. He collected a fine library and he composed glees. As
most of his pastimes were expensive his parents kept him on a tight
allowance. But he was a spoilt child and if he coveted some object he
saw no reason not to have it. 'But I can't help it; I must live', he
explained petulantly when showing off his possessions. So helpless
was he that most of his acquisitions were sold – at a loss – during his
lifetime. But his garden at White Knights, for a time, was legendary.

As an eligible bachelor he was subjected to what was known as 'the
New Art of Gunning'. It was the kind of scandal that society loved.
A certain Mrs Gunning decided that her daughter, Miss Gunnilda
Gunning, would marry a duke. Her eye lit on Blandford, heir to the
dukedom of Marlborough. In her ruse she forged love letters from
Blandford to Gunnilda. General Gunning, her husband, observing
Blandford's apparent attentions to his daughter taxed the Marl-
boroughs about their son's intentions. They were in favour of the
match. The unwitting Blandford denied the letters; their forgery by
Mrs Gunning was revealed and her plot unmasked. The General,
who had not been party to it, turned his scheming wife and daughter
out of the house, and Blandford was swiftly married to Lady Susan
Stewart, the daughter of the Earl of Galloway, in order to avoid any
similar pitfalls.

Blandford succeeded to the dukedom with great fanfare in 1817.
An elaborate celebration was held at Blenheim and soon after he
received royal licence to add Churchill to the family surname. He
soon set to work in the garden to add a touch of the exotic to Brown's
English lawns. He planned grottoes, rustic bridges, a Chinese garden,
an aviary and much more fantastic ornamentation. But the ostentation
was short-lived and his dream faded as debtors nagged. One after the
other treasures were sold, shooting and other rights let, plans
abandoned, rooms shut up. It was even reported that he melted
down the gold plate given to his great-great-grandfather. Mrs
Arbuthnot, who accompanied the Duke of Wellington on a visit
there in 1724, remarked: 'The family of our great general is, however, gone sadly to decay and are but a disgrace to the illustrious
name of Churchill, which they have chosen at this moment to resume. The present Duke is overloaded with debt, is very little
better than a common swindler, and lets everything about Blen-

heim' She regretted, however, that a similar palace could not be erected for Wellington.

George, the fifth Duke, was compelled by debt to lead a shabby existence in a few rooms of his pile. Susan, his wife, had left him, as had Lady Mary Ann Sturt, his mistress, whom he considered his spiritual wife. He died in 1840 and in his will left what he could to Matilda Glover. There is a snippet of information about Miss Glover, who lived at the Home Lodge: 'The Duke have given Miss Glover a poney and gig and Miss takes her eldest daughter there every morning and fetches them at night. The woman and Miss seem very comfortable companions. Both the Misses and the Duke are at the Home lodge most nights to a late hour playing on music and they say she is finer singer . . . We hear she is in the familey way, and Miss Glover quite forward in the same way'. The Duke was described in the *Annual Register* as a 'melancholy instance of the results of extravagance'. It was not a very glorious return for the name of Churchill.

George's son, the third George, was a better fellow, but made a muddle over his marriages. At the age of twenty-three he married a seventeen-year-old girl. The 'clergyman' who performed the wedding ceremony was his brother, who was in fact an army officer. The matter later went to court; the marriage was ruled invalid and their daughter illegitimate. By that time George had married, more appropriately, in St George's Hanover Square, his cousin, Lady Jane Stewart. She bore him four children, but then died. His next wife, Charlotte Flower, supplied two more children before she too died. His last wife, also called Jane Stewart, took him to the courts again. It was a curious story; 'most singular', said the Solicitor-General. At the time of their marriage the Duke was fifty-eight and a cripple. Like Sarah, more than one hundred years earlier, gout had robbed him of the use of his legs and he had to be carried or wheeled round Blenheim. His bride was thirty-four. Soon after their marriage she became pregnant. After giving birth to a son she ran off to Brighton with the child, but the boy was returned to Blenheim. She applied to the courts for custody and accused the Duke of kidnapping the baby and made charges of adultery. The Duke said she could return to Blenheim whenever she liked and denied refusing her access to the child (although it is unclear how the boy was returned from Brighton to Blenheim). He also denied her charge of adultery. His alleged mistress was his housekeeper and nurse, Sarah Licence, who had been in his service for twenty-eight years. The Duchess said she would return to Blenheim if the Duke dismissed Licence. The Duke refused: 'as an infirm valetudinarian', he was too de-

George Spencer Churchill,
sixth Duke of Marlborough
(1793–1857). He married
three times and had
seven children.

pendent on her, he said. It transpired that Licence slept in an adjoining room to the Duke's, so that she could be quickly summoned in the event of an attack of gout. He kept the door from his room to the passage bolted for fear of pryers. Licence was a trusted, loyal and invaluable servant. The Duchess – 'this infuriate lady' – accused the Duke of attempting to make her miscarry and of lying about his relationship with Licence. The upshot was that the Duke allowed the Duchess access to the child at all times – he had never withheld it – but he did not dismiss Licence. The case of the Duke and the Old Domestic rested there. How amicable relations were between the Duke and the Duchess after that is not known.

Four years later in 1857 the Duke died. To Sarah Licence he left £50 down, £3 a week for life, his brass bedstead, a marble clock, a rosewood writing table and an armchair; he also provided her with a house for life. To the Duchess he left nothing.

A 'full-blown Victorian prig' is how A. L. Rowse describes John Winston, seventh Duke of Marlborough. Although it is hard to determine his priggishness he does conform to the image of the

Victorian pater-familias. Stiff, whiskered and forbidding, he had a fierce wife, a large brood of children and a greater number of servants. His wife, Frances, had 'large prominent eyes', a characteristic whose genetic bequest later caused an American visitor, looking at the family portraits on a tour of Blenheim, loudly to remark: 'My, what poppy eyes those Churchills have!' Frances, the daughter of the Marquess of Londonderry, was a strict chatelaine. 'At the rustle of her silk dress, the household trembled', wrote Jennie, her American daughter-in-law, who described the routine of the day at Blenheim in the 1860s thus:

In the morning an hour or more was devoted to the reading of newspapers, which was a necessity if one wanted to show an intelligent interest in the questions of the day, for at dinner conversation invariably turned on politics . . . At luncheon rows of entrée dishes adorned the table, joints beneath massive silver covers being placed before the Duke and Duchess, who each carved for the whole company, and as this included governesses, tutors and children, it was no sinecure . . . After dinner, which was a rather solemn full dress affair, we all repaired to what was called the Vandyke room. There one might read one's book or play for love a mild game of whist. Many a glance would be cast at the clock, which sometimes would be surreptitiously advanced a quarter of an hour by some sleepy member of the family. No one dared suggest bed until the sacred hour of eleven had struck. Then we would all troop out into a small anteroom, and, lighting our candles, each in turn would kiss the Duke and Duchess and depart to our own rooms.

John Winston was a very religious man: he took his position in life seriously. As Marquis of Blandford he was MP for Woodstock. He moved to the Lords in 1857 on the death of his gouty father. In both Houses his prime concern was the Church of England and he toiled persistently for the reforms of its administration. He cared deeply about the moral details of life. He deplored, for instance, any infringement of the Sabbath. In 1855 a motion was put forward that 'it would promote the moral and intellectual improvement of the working classes of this metropolis if the collections of natural history and of art in the British Museum and the National Gallery were open to the public inspection after morning service on Sundays'. John Winston abhorred the idea. Similarly, he objected to military bands playing in the parks on Sunday. He thought that 'affording amusement to the public' on Sunday was wrong: 'some colonels would rather cut their right hand off than offend their religious scruples', he said sweepingly. That drink was obtainable on the Sabbath from six to ten was most regrettable; it led to no good at all. Indeed it reduced people 'to the level of beasts'. Such was the colour of his convictions. So worried was he by the lax way things were going that in 1858 he supported a motion for a Select Committee to inquire into the Spiritual Destitution of England and Wales. His last speech in the House of Lords was on a bill to legalise marriage with a deceased wife's sister. He spoke against the measure. He thought it would be deleterious to the Church of England, and the House must have agreed with him for the bill was defeated by 145 votes to 140. After his death the matter was brought up again in 1901 but was resisted stalwartly by Lord Hugh Cecil, supported by Winston Churchill. Not until 1907 could men make honest women of their deceased wives' sisters – should they have wanted to.

John Winston's efforts were not unrewarded. He became Lord Steward of the Household and Lord President of the Council under Lord Derby. When Disraeli became Prime Minister in 1868 he wanted Marlborough to lead the Lords. 'He has culture, intellectual grasp and moral energy – great qualities, though in him they may have been developed in too contracted a sphere' was Disraeli's opinion. But the Duke stood down in favour of the more experienced Lord Malmesbury. In 1874 Disraeli offered him the Vice-regency of Ireland, but the Duke declined. He had enough to contend with at Blenheim and lacked the resources for a job entailing much expense in entertainment and duties; those careless Georgian dukes had not left him with an unlimited income.

Disraeli – then Lord Beaconsfield – again offered him the post in 1876. This time the Duke accepted. Winston Churchill in *My Early Life* said he did so because 'he always did what Lord Beaconsfield told him'. But that was not the true reason. Nor was it because he now had some cash in hand, having sold the Marlborough gems the year before for 35,000 guineas. The main reason was that the Duke's younger son, Lord Randolph Churchill, had fallen foul of the Prince of Wales over a scandal involving his brother, the Marquis of Blandford, and it was generally thought judicious to remove Randolph from London until the storm blew over. He accompanied his father to Dublin as unpaid Private Secretary. He took with him his young American wife, Jennie, and their two-year old son. This event marked the beginning of Lord Randolph's development as a serious politician, the beginning of Winston Churchill's long life and the end of Randolph and Jennie's marriage as anything other than a token partnership.

In Ireland the old Duke performed his duties as assiduously and stiffly as ever. His wife instituted a Famine Fund for Ireland and was proud to raise more than £110,000. When Gladstone returned to power in 1880 the Marlboroughs came home from Ireland. They must have been short of money again, for in 1881 they sold the

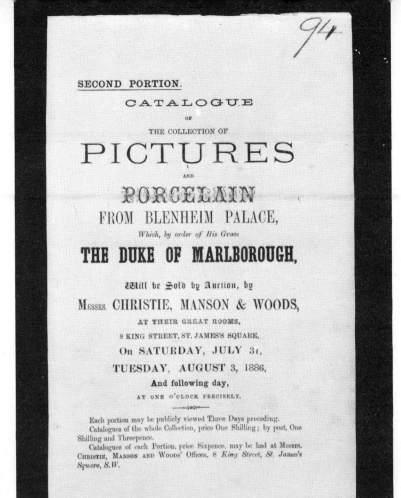

SECOND PORTION.

CATALOGUE

OF

THE COLLECTION OF

PICTURES

AND

PORCELAIN

FROM BLENHEIM PALACE,

Which, by order of His Grace

THE DUKE OF MARLBOROUGH,

Will be Sold by Auction, by

Messrs. CHRISTIE, MANSON & WOODS,

AT THEIR GREAT ROOMS,

8 KING STREET, ST. JAMES'S SQUARE,

On SATURDAY, JULY 31,

TUESDAY, AUGUST 3, 1886,

And following day,

AT ONE O'CLOCK PRECISELY.

Each portion may be publicly viewed Three Days preceding.
Catalogues of the whole Collection, price One Shilling; by post, One
Shilling and Threepence.
Catalogues of each Portion, price Sixpence, may be had at Messrs.
CHRISTIE, MANSON AND WOODS' Offices, 8 *King Street, St. James's
Square, S.W.*

Lack of money with which to preserve Blenheim placed a financial strain on successive dukes. The sale of porcelain advertised on this catalogue was but one of many occasions when the Churchill treasures were put up for sale. The collection of Bow, Bristol, Derby, Wedgwood and Worcester in this catalogue sold for £3646 12s.

Sunderland Library for £56,581. 6s. Despite the Duke's primness, his church-going, his killjoy measures in the House of Lords and his lack of money, life at Blenheim flourished as it had not for many years. Balls, parties and shoots were often held. The house was full. That depressing introspection of the fifth and sixth Dukes was dispelled and Blenheim's doors were open again to the outside world. It was unfortunate for the family that, with all his good intentions, John Winston was not an aesthete. There was a constant traffic of objects from Blenheim to the sale rooms. He was more interested in forestry. When his son became Duke in 1883 the traffic continued. Van Dyck's equestrian portrait of Charles 1 and Raphael's *Ansidei Madonna* were sold for £17,500 and £70,000 respectively to the National Gallery where, despite John Winston's efforts, they can now be seen on Sundays before, during and after morning service.

6
Randolph
and Jennie

RIGHT Lord Randolph
Churchill (1849–95),
second son of the seventh
Duke of Marlborough.
LEFT Jennie Churchill
in 1880 when she was
twenty-six.

JOHN WINSTON and his Duchess had five sons and six daughters.
All the daughters survived childhood, but only two sons did –
George Charles, Marquis of Blandford, and Lord Randolph Henry
Spencer-Churchill. Neither lived to an old age; both died before
their mother. Randolph was the more interesting of the two.

Born somewhat ominously on 13 February 1849, he was a wild
child who adored his parents, especially his mother, and who revelled
in the life at Blenheim with all the amusements it had to offer a young
boy. Eton he regarded as an unwelcome intrusion into that enjoyment. At Oxford he spent most of his time following the Blenheim
Harriers – a pack of hounds that he had formed himself. As Oxford is
only eight miles from Blenheim they were an easy temptation. Perhaps his father – or more likely his mother – persuaded him to give
up his Harriers and pay attention to his studies; certainly, in his last
year at Oxford he worked hard and only narrowly missed a first.

Whereas his brother, Blandford, spent his time in a fairly dissolute manner Randolph's life, though frivolous, showed greater promise. His parents therefore planned that he should be the next Member of Parliament for Woodstock. While he awaited the next election Lord Randolph led a merry life in the wake of the Prince of Wales, whose espousal of good living set the tone for his generation. The gaiety of the Marlborough House Set, as they were known, bubbled from under the austere canopy of Queen Victoria's reign. The London season then was 'a very serious matter which no self-respecting persons who considered themselves "in society" would forego, nor of which a votary of fashion would willingly miss a week or so'.

In 1873 Lord Randolph was following the fashionable trail and at the appropriate time of year found himself with the Marlborough House Set and many others at Cowes. A reception was held to meet the Russian Tsarevich and Tsarevna on board HMS *Ariadne*. It was not, however, the Russian royalty who impressed Randolph so much on this occasion as a young American girl, Miss Jeannette Jerome. She had black hair, a well-defined and lively face and, dressed for the party in white tulle, she was most striking. Randolph was mesmerised by her. They met again the following day and were still more delighted with each other. By the third day they had decided to marry. Randolph was twenty-four, Jennie nineteen. They set about lobbying their parents. Certain of the sense in their decision, they were genuinely surprised at others' lack of enthusiasm for their precipitate engagement.

Randolph sent his father Miss Jerome's photograph and added that 'She is as nice, as lovable, and amiable and charming in every way as she is beautiful, and that by her education and bringing-up she is in every way qualified to fill any position'. The Duke had his doubts. 'Under any circumstances an American connection is not one we would like', he said. 'You must allow it is a slight coming down in pride for us to contemplate the connection. From what you tell me and what I have heard this Mr Jerome seems to be a sporting, and I should think, vulgar sort of man. I hear he owns about six or eight houses in New York (One may take this as an indication of what the man is).' He added: 'It is evident he is of the class of speculators'.

Leonard Jerome was a flamboyant entrepreneur of great charm. It was said that he had made and lost two fortunes. Certainly he dabbled in publishing, in the press, in the telegraph business and in railroads. Sometimes he was very very rich and sometimes very much less so. Apart from speculating on Wall Street, what he most enjoyed was having a good time. This he did with a splash and an

Leonard Jerome (1818–91), father of Jennie Churchill, painted by an unknown American artist. His 'Wall Street career was remarkable alike for its alternation of enormous gains and losses.'

enthusiasm that were rare in his European counterparts. Above all, he loved horses. He determined to make racing a respectable business and he founded the New York Jockey Club. He then built the Jerome Park Racecourse, the opening of which 'proved the social event of all time and started a new era in the horse-racing world'. He built himself a mansion on the corner of Madison Square. 'It was of brick, faced with marble, three stories high, with a mansard roof' – that was the stable. The house itself was no less sumptuous. At the house-warming party he threw the fountains played champagne and cologne. On top of the stables there was a small theatre, for his other passion was music. He encouraged and patronised many young singers. He was particularly fond of Jennie Lind and when in 1857 his wife, Clara, gave birth to a second daughter he suggested the name Jennie.

Clara was a stolid, dark, good-looking, fashion-conscious woman, said to be a quarter Iroquois. In 1858, exasperated by Leonard's philandering, she had moved to Paris and settled there with her daughters, Clara, Jennie and Leonie. Paris was packed with European nobility in those years before the Franco-Prussian war, and as *la belle Américaine* and a roaring snob Clara had a wonderful time. When the French armies were retreating before the Prussians in 1870 and the collapse of the Second Empire looked imminent she hurried off to London with her daughters and there provided a warm welcome for refugee *comtes*, *vicomtes* and even the *Impératrice*. Thus when her second daughter announced her intention of marrying the needy younger son of an English duke, she was not pleased. She had set her sights higher than that. Leonard, on the other hand, was delighted, but he told his daughter to take care: 'You were never born to love lightly. It must be *way* down or nothing'. He added: 'You are no heiress' (his fortunes were low at the time) 'and it must have taken heaps of love to overcome an Englishman's prejudice against "those horrid Americans"'. However when he learnt of the extent of the Duke of Marlborough's prejudice against himself he withdrew his approval of the match.

The Duke insisted on a cooling-off period for the young couple, but as they remained infatuated throughout their enforced separation he had to relent. After somewhat ungentlemanly haggling over the dowry Leonard Jerome and the Duke came to a mutually satisfactory agreement. Just as Randolph and Jennie were on the point of being reunited with each other in Paris, the Grand Old Man, Mr Gladstone, called a general election and Randolph was deflected from Paris to campaign at Woodstock. On 1 April 1874 he was elected to Parliament. The announcement of the result in Woodstock brought 'such a burst of cheers that must have made the Old Dukes in the vault jump'. A fortnight later Randolph and Jennie were married in the British embassy in Paris. The Duke and Duchess did not attend.

Randolph and Jennie Churchill settled in London and flung themselves into the social round. Jennie in particular brought new zest and prettier clothes to the drawing-rooms of Belgravia. Randolph, small, with popping eyes and a thick moustache 'which had an emotion of its own', also dressed colourfully. He had, as Lord Rosebery put it, 'a fascination of manner' and could be most charming when he wished. When he made his maiden speech in the House of Commons Disraeli said that 'it was a speech of great promise'. Benjamin Jowett, the sagacious Master of Balliol, disagreed: 'It is only the speech of a foolish young man who will never come to any good'. From Randolph's infrequent appearances in the Commons at that time it looked as if Jowett was nearer the mark. Society claimed Randolph's time. Jennie's and his attendance at every fashionable function was only briefly interrupted by the birth of a son in November 1874. The baby, born at Blenheim, was premature. Nothing was prepared for its arrival and the layette had to be borrowed from the local doctor's wife, who was also pregnant. The baby was named Winston Leonard after its grandfathers. The Churchills' gay life continued – that is, until the row.

The facts of the row were these. Blandford, Randolph's brother, had married Lady Albertha Hamilton. The Marquis could not stand her. In particular he disliked the crude practical jokes that she enjoyed. She would place bars of soap among the cheese and watch with glee polite guests munching through them, or she would lodge an ink pot on top of a partly opened door and wait for her husband to open it further. He spent as little time as possible with her. In 1876 his mistress was Lady Aylesford. Her husband, Lord Aylesford – known as Sporting Joe – was with the Prince of Wales in India. News reached Aylesford of his wife's affair. The Prince of Wales, when he was told, insisted that both the Blandfords and the Aylesfords divorce and that Blandford marry Lady Aylesford. But divorce was still difficult and undesirable except in extreme circumstances. Lord Randolph thought the Prince's demand most unreasonable and, happening to know that the Prince of Wales had himself had an earlier flirtation with Lady Aylesford, and happening also to possess some compromising letters from the Prince, threatened to publish them unless the Prince withdrew his demand for divorce. Such blackmail was not the kind of behaviour that either the Queen or her heir would tolerate; they were not amused. The Prince let it be known that he would not enter any house in which the Churchills were present. His word went in society. Invitations to Lord Randolph and his wife dried up. Randolph's father thought it a good moment to accept Disraeli's offer of the Viceregency of Ireland.

Blandford did not marry Lady Aylesford, although she did give birth to his child. At about the time of its birth his wife, Albertha, substituted a pink baby doll for bacon and eggs under the salver at Blandford's breakfast table. It was the last straw. He left at speed and did not return. After a divorce Blandford eventually married again, this time a rich American widow, Mrs Lilian Hammersley. She preferred the name of Lily to Lilian, because she thought the latter rhymed too neatly with million. Duchess Lily was a jolly, gushing lady whom some of the family clearly considered vulgar, and others – the more American-minded ones – liked.

Before they went to Ireland the Churchills made a journey to America to visit Jennie's father. They arrived downcast by their ostracism in London. Leonard Jerome welcomed and consoled them: 'Forget it', he said, 'Let us go off to Newport to sail and drive and see what I have got left of a racing stable'. In his good-hearted way he kept them diverted. America proved, as so often it can, an invigorating experience.

It is thought that the social ostracism that Lord Randolph met at this time gave an impetus and a hard edge to his ambition. It is also said that it made him bitter. But he was not a vindictive man and when he returned after four interesting years in Ireland he was not so much bitter as simply a tougher, more mature and more aggressive political animal. His performances in the House of Commons had bite.

Lord Randolph's colleagues were surprised at the accuracy of his attacks and the political weight of his arguments. They had thought he was just a dandy. H. W. Lucy said within a year of Randolph's return from Ireland: 'Few spectacles have been more sublime than that of this young man of fashion devoting himself to the affairs of the State'. That was in October 1880. In April of that year there had been a general election. The Liberals had won, Lord Beaconsfield had resigned and Mr Gladstone had become Prime Minister for the second time. The Duke of Marlborough and his unpaid Private Secretary duly returned from Ireland.

The Leader of the Opposition in the House of Commons at this time was Sir Stafford Northcote. He was a commendable, sensible and moderate politician. 'Where he failed', said Lord Rosebery, 'was in his manner. His voice, his diction, his delivery, were all inadequate.' He had an 'academic twang' that irritated the House. Lord Randolph held a dim view of him, not so much on account of his manner, more for his failure to oppose. When attacks on the Government were called for from the Opposition none was forthcoming; the Tory leader remained mute. Northcote had been Gladstone's private secretary and it is possible that he had never shaken off his deference for the great Liberal leader. Indeed the whole House revered the Grand Old Man – even Lord Randolph.

But Randolph could not bear such spineless politics; as the Opposition, the Tories must oppose. So he took it on himself to attack the Liberals. Together with three other backbenchers – Sir Henry Wolff, John Gorst and A. J. Balfour – he persistently obstructed Mr Gladstone's business. So vigorous, obstreperous and effective were they that they were referred to as the Fourth Party. They despised Northcote and nicknamed him 'the Goat'. They did not despise Gladstone, but they pestered him mercilessly. They went into the details of every Bill and raised any relevant question. Gladstone responded to the challenge and the rallies between him and the Fourth Party brought to the House a dynamism and an interest that had long been lacking. The four friends sat on the front bench below the gangway and from there pressed their attacks with the greatest gaiety and good humour. They enjoyed the battle and were more like irreverent schoolboys (although Gorst was in his late forties and Wolff over fifty) than responsible men of state. Unlike many schoolboys, they did their homework and their arguments had point and weight.

Lady Randolph enjoyed it too. She often sat in the Ladies' Gallery and watched the debates. Their house in St James's Place (next door, ironically, to Northcote's) 'became the rendez-vous of all shades of politicians' she wrote later. 'Many were the plots and plans which were hatched in my presence by the Fourth Party, who, notwithstanding the seriousness of their endeavours, found time to laugh heartily and often at their own frustrated machinations. How we used to chaff at the "goats" as we called the ultra-Tories and followers of Sir Stafford Northcote!'

Lord Beaconsfield advised them to support Northcote, but they were reluctant to do so. Beaconsfield died in 1881. Not long before his death he had been asked his opinion of Lord Randolph, who, although only thirty-two, was already an estimable figure in the Commons. Beaconsfield said that when the Tories came to power 'they will have to give him anything he chooses to ask for and in a very short time they will have to take anything he chooses to give them'.

Lord Randolph's reputation was considerable. He had a flair for Parliamentary business and an intuitive sense of the mood of the Chamber. His speeches were original, lively and funny; they skirted downright rudeness. Their impact was to exhilarate. At that time he and his colleagues of the Fourth Party were the life-blood of the Tory Party. And as his reputation grew in the House of Commons, so word of his ability spread throughout the country. He began to enjoy great popularity in the provinces, especially in the Midlands. 'Little Randy', 'Cheeky Randy', 'the Champagne Charley of Politics', he was called with affection. The Old Gang of the Conservative Party were uncertain of their new commodity. He could not be relied on to toe the party line. He did not treat their leader in the House of Commons with respect. Yet, they had to admit, almost single-handed he was reviving a flagging party, and he was undermining the rock of the Grand Old Man.

One of Randolph's prime beliefs was that the Tory Party could and must appeal to the working classes. Their loyal support was

A *Vanity Fair* cartoon of 'the Fourth Party', the four Tory backbenchers who in the early 1880s were renowned for their spirited opposition to Gladstone and the Liberals. They always sat on the front bench below the gangway. From left to right: Lord Randolph, A. J. Balfour, Sir Henry Wolff and John Gorst.

not necessarily the prerogative of the Liberals. To gain their trust and confidence the working classes must be represented on the Executive of the Party. But the National Union of Conservative Associations, a self-elected body controlled by the Old Gang, was the machine that ran the party throughout the constituences. Lord Randolph suggested that its council should be responsible, representative and elected annually. He intended to wriggle himself into the administration and then put his suggestions into effect. Before long he emerged as chairman of a council in which his supporters were in the majority. All was set for the reforms to turn it into a democratic institution. But the other big party machine – the Central Committee – was still manned by the Old Gang. Lord Salisbury, the party leader, began to by-pass the Council of the National Union and conduct his business solely with the Central Committee. Lord Randolph was furious – and resigned. This rattled the Tory ranks and they soon had him back as Chairman of the Council. The National Union of Conservative Associations became a democratic institution as advocated by Lord Randolph. His resignation had been effective.

At first wary of the Reform Bill of 1884, which gave the franchise to country householders and thereby added two million voters to the register, Randolph came to support it. For in his journeys to the Midlands and the North he saw how popular a measure it was. His growing acquaintance with the working classes and their needs led him to the brand of Tory Democracy with which he became associated. His dictum was: 'Trust the people'. Lord Salisbury, his leader, had not come to the same conclusion; he was sincerely anti-democratic in the old Tory tradition.

Lord Randolph made one other notable bid to promote the Tory party throughout the country. He and Wolff founded the Primrose League. After the ceremony for the unveiling of the statue of Lord Beaconsfield, Wolff had noticed on his way back to the Commons that a lot of MPs were wearing primroses – Disraeli's favourite flower – in their buttonholes. He thought it would be a suitable emblem for a Tory organisation, and the League, still alive today, grew from there. Lord Salisbury doubted its success. Lady Salisbury – a keen member of the Ladies' Grand Council – was asked if it were not all rather vulgar. 'Vulgar?' she said, 'Of course it is. That is why we have got on so well.'

Interruptions in Lord Randolph's parliamentary life were caused by the sudden death of his father in 1883 – a sad blow – and by his own bouts of illness. His slight frame was propelled by nervous energy. He was, as his son Winston was later to put it, 'of the temper that gallops till it falls'. He was cursed with unreliable health. Yet it was more serious than just nervous exhaustion and a weak constitution. His periods of collapse were precursors of the creeping paralysis that is caused by syphilis. When and how he contracted the disease, and when Jennie got to know about it, are uncertain. When she did, it must have been a dampener, to say the least, on their relationship. She was young, beautiful and sensual, admired and escorted by many. However she reached some kind of accommodating *modus vivendi* with Randolph.

In the winter of 1884–5, for reasons of health, Randolph went on a long trip to India. He returned in April in time to see Gladstone's administration topple and fall. The Liberals had tripped over an amendment to the budget. As Parliament could not be dissolved until the autumn because of the new, expanded franchise, Queen Victoria asked Lord Salisbury to form an interim administration. Lord Randolph was thirty-six; he had no experience of office, but such was his stature, his 'natural ascendancy', that Lord Salisbury was obliged to include him in his team. He was asked to be Secretary of State for India. It was a highly responsible and important position and the offer was a measure of Lord Randolph's meteoric success. Lord Randolph, however, refused. He would not serve unless his old enemy, Sir Stafford Northcote, whom Salisbury had appointed Leader of the House of Commons and Chancellor of the Exchequer, were removed. It was an arrogant demand and one that he later admitted was probably an error. But again his threat brought the desired results: Sir Stafford Northcote went to the House of Lords as Lord Iddesleigh, Sir Michael Hicks-Beach became Leader of the House of Commons and Lord Randolph took over the India Office.

On taking office he had to fight a by-election at Woodstock. Such was the pressure of work at the India Office that he entrusted the campaigning at Woodstock to his wife and to his sister, Lady Curzon. They sped about on a tandem flying Lord Randolph's racing colours of pink and brown. Mr Henry James rebuked Jennie for her rather risqué ascent and descent of the tandem. But the constituents enjoyed the spectacle.

> Bless my soul! That Yankee Lady,
> Whether day was bright or shady,
> Dashed about the district like an oriflamme of war.
> When the voters saw her bonnet
> With the bright pink roses on it,
> They followed as the soldiers did the Helmet of Navarre.

With her energetic charm Jennie persuaded the electorate and they duly returned Lord Randolph again.

At the India Office not only had Lord Randolph to master the complexities of an entire sub-continent of three hundred millions of the Queen's subjects, but he also had to preside over the India Council. This was a body of fifteen old or elderly men who had spent most of their lives in India. Randolph had spent barely four months there – and those as a tourist not an administrator. Queen Victoria, who had sanctioned his appointment with reluctance, was reassured by the fact that 'the India Council would be a check on him'.

The responsibilities were daunting, but he set to work hard. Where he had previously shown impatience and arrogance he now displayed patience and humility. He treated the India Council with respect but not subservience and revealed the greatest powers of concentration and a talent for getting things done. These qualities enabled him to triumph beyond anybody's expectations, not least those of the civil servants over whom he presided. At the first meeting of the India Council he felt, he said, 'like an Eton boy presiding at a meeting of the Masters'. But the old men soon appreciated his lack of pomposity and his ability to get straight to the point. He listened, he absorbed, he executed.

The honeymoon came to an abrupt end. The Bombay command had fallen vacant and the Queen wanted her son, the Duke of Connaught, to fill the vacancy. Lord Randolph told Lord Salisbury that in his opinion it was unsuitable to appoint a royal duke to a post that was not only dangerous and difficult but also carried political responsibilities. Furthermore the army and navy might well resent such a lucrative post going to a member of the royal family. The Queen asked Lord Salisbury to send a telegram to Lord Dufferin, the Viceroy, to find out his opinion on the matter. Lord Randolph, being told of the exchange of telegrams, felt that he had been excluded from what was essentially his business and took offence. His umbrage took the form of a letter of resignation to Lord Salisbury. 'A first-class question of Indian administration has been taken out of my hands', he expostulated. So Lord Salisbury sent another telegram to Lord Dufferin explaining that the first he had sent was from the Queen and that he had merely acted as transmitter. This soothed Lord Randolph. The extreme touchiness he showed in this matter has generally been attributed to his health, which was poor at the time. The Duke of Connaught was not appointed and the post remained vacant. But Lord Randolph had now used the weapon of resignation or withdrawal to carry a point for the third time, and although for the third time he had been successful, Lord Salisbury, who had to parry these attacks, was exasperated. He complained that he was in charge not of two departments but of four: 'the Prime Ministership, the Foreign Office, the Queen and Randolph Churchill – and,' he added, 'the burden of them increases in that order.'

The end of Lord Randolph's short period at the India Office was devoted to the affairs of Upper Burma, the annexation of which he formally and proudly announced on 1 January 1886. Within a month Lord Randolph had left the India Office, not because he had resigned, but simply because Lord Salisbury's administration had fallen and the Liberals were back in power. A minor amendment to the Coercion Bill for Ireland had ostensibly brought the Tories down, but as Lord Rosebery wrote: 'In the midst of all there loomed the stark form of the Irish question. That was the issue on which every mind was silently fixed, while the audible talk was of the area necessary to support a cow'.

Mr Gladstone had plumped for Home Rule for Ireland. The Irish members in the House of Commons, led by Parnell, had given him their support and enabled him to defeat the Government. But he was back in power for only five months and during that short term the impossible Irish question overshadowed all other business. Lord Randolph was passionately opposed to Home Rule. He was accused

A cartoon entitled 'The Home Rule Card Game'. The players from left to right are Lord Randolph Churchill, Lord Salisbury, Charles Parnell, William Gladstone and Joseph Chamberlain.

6. The Home Rule Card Game.

Churchill   Salisbury   Parnell   Gladstone   Chamberlain

Lord Randolph speaking
against Home Rule in
Belfast from the *Graphic*,
6 March 1886. It was about
this time that he coined the
phrase – 'Ulster will fight,
and Ulster will be right'.

THE

CHAIRED

IN THE ULSTER HALL, BELFAST

IN THE STREETS

of being inconsistent, because when in Ireland he had met and junketed with Parnell and other Irish nationalists; he also held liberal views on certain aspects of the problem, such as education and coercion. Whether he opposed Home Rule through conviction or whether simply to beat the Grand Old Man is arguable; but he picked up the anti-Home Rule stick, and thus armed threw himself into the fray. In February he wrote to his old Irish friend, Lord Justice Fitzgibbon, that he had 'decided some time ago that if the GOM went for Home Rule, the Orange card would be the one to play. Please God,' he wrote, 'it may turn out the ace of trumps and not the two.' He had enormous popular appeal in Ulster, to which he responded when he went to Belfast in February with strong and rousing speeches. Shortly after his visit, he coined those famous words: 'Ulster will fight and Ulster will be right!'

Meanwhile Mr Gladstone had introduced the Home Rule Bill. His party was not united. Many had defected to the Unionist cause – a term coined by Lord Randolph to include all those opposed to Home Rule. It was unlikely that the bill would get through, but such was Gladstone's eloquence that members knew that the case he put before them would be the very best that could be stated. 'From my knowledge of the House of Commons under the Gladstone spell,' said Lord Randolph, 'if the Angel Gabriel was to follow the GOM tomorrow, nobody would report him or care a damn what he said.' When the time came for the division on the second reading of the bill John Bright was found already sitting in the 'No' lobby. He said that he could not have trusted himself to oppose the bill if he had heard Gladstone speak. The result was 341 noes to 311 ayes. The Grand Old Man was out. Home Rule had to wait until 1922 when Lord Randolph's son, Winston, helped negotiate the treaty with Ireland. The electorate was asked to vote again.

In Paddington it was asked to vote for Lord Randolph; that was now his constituency. He hankered after a large Midlands seat and had fought the previous election in Birmingham. But on being beaten by the Radical John Bright he had declared: 'Gentlemen, the man who cannot stand a knock-down blow isn't worth a damn,' and had hurried off to Paddington where a seat had been kept warm for him in case of such eventuality. In his election address to the Paddington voters this time he deplored the plan to separate Ireland from England. He called it 'this monstrous mixture of imbecility, extravagance, and political hysterics . . . And why? For this reason and no other: to gratify the ambitions of an old man in a hurry'.

The election returned 316 Tories, 78 Liberal Unionists, 191 Gladstonian Liberals and 85 Irish Nationalists. It was Salisbury's turn to form an administration and he went to see the Queen. She wrote in her journal: 'Lord Salisbury came to see me again at four, and we talked over everything ... He feared Lord Randolph Churchill must be Chancellor of the Exchequer and Leader [of the House of Commons] which I did not like. He is so mad and odd, and has also bad health'.

Lord Randolph's enemies, who considered him wicked, were horrified by his appointment. Even his supporters were apprehensive for it was a daring appointment. Only his mother, his political confidante, was unequivocally pleased. The fact was that as Lord Randolph led the House of Commons in all but name he might as well do so officially. That was the opinion of Sir Michael Hicks-Beach, who had been offered the job first, but who had declined in favour of Lord Randolph. When asked how long he would stay at the job, Lord Randolph answered: 'Six months'. His forecast was out by a couple of months.

As at the India Office, so as Leader of the House, he again surpassed all expectations. He dealt with the business in hand with speed and agility. He showed great aptitude for the complicated work he had to do. Things moved forward. At the end of the first session he was considered a success. Queen Victoria thanked him and said that he had 'shown much skill and judgment in his leadership during this exceptional session of Parliament'.

The Treasury too was nervous of its new chief. *The Times* urged caution in his care of the public purse. His friends encouraged him not to take rash measures. The Cabinet wondered what sort of budget he would present. Before he had finished hacking it out, he gave an important speech to a large audience at Dartford, which amounted to a personal manifesto. He spoke in favour of local government reform, changes in the House of Commons procedure, allotments for agricultural workers, various government economies, and support for the liberties of the Balkan peoples. Radicals accused him of stealing their ideas and Conservatives complained that they had a radical Chancellor. He was proving a wilful and recalcitrant colleague. The Dartford speech provoked a series of dissensions within the Cabinet. On almost every issue Lord Randolph stood alone. He grew more and more irritated as his proposals met further rebuffs. 'I am afraid it is an idle schoolboy's dream to suppose that the Tories can legislate, which I did stupidly,' he wrote to Lord Salisbury. 'They can govern and make war and increase taxation and expenditure *à merveille*, but legislation is not their province in a democratic constitution.'

Lord Salisbury had the unenviable task of keeping the Cabinet united and Lord Randolph happy, of deferring to both sides. Naturally neither was satisfied. The Prime Minister explained his difficult position and justified his laissez-faire attitude to Lord Cranbrook:

What you call my self-renunciation is merely an effort to deal with an abnormal and very difficult state of things. It arises from the peculiarities of Churchill. Beach having absolutely refused to lead, Churchill is the only possible leader in the House of Commons – and his ability is unquestionable. But he is wholly out of sympathy with the rest of the Cabinet, and, being besides of a wayward and headstrong disposition, he is far from mitigating his resistance by the method of it. As his office of Leader of the House gives him a claim to be heard on every question, the machine is moving along with the utmost friction both in home and foreign affairs. My self-renunciation is only an attempt – a vain attempt – to pour oil upon the creaking machinery. Like you, I am penetrated with a sense of the danger which the collapse of the Government would bring about: otherwise I should not have undertaken – or should have quickly abandoned – the task of leading an orchestra in which the first fiddle plays one tune and everybody else, including myself, wishes to play another.

Meanwhile the 'first fiddle' was working on his budget. His proposals were unorthodox, daring and intelligent; he described them as 'unpolished gems'. Most of the ways for pruning the government expenditure had been exhausted, so Lord Randolph planned a reconstruction of the revenue. His general intentions were to transfer tax burdens from comforts to luxuries, from necessities to pleasures. He toyed with a tax evaluated according to the citizen's ability to pay. He had a new and simplified scheme for death duty. He proposed to reduce the Sinking Fund by four-and-a-half million pounds. There were many details, including an imaginative one to put a penny stamp on the shot end of cartridges, so that the surer the eye of the sportsman the less he would have to pay. When he delivered his mixed bag to the Cabinet they saw the point of it but made no comment. 'They said nothing,' he complained, 'nothing at all; but you should have seen the look on their faces!' Whereas the Treasury heaved a sigh of relief that it had been so smoothly received Lord Randolph sounded disappointed. It was as if he had wanted to shock them. But if a quarrel was what he wanted it was not long before he found one.

Friction had been growing between W. H. Smith, the Minister of War, and Lord Randolph. In increasingly querulous letters Lord Randolph had been chiding W. H. Smith for his extravagance and his reluctance to make cuts in his ministry. Smith had missed the Cabinet meeting at which Lord Randolph had presented his budget proposals, so he wrote and asked him for a short memorandum on them. He got back a hot-tempered and rude letter which said that his

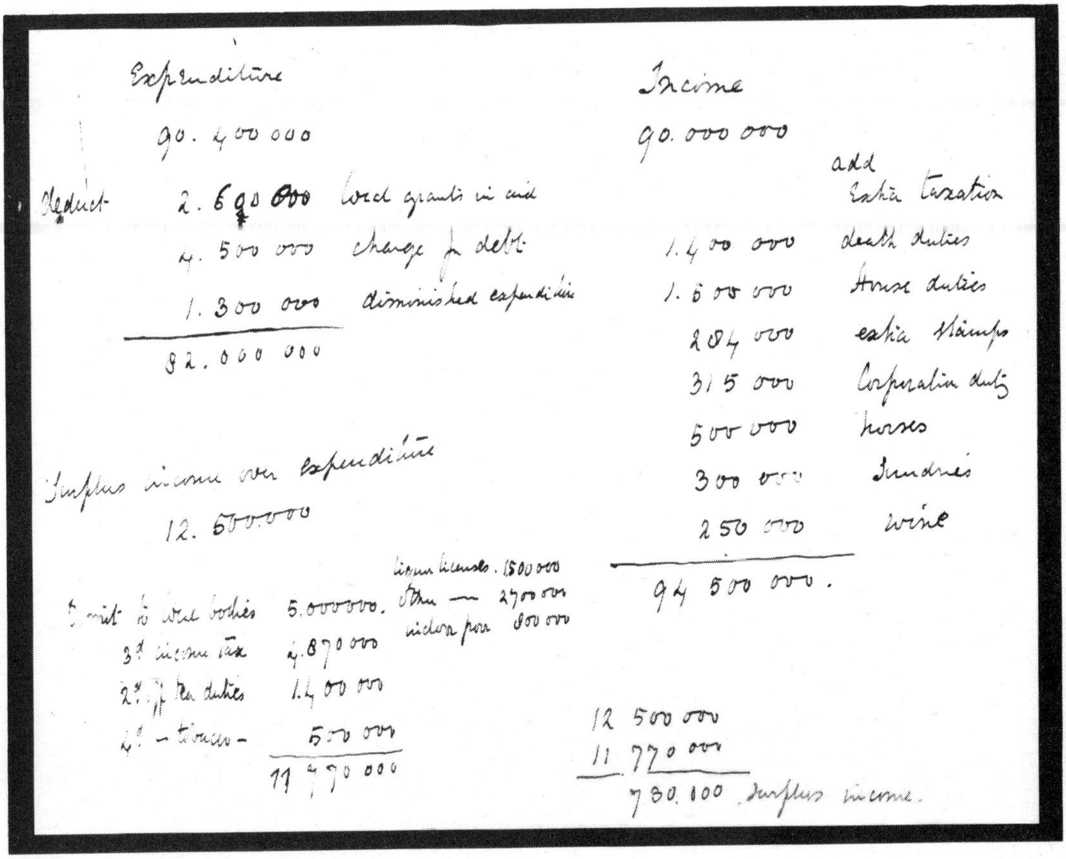

Expenditure
90.400 000
Deduct
2.600 000 local grants in aid
4.500 000 charge for debt
1.300 000 diminished expenditure
82.000 000
Surplus income over expenditure
12.500 000
liquor licenses. 1500 000
Other — 2700 000
widow pow 800 000
Remit to local bodies 5.000000.
3d income tax 4.870 000
2d off tea duties 1.400 000
4d – tobacco – 500 000
11 770 000
Income
90.000 000
add
Extra taxation
1.400 000 death duties
1.600 000 House duties
284 000 extra stamps
315 000 Corporation duty
500 000 horses
300 000 Sundries
250 000 wine
94 500 000.
12 500 000
11 770 000
730.100 Surplus income.

Lord Randolph's manuscript notes for the budget of 1886; he resigned before it was presented.

request was most unreasonable. They met on 20 December 1886 to hammer out the estimates for the army and navy. Smith said he needed thirty-one million pounds. Lord Randolph said he must do with less. That same night Lord Randolph wrote to Lord Salisbury from Windsor Castle, where he was spending the night as a guest of the Queen, and tendered his resignation on the grounds that the army and navy estimates were greatly in excess of what he could consent to. The following morning he returned to London. At an official luncheon party he was on good form and gave no hint of the step he had taken. Afterwards his former colleague in the Fourth Party, Sir Henry Wolff, asked a question about the Chancellorship. 'Between ourselves,' Lord Randolph replied, 'I do not know at this moment whether I am Chancellor of the Exchequer or not.'

In fact he was not: Lord Salisbury had accepted his resignation. He might have pressed him to stay on; he might have worked out an agreement between the two ministers and forced them to reach a

compromise. But he did not, and he gave Lord Randolph no chance to change his mind. By the evening of 22 December he was out of office. He did not tell Jennie; she read it in the newspaper the next morning. 'Quite a surprise for you,' he said. His mother, who had been staying with the Salisburys at Hatfield, 'left the house in tears. "Why, oh, why are my sons so unlike other people's sons?" she was heard lamenting as she was assisted down the Grand Staircase'.

Of course the news caused a sensation. The *Irish Times* wrote: 'Lord Randolph has burnt his boots'. His action was irrevocable whether he had intended it to be or not. Probably he had not. Nobody thought the comparatively trivial matter of the defence estimates was the whole truth behind his resignation, but nobody knew what was. Had it been an impatient bid for power? If so the moment was ill-timed: Parliament had dispersed for Christmas. And the ground was ill-considered: none of the Cabinet would support him and the issue was not popular in the country. 'Economy has no friends,' as Lord Rosebery put it. Was it a neurotic expression of exasperation at the gap between himself and his colleagues on so many issues, at their stubborn reluctance to adopt any of his progressive proposals? Or a petulant 'shan't' in the face of the Old Gang? Had he misjudged the power of his trusty weapon – resignation and withdrawal? It had served him well three times already. Perhaps he had just grown careless with it. Perhaps Rosebery was right that 'his nature required a relief for its high strung irritability in some sort of violence, and resignation was the only form that violence could take'. Or was Jennie nearer the mark?: 'In the bottom of my heart I sometimes think his head was quite turned at the moment and that he thought he could do *anything*'.

Whatever the reason he soon realised the extent of the damage done to his political career: it was shattered irreparably. 'In inflicting on the Old Gang this final blow I have mortally wounded myself,' he said. His son, Winston Churchill, claimed that although he regretted the consequences he never repented the course he had taken. The holes in the administration created by his resignation were soon filled. W. H. Smith became Leader of the House of Commons and Sir Edward Goschen, the Whig financial wizard, Chancellor of the Exchequer. Lord Randolph was variously reported to have made the laconic remark: 'I forgot Goschen'.

As Lord Randolph once again took his place on the backbenches two sad events occurred. A. W. Moore, his devoted private secretary at the India Office, died more or less of a broken heart at the age of forty-six. He had been deeply affected by Randolph's resignation – 'a calamity', he said. Lord Randolph, he told Jennie, 'has thrown himself from the top of the ladder and will never reach it again'. The second event concerned Lord Iddesleigh, who, as Sir Stafford North-cote, had suffered more than his fair share of Randolph's political savagery. Yet he had reason to regret his critic's downfall. Goschen, the new Chancellor, insisted on Iddesleigh's removal from the Foreign Office. Lord Salisbury, with no alternative chancellor, complied and sacked Iddesleigh. The sacking was a little vague and Iddesleigh did not realise it was final until he read it in the news-papers. Very upset, he hurried off to Lord Salisbury for an explana-tion. On arrival, 'he sank into a chair, and after breathing with diffi-culty for a while, he died at five past three in the presence of two doctors, Lord Salisbury and Mr Manners'. The poor 'Goat' was dead.

Lord Randolph remained on the backbenches for the rest of his parliamentary life. Although Lord Rosebery claimed that 'he was never the same man again', for the time being his speeches were as brilliant and his audience in the House of Commons as captive as ever. He pledged support to the administration, but was not re-strained from attacking it when he saw fit – no Tory cow was sacred. Nevertheless Salisbury and his Government had an easier time of things. 'Did you ever know a man who, having a boil on his neck, wanted another?' said Lord Salisbury, when asked if he would em-ploy Lord Randolph again. The irony was that by the end of their term in office the Tories had adopted many of Lord Randolph's measures, including those for cuts in expenditure on defence. From the backbenches Lord Randolph bullied the Government about the wastefulness at the War Office, and he continued to champion Tory Democracy. He moved closer politically to Joseph Chamberlain and thought of forming a Centre Party. 'All centre and no circumfer-ence,' commented Sir William Harcourt.

Although he had many enemies who eyed him with the darkest suspicion Lord Randolph still commanded an enormous following. There was a stock of goodwill behind him: from Members of Parlia-ment, who exulted when he combined his brilliance with conformity to his party (often he would disappoint them by following an appro-priate speech with a less appropriate one); and from working people throughout the country, many of whom saw him as the champion of their interests. Two or three times situations arose that he could have exploited to his own political advantage. Yet each time he let the opportunity go. He remained a critical and powerless supporter of the Government.

'I have tried all forms of excitement from tip-cat to tiger-shooting; all degrees of gambling from beggar-my-neighbour to Monte Carlo; but have found no gambling like politics, and no excitement like a big division,' he had said. But the fun had gone out of it now and he needed other entertainment. He took to the turf and to travel. His greatest success at the races was to win the Oaks with a filly he had bought for £300 called L'Abbesse de Jouarre. Jennie, who was boating on the Thames at the time of the race, asked a lock-keeper if he had heard who won. 'Abscess on the Jaw,' he said, and she regretted not having backed it.

Lord Randolph had always travelled a lot, partly for his health and partly out of curiosity. The aftermath of the resignation made him feel 'rather seedy' so, for distraction, he went to North Africa with his friend, Harry Tyrwhitt. His letters home profess his relief to be rid of politics, but the sentiment did not ring very true. As Winston Churchill commented: 'When a politician dwells on the fact that he is thankful to be rid of public cares, and finds serene contentment in private life, it may usually be concluded that he is extremely unhappy'. And Harry Tyrwhitt reported how he would brood gloomily for hours on end on their sunny balcony.

Sadly for his children he did not turn to his family for consolation. Since the Prince of Wales had forgiven them in 1883, Randolph and Jennie had been swept up again into society. Jennie flourished in its glare. Her vitality and allure had never been greater and while Randolph had been in office they had never been further apart. Count Kinsky, an Austrian nobleman of great suavity, laid the greatest claim to her heart. (He was especially popular in London for having ridden in the Grand National – and won.) But she was in demand everywhere, for she had a personality that enriched all occasions. 'One never thought of giving a party without her,' wrote Lady Warwick, the Prince of Wales's 'Darling Daisy'. 'She was like a marvellous diamond – a host of facets seemed to sparkle at once. Winston and his younger brother Jack were largely ignored. Jennie's sister, Leonie, described how Randolph would shoo his sons away when they came to the dining room to say good morning: 'The two pairs of round eyes, peeping round the screen, longed for a kind word'. Winston, in *My Early Life*, could remember having only 'three or four long intimate conversations' with his father. Both he and Jack were neglected at Harrow. They would ask their parents to come and visit them. 'You have never been to see me,' wrote Winston to his father after more than a year at school, 'and so everything will be new to you. P.S. I shall be awfully disappointed if you don't come'. But he did not come. Yet it seems that Lord Randolph's inability to form any warm relationship with his children and his utter lack of effort in that direction did not stem from cruelty or natural unkindness so much as from some psychological block that might in time have been dislodged. But the time was not there and the bad record of paternal callousness is unmitigated.

Jennie loved her sons, especially when they were grown up

While they passed through the less interesting state of childhood she confided them almost exclusively to the care of an old nurse, Mrs Everest. Winston adored this dependable and comfortable old lady who was, in his mind, 'associated more than anything else with *home*'. 'My nurse was my confidante,' he wrote. She was his 'dearest and most intimate friend', to be immortalised by him in *My Early Life*. Jennie too often found that the pull of a house party or a fashionable occasion was greater than that of her sons, and she often let them down. 'I would go down to you,' she wrote in June 1890 to Winston at Harrow, 'but I have so many things to arrange about the Ascot party next week that I can't manage it.' On another occasion her excuse was that she was '*really* obliged to go to Stowe on Saturday'. However Winston's letters to his mother are frank and it is clear that he often could get his way with her. She treated her sons as equals and encouraged them to treat her likewise. She told them to speak up and speak their minds however much older and wiser the rest of the company. It was an American habit and not one fostered by Victorian mothers or found in the manuals of Victorian etiquette. The result was that when the boys grew up they were warm and open with their mother and were never shy in company.

There was no relenting in the slow progress of Randolph's illness. As it took a firmer hold his grip on affairs began to loosen. His speeches lost their exceptional quality. He trembled. His face grew ashen and his mood irritable. He went abroad more often and, in 1887, annoyed Queen Victoria by going to Russia. 'He really is *not* to be trusted,' she said. Jennie went too and in her *Reminiscences* described the magnificent Tsarist functions they attended. Both regretted seeing Blenheim pictures by Raphael and by Rubens in foreign hands. (The pictures had been sold by Randolph's brother, the Duke, and had caused a rift in the family.) Winston wrote to his mother in Russia and described the Christmas he and Jack had spent in London: 'Auntie Clara was too ill to come so Auntie Leonie & Uncle Jack were our only visitors. We drank the Queen's health and Your health & Papa's. Then Everest's and Auntie Clara and Uncle Moreton'.

Lord Randolph went to South Africa in 1891 hoping to make some money. He had never had very much and Jennie was a consistently hopeless housekeeper. Both had expensive tastes. If depressed Jennie might hurry over to Paris for a £200 dress by Worth. As Edward Marsh wrote: 'Life didn't begin for her on a basis of less than forty pairs of shoes'. Randolph would demand *oeufs brouillés aux truffes*. A recurrent theme in their sons' letters from school was the demand for money; the usual answer was that there was none. Winston asked for an allowance: 'It would be much better than the present arrangements which are "Spend as much as I can get. Get as much as I can"'. On his widely publicised tour of South Africa Lord Randolph bought some gold-mining shares, which did appreciate handsomely, but not in time for him to enjoy the income from the investment.

W. H. Smith died later that year and A. J. Balfour became Leader of the House of Commons. 'I have waited with great patience for the tide to turn, but it has not turned, and will not now turn in time,' Lord Randolph commented. The following year Mr Gladstone and the Liberals were once again returned to power. Back in opposition, Salisbury and his colleagues began to make overtures to Randolph again. A. J. Balfour urged him to come and sit on the front bench. They knew that Randolph was the man to tackle the Grand Old Man. But the moment for such a battle had passed, Lord Randolph's nerve had gone. There was one moment on the introduction of that old tortoise, the Home Rule Bill, when he delivered an excellent speech, which, as his words had so often done before in the days of the Fourth Party, provoked a dazzling response from Mr Gladstone. But it was just a spark; there was no fire. Gladstone was ageing, Lord Randolph was ill. His colleagues were horrified to see just how sick he was. His white, drawn face and shaking hands were a shock to them. As the new session in the Commons progressed his condition deteriorated. He often lost the thread of what he was saying. He stopped making sense. Where previously he could fill the House members now dreaded him rising to speak and cried 'Divide! Divide!' when he did. It was pitiable. What made it more so was that he was to some extent oblivious of his decay. 'There was no retirement, no concealment. He died by inches in public.'

In 1894 he was told to take a rest from politics. He decided to go round the world. Nobody thought it a good idea but he was determined. Jennie and a young doctor were to accompany him. Before he left he gave a farewell dinner party for his friends, an occasion which was, Lord Rosebery said, 'all pain and yet one would not have liked to miss his goodbye'.

Jennie described the trip to America and the Far East in her *Reminiscences*, but she made very few references to Randolph or his condition. However she wrote privately to her sister that he was 'quite unfit for society . . . you cannot imagine anything *more* distracting and desperate than to watch it and to see him as he is and to think of him as he was'. At Singapore he became very ill indeed, but refused to return until he had seen Burma, 'which I annexed'. After Burma they hurried home to arrive at the end of December. 'Physically he is better but mentally he is a thousand times worse,' Jennie told her sister. 'Even his mother wishes now that he had died the other day.' His body slowly succumbed to the final paralysis. He died in his sleep on 24 January 1895. 'Summoned from a neighbouring house where I was sleeping,' wrote Winston, 'I ran in the darkness across Grosvenor Square, then lapped in snow. His end was quite painless. Indeed he had long been in a stupor. All my dreams of comradeship with him, of entering Parliament at his side and in his support were ended. There remained for me only to pursue his aims and vindicate his memory.'

'The most tragic career in British politics of the nineteenth century,' is A. L. Rowse's verdict. For all its brilliance it had lasted only six of Lord Randolph's forty-six years; and of those only twelve months had been spent in office. Yet the slight, dandified figure with the stiff frock coat and elegant diamond-studded amber cigarette-holder and poached egg eyes had hogged the limelight. Although he flirted with radical ideas and had a realistic and forward view of the importance of labour interests, and although he propounded the concept of Tory Democracy, it was not his politics that had appeal so much as some emotional empathy. His speeches 'tickled the popular palate'. Had he lived he might have found his way into the Liberal Party and been more comfortable there. But it is unlikely. His attachment to the Tory Party was deep. He had inherited strong Toryism from both his father and his mother and even at the end of his life his mother was still a powerful influence. The aristocrat in him was a Tory. In this he was almost a snob. His prejudice against the opulent middle class was manifested in his unreasonable attack on W. H. Smith, the bookseller and politician. The issue was votes for householders. Smith had argued against giving the Irish peasant in his log cabin the vote. Lord Randolph said:

I suppose that in the minds of the lords of suburban villas, of the owners of vineries and pineries, the mud-cabin represents the climax of physical and social degradation. But the franchise in England has never been determined by Parliament with respect to the character of the dwellings. The difference between the cabin of the Irish peasant and the cottage of the English agricultural worker is not so great as that which exists between the abode of the Right Honourable Member for Westminster [Smith] and the humble roof which shelters from the storm the individual who now has the honour to address the Committee.

Although Lord Randolph later apologised, 'vineries and pineries' stuck.

He was persistently scornful of his party, which he felt failed to enact enlightened and progressive measures; its members were 'ungrateful, short-sighted beasts'. The trouble was, as Winston Churchill said, 'that he regarded Liberal measures as things good and desirable in themselves; while many of his colleagues, and certainly his chief, looked upon them as so many unholy surrenders to the powers of evil'. After his resignation he wrote to Chamberlain saying that he had done his best, but that he 'had ceased to be useful . . . Their innate Toryism is rampant and irrepressible'. In Opposition his colleagues found him a useful and popular propagandist, but when in power he was an embarrassment, his ideas too radical to be put into effect. 'Though honourable members do not in the least object to my winning applause at great mass meetings in the country,' he said, 'there seems to be considerable difference of opinion when I attempt to carry these opinions to a practical conclusion.'

He was difficult. He was naturally rebellious and he liked to shock, he liked to be contrary. He had 'a certain perversity of character not unlike that popularly attributed to the ostrich'. He himself declared that he could not divest himself of his independent nature – it was both his strength and his weakness. He could be rude, he could be charming, he was a brilliant talker; on form 'he produced table-talk which would have strained a Boswell to bursting'. 'I remember . . . the generous lovable nature of the man,' wrote Lord Rosebery. 'I cannot forget the pathos of the story.'

For Jennie, who had shown resilience and courage over the last years, his death was a relief. In one sense it came two weeks too late for her to benefit from the release it gave her. As they approached Burma on that ghastly final voyage the news reached her that Count Kinsky was engaged to be married. His parents, for dynastic reasons, had found him a young bride. 'I hate it,' she wrote in despair to her sister. It was sad that circumstances prevented their marriage. Their mutual attraction was strong: 'I care for him as some people like opium or drink although they would like not to,' she said. Kinsky would have made a good father to the two boys deprived of paternal love and guidance. To the end of their days both Kinsky and Jennie felt that they had missed out on something and when Kinsky died in 1919 a friend said: 'If ever a man died of a broken heart, Charles Kinsky did'.

From the emotional exhaustion of these two events Jennie rallied, as she always would. With her dark looks, her 'forehead like a panther's and great wild eyes,' she was as attractive as ever. Her health was magnificent. People had always accused her and her sister of using rouge, so well did they look. 'We never did use rouge. It was our circulation,' Clara said. Jennie began to take a greater interest in her sons: Winston was twenty and Jack sixteen. Indeed when Winston was in India the following year she wrote: 'I am looking forward to

The many-sided character of Lord Randolph portrayed in a cartoon by Tom Merry c. 1880.

RANDOLPH,

The Marvellous Protean Artiste,

APPEARING NIGHTLY IN COUNTLESS

DIFFERENT CHARACTERS

AS SEEN BY

DIFFERENT PEOPLE.

140

Lord Randolph (centre) and
Jennie Churchill in Japan in
1894, a few months before
Lord Randolph's death.
On the right is his doctor,
George Keith, who found
his patient very difficult.
'One hour he is quiet and
good-tempered, the next
hour violent and cross.'

In 1896 Jenny was among the guests at a Blenheim shooting party photographed in the grounds at High Lodge. Back row, left to right: Earl of Gosford, Lady Emily Kingscote, Hon. Sydney Greville, G. Curzon, General Ellis, Countess of Gosford, Arthur Balfour, Mrs Grenfell, Sir Samuel Scott, Lord Londonderry, Lady Helen Stewart, Lady Lilian Spencer-Churchill, Mr Grenfell, Prince Charles of Denmark, Viscount Curzon. Middle row: Earl of Chesterfield, Lady Randolph Churchill, Duchess of Marlborough, Princess Alexandra, Mr H. Chaplin, Prince of Wales, Mrs Curzon, Marchioness of Londonderry, Princess Victoria, Princess Charles of Denmark. Front row: Lady Sophie Scott, Duke of Marlborough, Viscountess Curzon.

the time when we shall be together again and all my political ambitions shall be centred in you'. And she gave him all the assistance she could in whatever he wanted to do. With her contacts there was always some string that could be pulled or a word that could be dropped in an appropriate ear. She also on occasion gave excellent moderating advice to that over-eager, egotistic young cavalry officer.

There was one problem that perpetually worried both mother and sons – money. Jennie could not help living as if she were rich, whereas in truth she was not. As J. H. Plumb put it: 'She squandered her inheritance with insouciant eagerness'. Although they moved in the grandest circles and entertained distinguished guests, they were far from wealthy. Randolph's South African investments had been swallowed up by the debts he left. His widow had no source of income. Jennie might have married a millionaire, but she was not keen. 'I am *not* going to marry anyone,' she told Lady Warwick. 'If a perfect darling with at least £40,000 a year wants me *very much* I might consider it ...'. Winston told her that he hated the idea of her remarrying: 'but that would of course be a solution', he added. Her solution for the time being was to start her own money-making enterprise. She founded a magazine, the *Anglo-Saxon Review*. Its contributors were celebrated and its readership – at a guinea an issue – select: too select, alas, for it to make any money.

When the Boer War broke out in 1899 Jennie shifted her energies to the equipping and manning of a hospital ship. She sailed on it to South Africa where both her sons were serving. Perhaps that is why she went. Or perhaps it was because her latest admirer, a good-looking young officer called George Cornwallis-West, was serving there. If so she was unlucky, for by the time she reached Cape Town he was already on his way home, suffering from sunstroke. On her return she decided to marry George Cornwallis-West. Friends cautioned her – he was after all only sixteen days older than her son, Winston, and he had no money. 'But I want him,' she declared to the Prince of Wales when he tried to discourage her. Winston strongly advised her to reflect on 'the business aspect, on which as you know, I lay paramount stress. Fine sentiments and empty stomachs do not accord'.

But sentiments prevailed. They were married in July 1900. Jennie was forty-five, George twenty-five. He quit the army in search of more lucrative employment. 'Unsuccessful Enterprises' was the sad chapter in his memoirs which records that search. Where he shone was on the salmon river and on the grouse moor, in the hunting field or in the Highlands with a stag in his sights. His letters to Jennie read more like the remarks column in a game book than the delicate

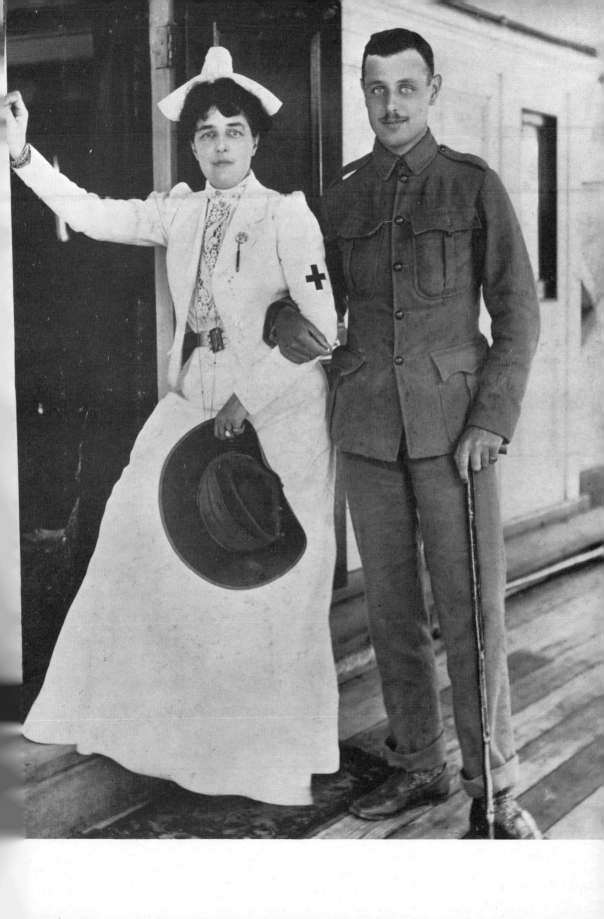

Jennie Churchill (by this time married to George Cornwallis-West) sitting in the
centre of the cast of her play *Borrowed Plumes*, which was performed in July 1909.
Behind her to the left is the woman for whom her husband was to leave her, Mrs Patrick Campbell.

expressions of passion. 'Just off for a stalk and try for a salmon on the way,' he would sign off. For a while, however, they were happy – money their only contention. But George lusted after other women and in the end left Jennie. After the demise of the *Anglo-Saxon Review* she had started to write plays. Ironically, the woman George decided to marry next – the legendary Mrs Patrick Campbell – was the star of Jennie's first play, *Borrowed Plumes*. 'This is the *real* parting of the ways,' Jennie wrote to George just before their decree nisi was made absolute, 'but for the sake of some of the happy days we had together – should you ever be in trouble and wanted to knock at my door it would not be shut to you . . . I say goodbye – a long, long goodbye.' The decree was made absolute on a Monday and on the Tuesday George married Stella Campbell who sighed, 'Ah, the peace of a double bed after the hurly burly of the *chaise longue*!'

It was 1912. Jennie's spirits, which could so often be relied upon to triumph, were low. 'I shall never get used to not being the most beautiful woman in the room,' she lamented. When war came she failed to find a satisfactory occupation. There was little comfort in society. Then Winston's career crashed. In 1918, however, she found another husband, Montagu Porch, who was younger than George, and younger even than Winston. He was forty-one and she was sixty-four. 'He has a future and I have a past so we should be all right,' she said. They were. Then three years after her third marriage she slipped down the stairs at Mells, the house in Somerset belonging to Lady Horner, and broke her leg. Gangrene set in and the leg had to be amputated. She showed the courage of which she was always capable, but a few days later an artery gave way and she fell into a coma and died. In death she looked, as her mother Clara had done, rather like a squaw.

7
His Early
Life

To WINSTON his mother had been 'young, beautiful, and fascinating'. 'We worked together on even terms, more like brother and sister, than mother and son.' The early neglect had, to some extent, been compensated for by her later comradeship. But she had never really provided an adequate home life for her sons. They had moved from house to house, often lodging with the old Duchess in Grosvenor Square. Soon after his father's death, when Winston was at Sandhurst, he had written to her: 'My darling Mamma – I am longing for the day when you will be able to have a little house of your own and when I can really feel that there is such a place as home'. He was twenty then.

Blenheim did represent some kind of stability, but he did not come to know the house or his cousins who lived there until after the death in 1892 of his uncle, the eighth Duke of Marlborough. A quarrel between Lord Randolph and his brother, the Duke, had precluded any social intercourse between their families. From 1892 until 1897 when his first cousin, the ninth Duke of Marlborough, produced a son (subsequently the tenth Duke of Marlborough) Winston was the heir to the dukedom and to Blenheim. Had some accident befallen 'Sunny' Marlborough in those years, the 'greatest commoner' would have become a peer of the realm at a tender age. His grandmother was aware of the situation and informed Sunny's wife, Consuelo, at their first meeting: 'Your first duty is to have a child and it must be a son, because it would be intolerable to have that little upstart Winston become Duke. Are you in the family way?'

Winston was very fond of his cousins, the Frewens and Leslies on the Jerome side, and the Spencer-Churchills on his father's side: they

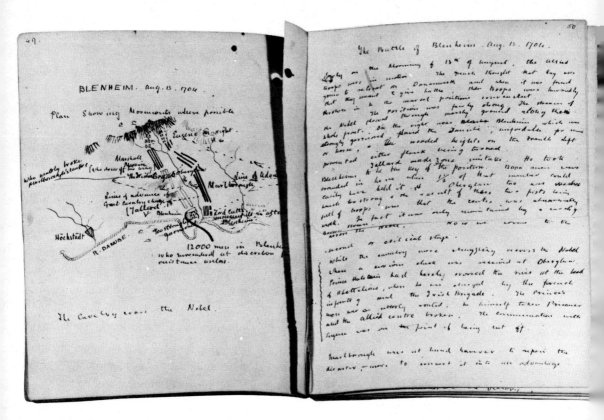

Winston Churchill's Harrow exercise book showing his map of the battle of Blenheim, won by his ancestor the Duke of Marlborough.

could do no wrong in his eyes. He had that strong sense of family loyalty that can colour the judgment. No doubt it had been nurtured by the inadequacies of his parents' attention. 'Sunny' Marlborough became and remained a close friend.

Churchill was fascinated by the historical bones of Blenheim. Not only did the house embody his ancestry it also represented two centuries of British history. Winston with his keen imagination of the past responded deeply to the glory of its origin and took pride in his association with it. The sense of British heritage, with which he was so thoroughly infused, accounts for much in his long life. He openly explored his relations with his forebears; he played them out on the open stage – and his fundamental affections and prejudices rebounded world wide. For instance, could that 'fortunate friendship', as Eleanor Roosevelt called it, between him and Franklin Roosevelt, have sprung up had Winston not had an unshakeable conviction that America was 'a good thing'? It was a belief that was genetically part of him.

Harrow, to which he had been sent because it was on a hill and thought to be better for his unstable health than Eton in the Thames valley, was hateful. He was a naughty, wilful child, unable to respect authority if he could not see the point of it. He failed to benefit from the teaching at school; nobody managed to stimulate his mind. He was often bottom of the form. In exams he complained: 'I should have liked to be asked to say what I knew. They always tried to ask what I did not know. When I would have willingly displayed my knowledge, they sought to expose my ignorance. This sort of treatment had only one result: I did not do well in examinations'. Which meant that he was constantly held back in Mr Somervell's English class – the class for dunces who were not clever enough to go on to Latin and Greek. Here they had to parse, reparse, break down and analyse every kind of sentence in the English language. 'Thus I got into my bones the essential structure of the ordinary English sentence – which is a noble thing.'

In the holidays he and his brother, Jack, were looked after by Mrs Everest. She was the only really warm support they had at home. His father's parliamentary career had, by this time, collapsed, but not a word of this was uttered in front of the children or the servants. However, 'one could not grow up in my father's house, and still less among his father and sisters, without understanding that there had been a great political disaster'. The political proclivities of the nursery were staunchly on Lord Randolph's side: 'Of course I was his vehement partisan,' wrote Winston, 'and so in her mild way was Mrs Everest.'

University was out of the question for the academically dim boy. A career in the army was decided upon. Churchill later described how the decision was taken. He liked playing with toy soldiers:

The day came when my father himself paid a formal visit of inspection. All the troops were arranged in the correct formation of attack. He spent twenty minutes studying the scene – which was really impressive – with a keen eye and a captivating smile. At the end he asked me if I would like to go into the Army. I thought it would be splendid to command an Army, so I said 'Yes' at once: and immediately I was taken at my word. For years I thought my father with his experience and flair had discerned in me the qualities of military genius. But I was told later that he had only come to the conclusion that I was not clever enough to go to the Bar.

However at the Military Academy at Sandhurst he was happier. He enjoyed learning about Tactics, Fortification, Military Administration; he enjoyed the riding and the hard work. And at last his father began to treat him as a proper person and took him to meet interesting and distinguished people. 'But if ever I began to show the slightest idea of comradeship, he was immediately offended; and when once I suggested that I might help his private secretary to write some of his letters, he froze me into stone.' Occasionally Lord

Churchill photographed while serving on
the North West Frontier of India, 1897.

Randolph would write his son letters of unwarranted severity, deploring his 'idle, useless, unprofitable life', and said that unless he mended his ways he would become 'a mere social wastrel, one of the hundreds of public school failures', that he would 'degenerate into a shabby, unhappy and futile existence'. But Winston did well and passed twentieth out of 130. Whereupon the world 'opened like Aladdin's cave', he wrote in 1930. 'From the beginning of 1895 down to the present time of writing, I have never had time to turn round. I could count almost on my fingers the days when I have had nothing to do. An endless moving picture in which one was an actor. On the whole Great Fun!'

One month after his father's death Winston was gazetted to the Fourth Hussars at £120 a year. Like most young cavalry officers he thirsted for action, for gunfire and for medals. But the empire was peaceful and those eager lieutenants were restricted to the polo or the hunting field. Churchill, during his leave, scanned the world scene for a possible trouble spot. His eye landed on Cuba where a long guerilla war was rumbling on, and off he sailed. It was not long before he and a fellow officer had attached themselves to a Spanish division and were marching through the island. The young British officers came under gunfire; one bullet passed within a foot of Churchill's head and struck a chestnut horse behind him. Such action was what he had hoped for. He had not been disappointed and returned, after an illuminating and educative visit to America, delighted and with a medal to boot. One paper remarked that 'fighting other people's battles is rather an extraordinary proceeding, even for a Churchill'.

He exploited his leave the next year in a similar way. The Fourth Hussars had been stationed at Bangalore in the Madras province of Southern India. The life of the officers there was pleasant indeed: 'Princes could live no better than we', Churchill remarked. At 3,000 feet Bangalore had a pleasant climate and with many servants, good friends and a life devoted almost exclusively to polo the officers were in clover – except that they yearned for action. Luckily for Churchill, his next leave coincided with a rebellion of Pathan tribesmen on the northern frontier. Having tugged a string or two he was soon on the spot with a position on General Sir Bindon Blood's staff and a commission from the *Daily Telegraph* and the *Pioneer* for some articles about the campaign. There in a wide, steep, hot and sparsely populated valley the British and Indian troops had some vigorous clashes with the fierce tribesmen. It was close fighting, sometimes with swords, in precipitous terrain and Churchill was in the thick of it. 'Here everything is life size and flesh colour,' he wrote with glee to his mother, adding that he wanted to return 'and wear my medals at some big dinner or some other function'. He was keen to prove himself and for the proof to be seen. 'There is no ambition I cherish so keenly as to gain a reputation for personal courage,' he told his brother.

When his leave expired Churchill reluctantly returned to his regiment to be 'tethered' to his garrison at Bangalore. Not content only to play polo – at which he excelled – he began to read and to write. On idle sultry afternoons he began to flex his literary muscles. The articles he had sent to the *Daily Telegraph* from the northern frontier had been a success. But they had been published anonymously and he was furious, for they had been written, he explained, with the 'design ... of bringing my personality before the electorate ... I was proud of the letters and anxious to stake my reputation on them'. 'They are I believe of some literary interest,' he added immodestly.

Churchill was impatient for fame. He made a book out of his articles and saw to it that it was not published anonymously. Entitled *The Story of the Malakand Field Force*, it was favourably received and many people, including the Prince of Wales, wrote and congratulated him on his masterly and lucid account of the campaign. How exciting it was for Churchill, for as he later wrote in *My Early Life*: 'The reader must remember I had never been praised before. The only comments which had ever been made upon my work at school had been "Indifferent", "Untidy", "Slovenly", "Bad", "Very Bad", etc. Now here was the great world with its leading literary newspapers and vigilant erudite critics, writing columns of praise'. He was a little less modest at the time: 'My style is good,' he boasted, 'even in parts classic'.

The bulk of his education he acquired at Bangalore. His mother sent him books – Gibbon, Macaulay, Adam Smith, Hallam – all of which he gobbled up like a hungry animal. She also sent the recent volumes of the *Annual Register*. On these he tested his opinions and views by writing comments on events and then reading on to see how they transpired and whether his first opinion had been right or valid. An unorthodox education, but one on which his untutored mind thrived. He was particularly enthralled by history and by the contrast between Gibbon and Macaulay, both in style and attitude. Probably from them grew his great love of language. He relished words and began to appreciate their potential power. He wrote an article, which was never published, called *The Scaffolding of Rhetoric*. The article began: 'The orator wields a power more durable than that of a great king'. Another curious product of his days at Bangalore was *Savrola*, a politico-romantic novel. He was delighted at the time with the hero, Savrola, a popular liberal leader who in the cause of freedom overthrew the misguided military dictator of Laurania,

Antonio Molara, and at the same time lured away Molara's beautiful wife, Lucile. Formidable indeed were the qualities of the hero, whose magical oratory in which 'instinctively he alliterated' held crowds spellbound, and whose tastes were expensive: 'The supper was excellent: the champagne was dry and the quails fat.' And although he later preferred to forget about this jolly, rolling, pompous novel, he has always been identified with Savrola. Savrola had no self-doubt. Nor did Churchill. His self confidence and his ambition grew apace. His extrovert nature, his energy and his lust for adventure made him arrogant, bumptious and intolerable to many of his contemporaries. As for Savrola, 'Ambition was the motive force, and he was powerless to resist it.'

Since the outlook in India was 'I fear pacific', he hoped to get to the Sudan where it looked as if Kitchener was going to have fun. He was about to march with 20,000 men against the Dervishes at Omdurman. 'I was deeply anxious to share in this,' wrote Churchill. On his next leave he hurried back to London and bullied, lobbied and cajoled the right people. He even recruited the influence of the Prime Minister, Lord Salisbury, to secure a place in the expedition. His mother too made energetic efforts on his behalf; as often before 'she left no wire unpulled, no stone unturned, no cutlet uncooked.' All to no avail. Sir Herbert Kitchener was implacably opposed to including this irritating and arrogant young officer in his expedition. Churchill was not deterred by the Sirdar's veto and, several cutlets later, found himself attached a supernumerary lieutenant to the 21st Lancers – no expenses paid. A commission from the *Morning Post* for letters (at £15 a column) solved the money problem and he was off, soon to be riding up the Nile in search of Dervishes. Churchill's subsequent account in *The River War* of the campaign was excellent. He vividly described the scene of 60,000 ill-equipped, brave, dark Dervishes marching on 20,000 stiff, trained soldiers. 'Talk of fun! Where will you beat this,' he said. He described the jingling of the cavalry as they began to trot before the charge, and then how they broke into a fast gallop and thundered through thousands of crouching warriors, bristling with popping musketry. Then, once through, how he found himself separated from his regiment, wheeled around, surveyed the slaughter, avoided the snipers and rejoined the troop. He had shot some Dervishes – 'five for certain and two doubtful'. He was lucky not to have been killed and glad, he said, 'to have added the experience of a cavalry charge to my military repertoire'.

Despite the fun Churchill had already decided to leave the army, for, as he said, his books and journalism 'had already brought in about five times as much as the Queen had paid me for three years of assiduous and sometimes dangerous work'. He had no private income, he

A contemporary lithograph by R. Sutherland of the battle of Omdurman (1898) in which Churchill fought with the 21st Lancers, who are shown charging on the left of the picture. 'Nothing like the battle of Omdurman will ever be seen again', Churchill wrote. 'It was the last link in the long chain of those spectacular conflicts whose vivid and majestic splendour has done so much to invest war with glamour'.

needed to earn his living and he was no longer content to idle away his time on the army's polo fields. (The three campaigns he had taken part in had all been during his leave.) He had three medals and had been mentioned in despatches. But he was impatient. It was time to move on. He cast his eyes towards Parliament and decided to try public speaking. 'It appeared there were hundreds of indoor meetings and outdoor fêtes, of bazaars and rallies, all of which were clamant for speakers. I surveyed this prospect with the eye of an urchin looking through a pastry cook's window.' A meeting of the Primrose League at Bath was selected for his first effort. He rehearsed and rehearsed his speech until he knew it backwards, forwards, any way round. For all his trepidation it went well: the audience cheered at the right moments and clapped at the end. 'So I could do it after all! It seemed quite easy too.' A year later, after further experience, the conclusions he formed were these: 'With practice I shall attain great power on a public platform. My impediment is no hindrance. My voice sufficiently powerful, and – this is vital – my ideas and modes of thought are pleasing to men'. His impediment was a lisp, which he tried to overcome by repeating as an exercise, 'The Spanish ships I cannot see for they are not in sight'. But realising that he would never pronounce his S's properly, he decided instead to convert his lisping 'th' into the emphatic 'sh' that became such a strong characteristic of his war-time speeches.

Before the century turned he had fought as a Conservative a by-election at Oldham in Lancashire – and lost. 'I returned to London with those feelings of deflation which a bottle of champagne or even soda-water represents when it has been half-emptied and left uncorked for a night.' That was in July 1899. In October war was declared between Great Britain and the Boer republics of South Africa. ('I thought it very sporting of the Boers to take on the whole British Empire,' wrote Churchill later.) More fun was in the offing. Two days after the declaration Churchill 'in joyous expectation' was bound for South Africa as war correspondent for the *Morning Post* which, in paying him his expenses and £250 a month, was awarding him a record fee for a newspaper correspondent.

Though not much was happening he went straight to the front. He boarded an armoured train, which set off to do reconnaissance towards Ladysmith. But on the way there it was ambushed. Churchill, after valiant work under fire conducting operations to dislodge the engine from where it had stuck, was taken prisoner by a Boer horseman. Louis Botha, who became South Africa's first Prime Minister in 1910, claimed on a mission to England some years later that he had been that horseman. Both he and Churchill liked to believe this.

OPPOSITE The capture of Winston Churchill near Colenso during the Boer War was reported in the *Daily Mail*, 20 November 1899.

NEWS FROM LADYSMITH.

FIERCE FIGHTING ON TWO DAYS.

INFANTRY DUEL.

CRUSHING BLOW TO THE RAND VOLUNTEERS.

COLLAPSE OF AN ATTACK ON ESTCOURT.

SHARP FIGHTING AT KIMBERLEY.

RELIEF COLUMN ABOUT TO ADVANCE.

BOERS VERY ACTIVE.

MAFEKING AGAIN SERIOUSLY MENACED.

FATE OF WINSTON CHURCHILL.

General Buller's original plan was understood to be for an advance by three lines upon Bloemfontein and Pretoria. Three columns would have landed, one at Capetown, another at Port Elizabeth, and the third at East London, concentrating probably at Norval's Port and making preparatory to the invasion of the enemy's territory. This plan has been temporarily broken up by the despatch of a division to Natal, by the need to relieve Kimberley, and by the appearance of the enemy in some force in the strategic route indicated by the railways joining Naauwpoort Junction, Rosmead Junction, and Stormberg Junction.

present plan would seem to be:—
An advance in strong force in the direction of Kimberley by Lord Methuen.

A movement by a force which has been disembarked at East London past the Boers on the line from East London to Stormberg Junction. There is also be

An movement from De Aar on the Boers at Naauwpoort, with object of forcing the enemy back into British territory.

Unavailable British troops in Cape Colony are now about 18,000, of which are near East London. To these 12,000 Colonial troops, police, etc., may be added.

Despatch has been received from Ladysmith giving news up to the 15th, on which day all was well. On the 9th the Boers attacked the British camp early in morning, but were repulsed. Counter were delivered by the Rifle Brigade, King's Royal Rifles, and Manchesters, in which the enemy was heavily defeated and driven off the field with total loss. The Boers are estimated to have had 800 to 1,000 killed and wounded. On the same day twenty-one shells were fired at the enemy to honour the Prince of Wales's birthday. With a skirmish occurred on the same road, in which the Boers were driven back. The British loss was reported to be trifling. The Boer bombardment is stated to be ineffective.

has been skirmishing before East London at our correspondents at Pietermaritzburg and Capetown state that immediate news is to be expected shortly. The fact that all arrangements for the relief of the relief force have been completed. The Boers have destroyed the bridge over the Tugela, and will meet our troops on the further that river.

force of 10,000 men, under Joubert, is said to be moving south on the British advance from East London. General White will throw a force against them, however, will probably be enough, and therefore will be difficult if The relief column will evidently of task before it, if the enemy as he is reported to be.

Invasion of Cape Colony is apace. Aliwal North has been a Boer commando 600 strong; another at one of 600; at Burghersdorp 500. All these Boers have come to the Orange Free State, whose proclamations have been in the invaders ordering loyal people to leave the district unwilling to be commandeered. The fresh violation of the laws of nations the enemy, but it can best be some our arms reach Boer soil. It is still unmolested, and no doubt as yet been made on the British at Aar.

has been again shelled by the little damage has been done. A was killed. The British force Kimberley has been concentrated River and will by now have advance. Fighting is imminent.

EASTERN FRONTIER.

A CRUSHING REPULSE.

LADYSMITH REPELS A COMBINED BOER ATTACK.

WILINESS OF THE BOERS.

PUTTING RAND VOLUNTEERS IN THE VAN.

PIETERMARITZBURG, Nov. 18, 1.55 p.m.

News has been received here by despatch runner, dated Ladysmith, November 15, and duly passed by the censor, recording the events up to that date.

On November 9 the Boers began to shell our camp at four o'clock in the morning, at the same time advancing under cover of their guns, and taking every advantage of any shelter the ground afforded.

Our infantry met them with a hot fire, and although the Boers advanced from all sides they were beaten back.

The main attack was delivered by the Johannesburg Volunteers, who were met by the King's Royal Rifles and the Rifle Brigade. The enemy rallied again and again, but were driven back.

The Boers had dug a trench, which in their advance they had left unguarded. The Rifle Brigade advanced at the double, and captured the trench unobserved by the enemy, who, when they reached the edge of the trench on their return, were met with a murderous fire from the Brigade. They were driven back in great disorder with frightful loss, being played upon in their flight by our artillery.

Meanwhile a big artillery duel was going on. The Boers brought a mortar into action, but this was speedily silenced. The enemy returned to the mortar, but our lyddite drove them back.

By eleven the fighting was practically over.

At noon Sir George White celebrated the Prince of Wales's birthday by firing twenty-one lyddite shells at the enemy. This was followed by terrific cheering from our lines.

On the south-western side of the camp the Manchesters caught a body of Boers in a ditch, and cut them up.

The Boer loss during the day is estimated at from 800 to 1,000.

The lyddite completely demoralised the Boers, who had to be driven back to their guns.

Our loss was trifling.

So far, the semi-official despatch.

A reliable native employed in the Elands Laagte Colliery says the fighting on November 9 continued till sundown.

According to him three large camps surrounded the town. The Free State's forwards were at Besters. The main body, under Joubert, were at Pepworth's Farm, the general occupying the homestead, and the third camp was at Umbulwane.

The combined forces began their attack at dawn under cover of their guns, but were repeatedly repulsed, our cavalry doing immense execution.

The thickest of the fight was near Umbulwane, whose big gun fired only one shot, having been at once silenced by our fire.

The next morning the Boers took two trains of wounded away. The dead were buried on the field. The more prominent Boers were buried by themselves, but the others were buried by natives, 200 of whom were requisitioned from the Colliery for the purpose.

A British shell struck a Boer ammunition train and destroyed it. The British captured the stores conveyed by the Boers from Dundee to Ladysmith.

The Boers are disheartened, and many desire to return home.

General Joubert brought them back, and told them that as they insisted on coming, the border they must fight to the end.

On November 14—to continue the censored Press despatch—our cavalry and artillery met the enemy near the Colenso road and drove them back. Our loss was one wounded. Our shell fire was very effective.

Ladysmith is in the best of spirits.

Dysentery is reported among the Boers. Native runners from Ladysmith report that when they left there on the 15th the people were all cheerful, and the health of the town was good.

The Boer bombardment, they say, in Ladysmith and Kimberley would have been relieved before this. This was a sanguine view of the state of affairs, but it is likely that before the end of the month the Boers will be driven over the border.

A forward move is expected at Estcourt shortly.

OFFER FROM MAURITIUS.

PIETERMARITZBURG, Nov. 17.

French Mauritius is evidently as enthusiastically loyal as the French Canadians. The Legislative Council has just voted £2,000 in aid of the sick and wounded soldiers in Natal, and the health of the island are collecting private subscriptions for the same purpose.

M. Decroulis, Surveyor-General of Mauritius, writing to an official here, asks whether there is any possibility of local Volunteers being accepted to assist the Natal Volunteers. He offers to resign his position and place himself at the head of such a corps.

ANOTHER "LONG TOM."

DURBAN, Nov. 11.

According to the "Times of Natal," a private telegram from Lorenzo Marquez states that the Transvaal Government has despatched 300 empty trucks and another big gun to Ladysmith.

The enemy is reported to be seriously short of provisions.—Reuter.

The War Office has issued the following telegram from the general officer commanding in South Africa:—

CAPETOWN, Nov. 17.

Reports received from Ladysmith 12 November and 15 Nov. all well.

RAND HORSEMEN FOR THE FRONT.

DURBAN, Nov. 16.

Bethune's Horse, a mounted infantry regiment 500 strong, composed of Randmen, left the camp here to-day for the front to take part in the Ladysmith relief expedition. They were accorded the heartiest of send offs.

The regiment's colours were made at

FIVE MORE TRANSPORTS.

4,500 MORE TROOPS FOR GENERAL BULLER.

FURTHER REINFORCEMENTS SENT TO DURBAN.

Five more transports, bringing in all over 4,500 troops, have reached Capetown —viz.:—

MONGOLIAN (2nd Battalion Seaforth Highlanders, and No. 8 Company R.A.M. Corps, Field Hospital), 1,015 officers and men.

AMERICA (R Battery R.H.A., 1st Cavalry Brigade, Ammunition Column, and detachments R.E. and R.A.M.C.), 179 officers and men.

PAVONIA (2nd Battalion Royal Fusiliers, 3rd Battalion Royal Scotch Fusiliers, and No. 11 Company R.A.M.C.), 1,860 officers and men.

JAMAICAN (B Squadron 8th Dragoons, and No. 19 Company R.A.M.C.), 160 officers and men.

CEPHALONIA (4th Brigade Staff, 1st Battalion Durham Light Infantry, two companies Mounted Infantry, No. 9 nance Corps, and Reservists R.A.M. Corps), 1,316 officers and men.

The twenty-five trooopships now in South

WAR NOTES.

All the Transvaal officials, even the judges, have gone to the front.

Lieutenant Bridges, R.H.A., has been attached to the Imperial Light Horse.

The subscription in Paris for the American Ladies' Hospital Ship amounts to nearly £400.

H.M.S. Thetis has arrived at Lorenzo Marquez. The Magicienne is also in the harbour.

It is estimated that one in every sixty of Cheltenham's inhabitants is taking part in the war.

The regimental colours of the 2nd Royal Warwicks have been sent with their pet antelope to the depot.

The Salt Union of Liverpool offers 30,000 damp-proof packets of salt for the use of the troops in South Africa.

The general ineffectiveness of the Boer shells has aroused a belief that they are not filled with explosives.

The only colonial possession that is left at Johannesburg is the Rev. F. C. Rollin, who has obtained a special permit to remain.

Private Espeland, the Norwegian, who was crushed by a truck in the armoured train disaster, has been buried with military honours.

Speaking at Nuneaton on Saturday, Mr. Akers-Douglas declared that the old Convention of 1884 had been destroyed, never to be renewed.

Thousands of men belonging to the First Army Corps submitted themselves to inoculation for enteric fever before they left Aldershot.

When Sir Redvers Buller arrived at Capetown, flags on the Government buildings were conspicuous by their absence: a significant and unpleasant incident.

Joubert gives as the reason why the officers are picked off in battle that the Boers have no quarrel with the privates, who only fight under compulsion.

A soldier at the front writes home:— "It is rumoured that after the affair is over we shall march straight on to Cairo by the route they are going to lay 'by the line along."

Mr. A. Hirst is in charge of 200 carrier pigeons, Yorkshire racers, at Ladysmith. The pigeons cover the distance to Durban in five hours, and are then sent back to Ladysmith.

According to a Uitlander the Boers, on entering upon the war, were chiefly afraid of the Naval Brigade and the colonials who knew and could plan out the burghers' work, though we have tons of work to help us.

A splendid piece of thermalutation work was performed when the Hasworden Castle reached Capetown. Her cargo of 1,700 men and stores, ordnance, and rations for fourteen days were landed and returned in ten hours.

A private in the Gloucestershire Regiment writes that a good many of the Natal volunteers are up sent by the Boer authorities to enlist in the British Army and send all the information they can to General Joubert.

A "Gunner" points out that while the Regular regiments are being sent great supplies of tobacco, etc., the Reserve, Artillery, and Army Service and Army Ordnance Corps are apparently to be left to their own resources.

Here is a translation of a telegram posted up in the cafés of Rouen on October 31:— "Disaster to the English Army confirmed. Ladysmith capitulates. The Boers take 150 officers and 2,600 men prisoners and capture eighteen guns."

One of the "Devons" writes home from Ladysmith:—"The Boers are a brave lot of men, and are not half so bad as they are painted. All these outrages are committed by bands of outlaws, who resemble our own gangs of Hooligans."

The "Pioneer" of Allahabad regrets that the Hawkes siege train has not been ordered to the Cape, as the train has been officially reported to be splendidly efficient, and could reach the Cape earlier than the proposed English siege train.

The Sumatra, which left Capetown on Friday, has, among her passengers on board Captain Lambton Forbes, of the Imperial Light Horse, and Lieutenant W. G. H. Manley, of the 21st Battery R.F.A., both of whom were wounded at Elands Laagte.

Aldershot has been experiencing with a gigantic steam-plough, which can cut a trench four feet deep, and throw the earth aside, so affording perfect cover for infantry, who can follow immediately in the wake, whilst the great implements are to be seen out in the war.

In Paris yesterday the police pulled down a number of placards posted up by students, describing with much virulence:— "Down with the English. London at the mercy of 20,000 resolute men. A thousand students in already been enrolled to support the Boers."

Nathan Marks, whose safety is such a concern to the Boers, is said to be a man of between sixty and seventy years of age. A most respectable English family, who, after keeping a drinking saloon at Capetown, migrated to Pretoria, where he entered the service of the State Attorney.

PRISONERS WITH THE BOERS.

LORENZO MARQUEZ, Nov. 19.

The "Standard and Diggers' News" of Friday last states that cases of scurvy have made their appearance among some of the British prisoners at Pretoria.

The soldiers are being transferred to Waterfall Farm, and hate asked the Government raft to give them any more tinned food, as it is of very inferior quality.—Reuter's Special.

African waters have been disposed of as follows:—

At Capetown:—

	Officers and Men
Aurania	1,550
Nubia	1,540
Orient	1,304
Harlech Castle	725
Nomadic	66
Mohawk	259
Malta	1,316
City of Vienna	272
Oreana	1,019
Mongolian	1,015
*America	179
Pavonia	1,896
Jamaica	160
Cephalonia	1,316
	12,725

Ordered to Durban:—

	Officers and Men
Roslin Castle (arrived)	1,050
Lismore Castle (arrived)	1,070
Harwarden Castle (arrived)	1,084
Yorkshire (arrived)	1,050
Gascon	1,090
*Armenian (arrived)	789
Oriental (arrived)	1,293
Manila (arrived)	1,022
Goorkha	1,551
City of Cambridge	1,010
	10,624

*Bringing artillery.

The transport Britannic, with 908 officers and men, has arrived at East London.

The Zulu, Prah, and Caspian, presumably carrying mules, have arrived at Capetown.

BOUND FOR THE CAPE.

MONTFORT (half 61st Howitzer Battery R.F.A., 7th Battery R.F.A., detachment 13th Hussars, 6th Company R.E., and detachment No. 4 General Hospital) left Gibraltar on Saturday.

TEMPLEMORE (three squadrons 13th Hussars) left Las Palmas on Saturday.

ISMORE (part of 10th Hussars) left Las Palmas on Saturday.

GUELPH (82 officers and men Army Ordnance Corps, with two guns, ammunition, and stores) left Southampton on Saturday.

ALGERIA (14th Field Battery R.F.A. and 4th Brigade Division Staff) left St. Vincent yesterday.

CANNING (65th Howitzer Battery R.F.A., detachment R.F.A. ammunition column, one troop 2nd Dragoon Guards, and Detachment No. 4 General Hospital) arrived at Las Palmas on Saturday.

MORE TRANSPORTS WANTED.

WASHINGTON, Nov. 19.

Agents of the British Government are trying to purchase some colliers and supply ships bought by the United States Government during the war with Spain. They specially want the Arethusa, a big tank steamer of 6,000 tons.

It is believed that the ships are wanted to carry troops and supplies to South Africa. No action has yet been taken by the Navy Department.

ARMOURED TRAIN FIGHT.

BOER ACCOUNT OF THE ENGAGEMENT NEAR COLENSO.

MR. CHURCHILL WOUNDED AND A PRISONER.

LORENZO MARQUEZ, Nov. 18.

A despatch, dated Pretoria, November 16, says:—

"General Joubert advises the Government that a Transvaal force had a sharp engagement with the British near Chieveley on Tuesday between Colenso and Estcourt.

"An armoured train came out suddenly round a kopje and fired on the burghers with Nordenfelt and Maxims. The burghers on the other side of the kopje made a detour, and placed stones on the line. Three armoured trucks and two ordinary carriages were derailed. Firing ensued, during which the locomotive managed to uncouple, and retired with the rest of the train.

"The British lost two killed, ten wounded, and fifty-six taken prisoners. Among the latter was Mr. Winston Churchill, correspondent of the 'Morning Post.' The prisoners are being brought to Pretoria. Our loss was five slightly wounded."

Another telegram, dated Bloemfontein (headquarters camp), yesterday, says that the Estcourt column had a skirmish with the Natal Carabineers yesterday, and that two burghers were killed.

The following are the correct names and official numbers of the able seamen reported missing in connection with the attack on the armoured train at Estcourt on November 15:—Walter Thompson, 160,621; George Mong, 138,019; Ernest John Read, 187,682; and Christopher Connor, 142,561.—Reuter's Special.

Fifty-six prisoners, comprising Dublin Fusiliers and several bluejackets, arrived here at noon to-day. There were large crowds at the station, but no demonstration was made.

Mr. Winston Churchill, who is wounded in the hand, accompanied by two other officers, was taken to the Model School, where the rest of the British officers are confined, the rank and file being sent to the racecourse.

The wounded had been treated at Colenso.—Reuter's Special.

COL. SCHIEL'S COMPLAINT.

POINTED REMINDER BY SIR REDVERS BULLER.

CAPETOWN, Nov. 18.

Colonel Schiel, the German free-lance captured at Elands Laagte, in his letter to Sir Redvers Buller, written from the prison ship Penelope, complains that he gave his parole to General White, but is still detained as a prisoner, which he says is not in accordance with the rules of civilised war.

Sir Redvers Buller, in reply, declined to admit that there had been any breach of military etiquette, saying that no commander could give parole outside the limits of his own command.

The action of the Boer forces was limited to General White's army at Ladysmith, and for the present, therefore, the general commanding in Natal was justified in making any arrangements necessary for the safe custody of the prisoners.

The Boers, Sir Redvers Buller further intimated, had a tremendous advantage at the outset of the war, and must have taken into consideration that the British had but few men to spare, under the circumstances, to guard their prisoners, if the latter were allowed ashore.

Colonel Schiel admits that he is extremely well treated.

The British and Boer wounded are all removed to Wynberg.

GENERAL JOUBERT INDISPOSED.

PRETORIA, Nov. 12.

General Joubert has been slightly indisposed. He is now better.—Reuter.

General Joubert's wife arrived in the camp near Ladysmith yesterday.

WESTERN FRONTIER.

FIGHTING AT KIMBERLEY.

ENEMY'S SHELL-FIRE KILLS A KAFFIR WOMAN.

A NEW SEVERE FIGHT: BOER VERSION.

KIMBERLEY, Nov. 11.

The Boers recommenced shelling the town this morning from the neighbourhood of the lazaretto with three guns.

Our batteries retaliated, and a brisk duel ensued. Our shells fell fast in the immediate neighbourhood of the enemy's guns, and the latter retired.

The damage done to the town is comparatively trivial. One native woman was killed by a piece of a shell which exploded in the street, and a few buildings were slightly damaged.

This afternoon the firing was resumed for about three-quarters of an hour. The enemy's fire was directed at a battery of Diamond Fields artillery. No damage was done.

This evening, again, a few shots were fired.

The enemy also fired several shells into Wesselton township this morning without result.

This morning a portion of our mounted troops who had taken up an advanced position near Otto's Kopje for the purpose of reconnoitring were fired upon by the enemy's cordite nine-pounder at Kamperadam.

A party of Boers also advanced to meet our men, who poured a hot fire into them at 600 yards.

Six Boers were distinctly seen to fall from their saddles, four being shot in quick succession by the marksmen of the Cape Police. There is little doubt that there were other losses on the enemy's side.

A member of the Cape Police was mortally wounded and another slightly injured. These were the only casualties.

Another mounted party engaged the enemy in another direction, a Maxim being brought into action. The result is unknown, but our loss is nil.

KIMBERLEY, Nov. 11.

Our casualties at Otto's Kopje were one Cape policeman, named Algernon Parker, very seriously wounded in the back and not likely to survive, and John Stumke, Kimberley Light Horse, slightly wounded.

It is estimated that the Boers fired quite 300 shells to-day. Those found bear date marks varying from 1891 to 1896.

It is known that the enemy have eight guns—possibly more.

The wounded are progressing very satisfactorily.—Reuter's Special.

LORENZO MARQUEZ, Nov. 18.

Telegraphing to Pretoria on the 15th, Commandant Wessels states that at Tarantalrand, near Kimberley, thirty Bloemfontein burghers, who were afterwards reinforced with a gun from the Free State artillery, were attacked by four Maxims.

The fight lasted two hours. Commandant Wessels adds:—"The British are retreating with their dead and wounded. A burgher named Strauss was killed and two wounded, of whom one is since dead; but it is impossible to say everything. So far nine burghers are reported wounded and five dead."

A Pretoria despatch, dated the 16th, says:—

It is reported that the cannonading of Kimberley recommenced this morning.—Reuter's Special.

TO CHECK METHUEN.

ORANGE RIVER, Nov. 15.

The Boers are concentrating their forces outside Kimberley, at Spytfontein.—Reuter.

Spytfontein is on the railroad, a few miles only south of Kimberley.

"MARKED MEN."

DE AAR, Nov. 15.

A peculiar feature of the equipment of the infantry here is a large red patch on either side of the helmet.

It is easy to distinguish this patch at a considerable distance, when the men, by reason of their khaki uniforms, would otherwise be invisible.—Reuter's Special.

TO RELIEVE KIMBERLEY.

TROOPS RAPIDLY CONCENTRATING AT ORANGE RIVER.

LORD METHUEN'S PLAN FOR BAFFLING SHARPSHOOTERS.

ORANGE RIVER, Nov. 16.

The concentration is being rapidly completed, and everything points to an early move to relieve Kimberley.

The 2nd Coldstream and the Scots Guards have arrived; the latter are very fit. The Grenadiers and the 1st Coldstreams are shortly expected here.

Ample preparations have been made for the repair of the line, and a naval search-light is in position.

Sir Redvers Buller, in reply, declined to admit that there had been any breach of military etiquette, saying that no commander could give parole outside the limits of his own command.

Great activity prevails here. The Grenadiers and half of the Northamptons have arrived.

The Yorkshires are expected this afternoon, and the Coldstreams arrive to-morrow.

The transport is now crossing the river by the bridge.

The new arrivals are well and enthusiastic.

ORANGE RIVER, Nov. 16.

The column will be organised at the arrival of the Naval Brigade.—Reuter.

ORANGE RIVER, Nov. 17.

Lord Methuen has issued an order which is calculated to spoil the Boer plan of picking off British officers.

In going into action the dress of the officer will be so nearly alike that it is seen that it will puzzle the Boer marksmen to detect any difference.

The troops are to march as heavily laden as possible.

The Boers have taken possession of Barkly West and Douglas, and captured a few prisoners. Colonel Rhodes has escaped.—Central News.

Only four correspondents are permitted to accompany the advance, on baggage will be allowed, and only one horse will be allowed for two correspondents.

Only one American correspondent has re-

WESTERN FRONTIER. (continued)

received a permit to accompany the advance party. He is Mr. Julian Ralph.—Central N

Mr. Ralph does not rep... can paper. He has been e... by the "Daily Mail."

CLOSING IN ON...

BOERS AGAIN COMI... BIG FIG...

MAFEKING...

(By runner to Mochi...

An energetic bombardm... going on all day with the usual stoppage for meals...

The position of the... changed to a point south... and 400 yards nearer...

This is a much better... one previously chosen...

If it cannot damage... never will...

Most of the guns have... gether in that locality... that a big combined atta... will be delivered at our...

The Boers are thick... north-east, east, and s... town, about two miles a...

Mafeking is as confiden... confident, too, that our... through, but no news is...

I believe that a picked tectorate Regiment is... attack the Boer position the bayonet.

All well. No further...

CAP...

An official despatch... yesterday's date says th... Mafeking with big gun... result.—Reuter.

SKIRMISHING ROUN...

ORANGE...

A Pretoria telegram say... several skirmishes round S... day, and that the cordo... closer.—Reuter's Specia...

SURPRISED AND...

ORANGE...

The Boers dug a high... duct of our men at Bel... surprised at the accuracy and say they could not p... without being fired at...

The enemy are reported the stubborn resistance... Kimberley.—Reuter's Spe...

CAPE COI...

ON TO EAST...

THE TRIPLE INVAS... COLON...

WAITING FOR REIN... AND LOCAL...

NAAUW...

This morning at dayb... a mixed commando, with... two Nordenfelt guns an... into Colesberg and ass... name of the Free State... vaal.

A proclamation wa... Britishers seven days to... the oath of allegiance.

The Free State and T... floating over the magist... magistrate's books and... taken possession of by t...

The hotels have been... tial law will be proclaim...

The Boers are very i... disaffected villages the... tion is already threateni...

A large commando no... is expected to morrow w... advancing on Naauwpoo...

The three policemen... Goods are bought and... Transvaal coin, and a r...

All horses have been... the Boers, who are wo... look fit.

One object of the inv... a combined raid from I... Post, and Colesberg, th... isolate De Aar.

There is no truth in... Eckstein's buildings a... also at Johannesburg... stroyed.

The Boers are sanguin...

The whole population... in the market-square to... nation read.

The Boer commando... strong, well-armed and... through the town and h... The Commandant Gir... the meeting, making... speech, and calling on a... stand back to back and... British yoke. The loy... sullen silence.

The proclamation allo... molested, but all who w... in to within seven day... behaving well.

Later on a meeting... it was decided to... is merely a way of cover... ably confiscation.

Colesberg residents... mandeered right and left... An exodus has set in... have behaved well.

Lord Methuen has iss... Imperial proclamation... Mansel his assistant...

The collegiate cadets'... seized.

The magistrate, the po... staff have left.

A reliable estimate o... the Boer commandos fr... near Knap Daar station... gives the number at 1... field-pieces.

The Boers are slowly m... travelling only a few mi... Scouts in increasing n...

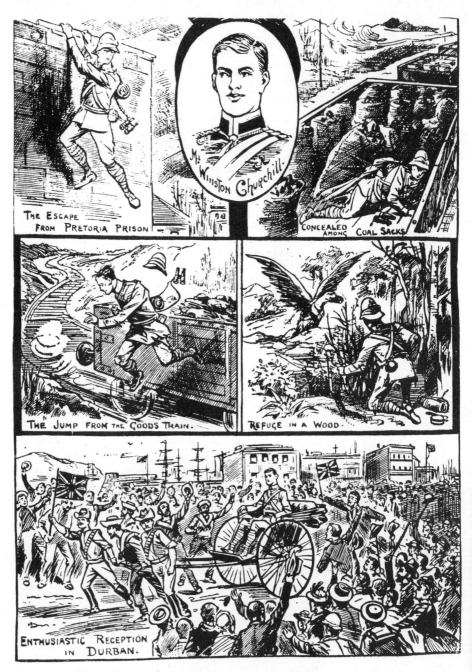

THE ESCAPE OF BRAVE WINSTON CHURCHILL FROM PRETORIA.

SIXTY HOURS OF TERRIBLE ANXIETY AND DARING ADVENTURES

Less than two weeks after his arrival in South Africa Churchill was in prison in Pretoria. He was not temperamentally suited to prison life – it was a waste of time and far too boring. 'It is terrible to think how little time remains,' he wrote on his twenty-fifth birthday there. He had to get out. With two others he made plans for escape, but only Churchill succeeded in climbing over the wall. The main difficulty however was that Pretoria was more than two hundred miles from the safe territory of Portuguese East Africa and he had no way of knowing in which direction that lay. He took pot luck and jumped a train that took him a little way in the right direction. By day he skulked in woods near the line and ate some chocolate. At night he again chanced his arm and knocked on the door of a house with lights on. By a stroke of fortune it was opened by one of the very few Englishmen for miles around. News of his escape was already out and posters offering a reward for his recapture had been issued. He was a hunted man. But the Englishman hid him in the mine of which he was manager until the outcry had lessened. There he spent several days in inky darkness while white rats ate his candles and ran over his body. At length his friend put him on a goods train bound for Lourenço Marques in Portuguese East Africa; he hid in some bales of wool and escaped the scrutiny of the guards at the frontier. It was a dramatic escape and when the news of it reached England Churchill became for a time a minor popular hero.

Attached to the South African Light Horse he stayed in South Africa another six months. Each was eventful. He was with the relief column that entered Ladysmith and fought gallantly at the battle of Diamond Hill. In a skirmish near Dewetsdorp he found himself in a position in which 'a disabling wound was the brightest prospect', and was only saved in the nick of time by a stranger on a pale horse. Later he marched into Pretoria where he witnessed the release of his former fellow prisoners.

He returned to England in July 1900 and in October Oldham triumphantly returned its hero to Parliament – the last of Queen Victoria's lifetime. Three months later she was dead.

By 1901 Churchill had made £10,000 from his literary and journalistic efforts. *Savrola*, *The River War* (his account of Kitchener's campaign), *London to Ladysmith* and *Ian Hamilton's March* (his books about his adventures in South Africa) had all been published. He bought a motor car and installed himself in a flat in Mount Street, Mayfair. He was a pudgy, piggy, redhaired fellow, who though only twenty-seven was already quite well known. His maiden speech in Parliament on the Boer War had a large audience and was favourably received. 'A very admirable speech,' said Joseph Chamberlain; the *Standard* reported: 'He spoke with great self-possession, modestly,

OPPOSITE Churchill's daring escape from prison in Pretoria, pictured here in the *Police News* brought him fame back in England. After his escape descriptions of him were circulated throughout South Africa, The first said he was 'about 5 ft 8 ins or 9 ins, blonde with light, thin, small moustache, walks with slight stoop, cannot speak any Dutch, during long conversations he occasionally makes a rattling noise in his throat.' A reward of £25 was offered for him, dead or alive.

and with a restraint of manner, and with no trace of a desire to be rhetorical.' Before the year was out he had made nine speeches in the House, thirty in the country and given twenty lectures in towns. He did not intend to mark time. His relationship with the Conservative Party was uneasy: he was unimpressed by Balfour, who became leader in July 1902 – a ditherer, he felt – and he was too much Lord Randolph's son to swallow Toryism whole. As he later said: 'I took my politics almost unquestioningly from him'. Lord Randolph's final resignation had been over the defence estimates, so when Mr Brodrick produced his estimates for the army in 1901 Winston picked up his father's 'tattered flag' and went into battle against them, whereupon Brodrick accused him of 'a hereditary desire to run imperialism on the cheap'. With Lord Hugh Cecil and two others he founded a quasi Fourth Party. Known as the Hughligans, or Hooligans, they had a jolly time. At their Thursday dinners they entertained the Liberal leaders more often than their own. They were, however, but a pale imitation of that earlier ginger group.

Winston was at this time engaged on a biography of Lord Randolph. He was finding out all he could of the father he had barely known, attempting to fathom his strange personality and peculiar brand of politics. He often referred to him in his speeches in the House of Commons. As J. H. Plumb has said, Lord Randolph 'seized the young Winston's imagination in a vice-like grip and at the same time totally over-awed him'. The biography was an attempt to come to terms with that grip. It was a great success: full, lucid, with a shrewd grasp of the politics of the 1880s, yet it failed perhaps to present the man. Many people thought it vulgar: to write openly of your father who had been dead but ten years was unseemly in an age when Queen Victoria's trend for lengthy mourning still prevailed.

Meanwhile Winston was veering further away from the Tories. Free trade was his largest bone of contention. 'I hate the Tory Party, their men, their words and their methods,' he declared. Then 'Why tarry?' asked his Liberal aunt, Lady Wimborne. So on 31 May 1904 he crossed the floor of the House to sit on the Liberal benches. No party takes kindly to defectors and the suspicion and antipathy that this action aroused were not dispelled for a very long time. 'I readily admit that my conduct is open to criticism,' he wrote to Lord Salisbury, 'not, thank heaven, on the score of its sincerity, but from the point of view of taste. I had to choose between fighting and standing aside. No doubt the latter was more decorous. But I wanted to fight.' He could not see that it was more than a matter of decorum.

In the general election in January 1906 he was returned as Liberal

MY AFRICAN JOURNEY

BY THE RT. HON.
WINSTON SPENCER CHURCHILL
M.P.

For the winter of 1907–8, as Under-Secretary of State for the Colonies, Churchill toured the East African territories. The articles he wrote on his travels were published in 1909 in *My African Journey* (left). One of his adventures was the hunting of the rare Burchell's White Rhinoceros (below).

member for North West Manchester. The Prime Minister, Campbell-Bannerman, made him Under-Secretary of State for the Colonies. Had he been a little impatient on those backwater Tory back-benches? If so he was now rewarded, for in his first Parliamentary job he was kept busy. Lord Elgin, his chief at the Colonial Office, liked to spend his time in Scotland, so the burden of work fell on Churchill's shoulders, which suited him well. He adored responsibility and greeted it with enthusiasm. He was always distressed, to put it mildly, when deprived of it – which he wasn't, fortunately, for ten years.

Churchill appointed an obscure clerk called Edward Marsh from the West African Department to be his Private Secretary. Their working association lasted more than twenty years and Marsh, who became a well-known patron of the arts, remained a friend of Churchill's until his death in 1953. At the Colonial Office Winston played a leading part in establishing constitutions of responsible government for the Boer republics of South Africa. He was able for the first time to put into practice his principle of magnanimity after victory. He held four such principles: 'In War, Resolution. In Defeat, Defiance. In Victory, Magnanimity. In Peace, Goodwill'. All stood him in good stead.

Churchill and Clementine
Hozier at their engagement
in 1908.

OPPOSITE The *Evening News*
reported every detail of the
Churchill wedding in
September 1908. Churchill's
marriage 'proved', wrote
his son Randolph, 'the
sheet-anchor of his career.'

Asquith, who had become Prime Minister on the resignation of
the dying Campbell-Bannerman, made Churchill President of the
Board of Trade and brought him into the Cabinet. It was still the
rule that a minister, on appointment, had to fight a by-election.
Churchill, in his North West Manchester seat, was beaten. The
Telegraph exulted, 'Churchill is out, OUT, OUT'. Another asked,
'What is the use of a WC without a seat?' Dundee came to the
rescue and swiftly returned him as its member.

Probably the best thing that happened to him that year, 1908, took
place not in the corridors of Whitehall nor on the hustings of
Dundee, but in an ornamental temple at Blenheim on 11 August.
There he proposed to Miss Clementine Hozier and was accepted.
She was very beautiful but not at all rich. But Churchill did not care
about her bank balance. He had known her some time, though not
well. His mother, Lady Randolph, realised how right Clementine
was for Winston and encouraged the courtship. Clemmie later re-
called their first meeting at a ball and how Winston 'just stared'. 'He
never uttered one word and was very gauche – he never asked me for

The Evening News

NO. 8,391. (TWENTY-EIGHTH YEAR.) LONDON: SATURDAY, SEPTEMBER 12, 1908.

TO-NIGHT'S GOSSIP.

BY THE end of this month most of the people who have gone abroad to take the waters at the different "cures" will have returned to town, and by the middle of October the autumn season in town will have begun. A great many weddings are expected to take place between now and Christmas.

SATURDAY is a red-letter day in the career of Mr. Winston Churchill, whose marriage this afternoon has engrossed the interest of all political parties. It was on a Saturday that he left for South Africa, where he earned so much fame. On a Saturday he opened his campaign against Mr. Brodrick's scheme of Army Reform, and he completed the severance from his old associates by assisting a Liberal candidate in a by-election.

WHEN MR. CHURCHILL contested North-West Manchester at the general election he won the seat on a Saturday, and when on his appointment as President of the Board of Trade he had to seek a "safe seat" in Scotland, he was returned on a Saturday. The offer of a position in the Cabinet also came on a Saturday, so that he has good reason for considering the day a lucky one.

IT IS interesting to note that already three members of the Government have entered into the matrimonial state while holding office, two of them being Cabinet Ministers. Mr. Churchill is therefore the third member of the present Cabinet to be married during his tenure of office.

THE EXPERIMENT of the West London Mission in taking the Lyceum Theatre for Sunday services recalls the fact that the history of the mission during recent years has been a curious record of flitting from place to place. Like Jo, it has constantly been "moved on." In the time of Mr. Hugh Price Hughes the mission had the old St. James's Hall, which was eventually pulled down, and it had to leave.

IT THEN went to the Exeter Hall. This was condemned, and it flitted to the Kingsway Hall. Not long ago the London County Council descended upon it there, and the building was once more condemned. Refuge was found in the new St. James's Hall, but this is too small for the people who flock to the mission.

EVENTUALLY a permanent abiding place is to be erected on the site of the building which was condemned in Kingsway. The work, however, is not to be started until a fund of £20,000 has been obtained. At present only £10,000 of this is in hand. It is hoped, however, to have the building [illegible]d in two or three years.

[illegible]TRE MANAGER SHOT

[illegible] Sequel to a Money Dispute in Paris.

PARIS, Saturday.

[illegible] sensation was caused at midnight [illegible] lieutenant in the Reserves shooting [illegible] manager of the Ambigu Theatre. The [illegible] now lies at the Lariboisière Hospital [illegible] serious condition.

[illegible] appears that the officer in question, Lieutenant Stein who is a shareholder in the theatre, had deposited £800 with M. Fraicheron, the Ambigu manager, and some dispute arose concerning it, with the result that the lieutenant fired four revolver shots at the manager.

The assailant has been arrested.

M. Fraicheron was formerly director of a London firm occupying premises on the Rue Notre Dame des Victoires.—Central News.

ANOTHER SAFE ROBBERY

Carried Off Bodily by Thieves from a West End Jeweller's Shop.

A remarkably daring burglary, in which a safe was carried away, took place last night at a jeweller's shop in New Oxford-street.

The proprietor, locking up his shop, went to a neighbouring restaurant for refreshment.

Returning in less than twenty minutes he noticed that the door had been opened, and found the place in disorder.

A large safe weighing some 5cwt, containing about eighty silver watches and a large amount of jewellery of all kinds had been carried off bodily from the shop.

From the weight of the safe it is thought that at least three men must have been engaged in the robbery.

The burglars left no clue, but the proprietor has his suspicions of two men whom he had noticed apparently watching the place for the past two or three days.

It was in consequence of this that he had put considerably more goods in the safe than was his custom.

MR. CHURCHILL'S WEDDING.

ENORMOUS CROWDS AT ST. MARGARET'S

THE BRIDEGROOM'S RECEPTION.

THE SCENE IN THE HISTORIC CHURCH.

The wedding of Mr. Winston Churchill and Miss Clementine Hozier, which has evoked such widespread interest, was celebrated this afternoon at St. Margaret's, Westminster.

The ceremony was attended by members of the Cabinet, members of Parliament, and a great number of distinguished personages from all over the country.

The popular interest in the event was evinced by the presence of an enormous crowd, which gathered outside the building, and watched the arrival and departure of the guests.

SCENE OUTSIDE.

Popular Desire to Get a Glimpse of the Proceedings.

Brilliant sunshine bathed Westminster this afternoon as people gathered at the scene of the ceremony.

For two hours before the time fixed for the event people were in the vicinity of St. Margaret's, coming, not in ones and twos at a time, but in scores.

By one o'clock the crowd numbered thousands, and during the next hour, from all directions, thousands more poured into the spaces about the church.

The pavements surrounding the gardens were packed, the throngs being kept back by a force of police.

Many clung to the railings or endeavoured to obtain a distant view from across the square.

A line of constables guarded each end of the roadway near the church, allowing only vehicles and privileged guests to go through.

So anxious also were the hundreds of the guests to secure admission that they lined up in a queue on the pavement long before the doors were opened. Smartly-dressed people in motors, carriages, and on foot arrived in a constant stream.

Mr. Joynson Hicks, M.P., who defeated Mr. Winston Churchill at the Manchester by-election, was one of the first to arrive.

THE BRIDEGROOM.

Mr. Churchill's Cordial Reception at the Hands of the Spectators.

Mr. Winston Churchill arrived at the door of St. Margaret's facing the Parliament buildings at a quarter to two.

As he sat in his electric brougham, all smiles and completely self-possessed, the crowd readily recognised him and cheers ran down the line of spectators, while the women waved handkerchiefs and some shouted "Good luck!"

At one point the crowd broke through the police and hands were extended in a vain attempt to seize his.

As the bridegroom alighted the click of a score of cameras greeted him. He seemed to hesitate a moment in order to afford the picture-takers their opportunity.

He was accompanied by Lord Hugh Cecil, his best man.

INSIDE THE CHURCH.

Historical Setting Adds to the Interest of the Ceremony.

It was fitting that the wedding of one whose family has been intimately connected with the affairs of Great Britain, and with the doings of the Houses of Parliament, should take place at St. Margaret's, Westminster.

The slight but effective decorations, combined with a sense of the historic interest of the edifice, made the scene a singularly impressive one.

Large palms, lilies, and other white flowers decorated the chancel and the rugged grey north porch, and palms bent gracefully over the west door, but the rich beauty of the body of the church was left without floral ornaments.

Milton was married to his second wife, in 1656, in this old parish church of the royal palaces and the House of Commons, and as the guests entered between the

MISS CLEMENTINE HOZIER PATTERSON

MR WINSTON CHURCHILL

THE BRIDE'S WHITE SATIN WEDDING DRESS

SOME OF THE BR[illegible]

MISS H SEYMOUR MISS M WHYTE M[illegible] THE HON. V. STANLEY MISS C. FREWEN

formally by practically the entire population of Woodstock.

But no special preparations in the direction of decoration or triumphal arches have been made, in deference to his vigorously expressed wishes in the matter.

The Duke of Marlborough is this year the Mayor of Woodstock, which is an ancient borough, and, of course, he would be the first to respect his cousin's wishes, apart from the fact that he is travelling, and will not be able to be present at the wedding to-day.

Mr. Churchill and his bride will take the 4.55 Paddington express to Oxford, which they reach at nine minutes past six.

The Birmingham portion of the train will go on, and an engine will be attached to their saloon, so that they will leave Oxford about 6.20.

The general public will, of course, not be admitted to the platform at Oxford, nor will Mr. Churchill and his bride be allowed to be inconvenienced by the public at any point of the route.

Very special instructions have been given to the Great Western officials on this point.

There will certainly be a large crowd at Paddington to see him off, and a few friends will accompany him on the journey as far as Oxford.

After spending three days at Blenheim Palace, Mr. and Mrs. Winston Churchill will go to Baveno, on Lake Maggiore, afterwards proceeding to Eichorn, near Brunn, in Austria, where Mr. Churchill will have some shooting over the estates of his friend, Baron de Forest.

THREE-DAYS-OLD WINSTON.

Amongst the birth announcements in the *Times* to-day was the following:—

HILLYARD.—On the 9th September, 1908, at 159, Dersingham-avenue, Manor Park, to Mr. and Mrs. Morris J. J. Hillyard, a son ("Winston").

Telegraphing to *The Evening News* this afternoon, the father of the three-days-old Winston said he selected the name:—

In appreciation of the President of the Board of Trade, a great Free Trader, and to honour the wedding function.

SQUANDERED A FORTUNE.

(From Our Own Correspondent.)

[illegible] GREAT [illegible]

London's [illegible] Catholic Ceremony.

Great crowds [illegible] witness the procession of the Blessed Sacrament in connection with the Eucharistic Congress to-morrow afternoon.

When the procession leaves the Cathedral it will traverse the following route, the various points [illegible] reached at the times stated below:—

Cathedral [illegible]
Ashley-place [illegible]
Carlisle-place [illegible]
Francis-street [illegible]
[illegible]-road [illegible]
Artillery-row [illegible]
Howick-place [illegible]
Ashley-gardens .... 4.30 p.m.
Ambrosden-avenue .... 4.35 p.m.

The order of procession is officially given as follows:—

Master of Ceremonies.
The Cathedral choir.
Cathedral chaplains.
The Sub-Deacon, carrying the Cross between candle-bearers.
The Canons.
The Abbots.
The Bishops.
The Archbishops.
A Chaplain bearing the crozier.
Two Thurifers.
The Cardinal Legate, carrying the Blessed Sacrament under a canopy borne by members of the Guild of St. Stephen, a cleric carrying a lantern walking at each corner.
The Chaplain of the Mitre.
Members of the Pontifical Mission.
Attendants of the Legate.
Vergers.
Masters of Ceremonies.
Cardinals.
Masters of Ceremonies.
The Archbishop of Westminster.
Masters of Ceremonies.
Protonotaries apostolic.
Domestic prelates.
The Pope's chamberlain.
Generals of religious orders.
Pro. Lireals of religious orders.
Superiors of religious congregations.
Representatives of absent bishops.

Upon returning to the Cathedral the Cardinal Celebrant will give the Benediction of the Blessed Sacrament to the people out-

HOLIDAY MYSTERY.

[illegible] Somerset House [illegible]k.

Mr. F. S. Boot, a clerk in the Inland Revenue Department, Somerset House, has mysteriously disappeared while on a holiday at Lourdes, in the South of France.

He left three weeks ago, but did not return to his office last Monday, as was expected, and nothing has since been heard of him.

Several telegrams have been sent to the hotel at which he was believed to have stayed, but no reply has been received.

Letters and postcards were received from Mr. Boot up to within a few days of the date on which he should have returned.

Two of his fellow clerks have been granted special leave, and left London last night to search for their friend.

THE KAISER'S THANKS.

Emperor Smilingly Shakes Hands with French Official on the Frontier.

PARIS, Saturday.

In expressing his thanks to the French Commissary of Epinal for the arrangements made to receive him should he visit French territory, the Emperor William, according to the *Petit Parisien*, said:—

"I am very grateful to the French authorities for their kind attentions. Please convey my cordial thanks to your superiors. I regret that I am not able to accept the hospitality of French soil to ascend the Hoheneck, as I am expected at Colmar. Perhaps I shall have an opportunity of doing so at some future time."

In taking his departure the Emperor smilingly shook hands with the French official.

The Imperial party subsequently passed quite close to the frontier, and was saluted by the French and German gendarmery drawn up in line.—Reuter.

OUT OF TOWN TO-DAY.

a dance, he never asked me to have supper with him. I had of course heard a great deal about him – nothing but ill. I had been told he was stuck-up, objectionable, etcetera. And on this occasion he just stood and stared.' At a later meeting they talked and Winston wrote to tell her 'what a comfort and pleasure it was to me to meet a girl with so much intellectual quality and such strong reserves of noble sentiment'. He added, 'I hope we shall meet again and come to know each other better and like each other more'. They were married on 12 September 1908 at St Margaret's, Westminister, and, as Churchill put it, 'lived happily ever after'. Certainly no wiser counsellor, nor more loyal companion could he have hoped to find.

At the Board of Trade Churchill grappled with social legislation and made considerable achievements in that field. He was largely responsible for introducing a system of labour exchanges, he vigorously promoted unemployment insurance and he passed legislation on sweated labour. The sphere was new to him and he was not well acquainted with the working classes. His reaction on a visit to a slum area was recorded by Edward Marsh: 'Fancy living in one of those streets,' he declared, 'never seeing anything beautiful – never eating anything savoury – *never saying anything clever!*' However his energy and his child-like quality of taking nothing for granted meant that problems, previously considered insoluble, were overcome. He and Lloyd George were known as 'the heavenly twins of social reform'. But Lloyd George was the more genuinely radical. Winston's radicalism was born of a paternalistic attitude, a generous nature and a dearth of preconceptions; it had an imperial twang. 'I see little glory in an Empire,' he said, 'which can rule the waves and is unable to flush its sewers.'

As Home Secretary in 1910 he introduced further measures for prison reform (his experiences in Pretoria had made him particularly aware of this problem), for improvement of conditions in mines, for early closing and so on. Women's suffrage he did not care for: 'This ridiculous movement' he had called it on the notes he had made on the pages of the *Annual Register* in India. Later, under his wife's tutelage and when three-quarters of the women of the country voted for him, he came round to it.

The siege of a group of anarchists in a small house in Sydney Street in 1910 brought Churchill scurrying to the scene. An irresponsible act, some said. 'He was, I understand, in military phrase, in what is known as the zone of fire,' said A. J. Balfour in the House of Commons. 'He and a photographer were both risking valuable lives. I understand what the photographer was doing, but what was the Right Honourable gentleman doing?' The Right Honourable gentleman was, of course, having fun. Later he was accused of using

In 1906 and 1909 Churchill
was invited to watch
German army manoeuvres.
In this photograph he is
shown with the Kaiser on
his second visit. He also
visited the French
manoeuvres in 1907 and the
English in 1908 and 1910.

the troops against the miners during a strike at Tonypandy in Wales.
It was a false accusation. It would not have been had it been levelled
at him over the railway strike in August 1911, but that for some reason was never remembered. He supported capital punishment as
being infinitely preferable to a life sentence, which he considered
boredom far worse than death, but found the decisions he had to
take as Home Secretary on this score painful.

The incident at Agadir in July 1911, when a German gunboat was
sent to the port, thus threatening Britain's presence on Gibraltar

and her vital trade routes, struck a chord of danger in him. Domestic troubles shrank in his eyes before the international peril that he fore-saw. He wrote an astonishingly prescient document for the Com-mittee of Imperial Defence, which stated with remarkable accuracy the course war would take in Europe. Asquith was impressed by his reasoning and asked him if he would like to replace McKenna as First Lord of the Admiralty. 'Indeed I would,' said Churchill.

He was fascinated by the Navy in all its aspects and not least by the fact that it was at that time Britain's supreme defence. From his earliest political awakening in India he had been aware of the Navy's all-important part in the security of the British Isles. 'The principle is clear,' he wrote to Asquith in September 1911, 'that the fleet con-centrated in the North Sea should be strong enough without further aid to fight a decisive battle with the German Navy.' With a less than supreme navy Britain was perilously vulnerable. 'The whole for-tunes of our race and Empire, the whole treasure accumulated during so many centuries of sacrifice and achievement would perish and be swept utterly away if our naval supremacy were to be impaired.' For the Germans, however, their navy 'was more in the nature of a luxury'. That rankled in Berlin.

Over the next few years, as the German forces grew, he worked to maintain that supremacy. He believed in keeping the fleet in home waters, not scattering it throughout the world as many people advocated. 'Dispersion of strength, frittering of money, empty parades of foolish little ships "displaying the flag" in unfrequented seas, are the certain features of a policy leading through extrava-gance to defeat.' He believed in 'overpowering strength at the deci-sive point'. Naturally he needed more money for his ships. His naval estimates for 1914–15, in which he sought an increase of nearly three million pounds, were considered by his cabinet colleagues extrava-gant and not in keeping with the Liberal principle of retrenchment. Despite a bitter row with Lloyd George, to whom Margot Asquith had written 'Don't let Winston have too much money', he was finally granted what he asked for in February 1914. He did make some economies: for instance, he scrapped the Grand Manoeuvres in favour of an exercise of general mobilisation of the fleet. 'The test is one of the most important that can be made, and it is surprising we should have continued for so many years without ever once making it.'

The first such exercise was held at Spithead 17–23 July 1914 – most fortunately as it turned out. On 24 July Austria sent Serbia an ulti-matum which was, Churchill wrote to his wife at the time, 'the most insolent document of its kind ever devised'. It meant that war was inevitable. As Europe's nations teetered on the brink, the First Sea

Lord, Prince Louis of Battenberg, backed by Churchill, halted the demobilisation of the fleet after its exercise. Other precautionary measures were taken. On 28 July he wrote to his wife: 'Everything tends towards catastrophe and collapse. I am interested, geared up and happy. Is it not horrible to be built like that? The preparations have a hideous fascination for me. I pray to God to forgive me for such fearful words of levity. Yet I would do my best for peace, and nothing would induce me wrongfully to strike the blow'. He added: 'Everything is ready as it has never been before. And we are awake to the tips of our fingers. But war is the Unknown and the Un-expected! God guard us and our long accumulated inheritance. You know how willingly I wd risk – or give if need be – my period of existence to keep this country great and famous and prosperous and free.'

The following night the fleet slipped swiftly and silently, without lights, to its battle stations in northern Scotland. Five days later the signal went out from the Admiralty to all His Majesty's ships and naval establishments: 'Commence hostilities against Germany'. 'Well, there is one thing at any rate, they cannot take from you,' said Kitchener to Winston later, 'the fleet was ready.'

Churchill was thirty-nine. He was stimulated by the war and set about his job with all the enormous energy and enthusiasm he could muster. J. L. Garvin of the *Observer*, who had long been his critic, appreciated his prompt executive actions and declared: 'We close the differences we have had with Mr Churchill.' There was general euphoria at the first naval success when, on 28 August, three German cruisers in the Heligoland Bight were destroyed. But censure was not far away.

Reinforcements were needed in October 1914 for the defence of Antwerp. Churchill had visited the city and although he had suc-ceeded in 'bucking up the Belges,' as Asquith put it, he saw the emergency of the situation and suggested sending two of his naval brigades to help the marines already there. These brigades were from the Royal Naval Division, a small naval army formed by Churchill. They were to be snatched from their training ground and sent to beleaguered Antwerp. And although Churchill had stipulated 'no recruits', some of the men had barely begun their training. Among the officers were Asquith's son, Oc, Rupert Brooke and the com-poser Denis Browne. They had been with the division three days, one week and one day respectively. The valiant action of these raw brigades probably did delay the German advance for a few days and did save Dunkirk and Calais. But there were many casualties and the soldiers became known as 'Churchill's Innocent Victims'. The press blamed him for the 'Antwerp Blunder'. The sinking of the *Audacious*

and the failure to track down the *Emden*, which was lashing out in the Indian Ocean, brought further criticism.

Churchill replaced Prince Louis of Battenberg with the wily, volcanic Lord Fisher as First Sea Lord. He was seventy-four and Churchill had long held him in high regard. Both respected the other's enthusiastic attitudes and fertile minds. 'Isn't it fun being back?' said Fisher, who had been First Sea Lord before. It was a reaction Churchill understood. 'Contact with you is like a breath of ozone,' Churchill had told him. Their mutual attraction was such that, as Violet Bonham Carter put it, 'they could not keep away from each other for long.' And the partnership was promising: Fisher's naval expertise was expected to complement Churchill's political energy. But Clemmie was a little sceptical: 'I hope he is not like the curate's egg!' she said.

By winter there was stalemate on the Western Front. The War Cabinet cast about for another theatre of action to relieve the pressure on Russia. The fleet was transfixed in the North Sea watching and waiting for the German fleet to come out. It was a frustrating vigil. Churchill was keen to make more positive use of his ships. He favoured the capture of the island of Borkum in the Baltic. An alternative plan was to capture the Dardanelles; the consequent fall of Constantinople would cause the Balkan states to fall in behind the Allies. They would then surge forward and strike a fatal blow to Germany. It was thought by the admiral on the spot that such an action could be carried out 'by ships alone' – and old redundant ships at that. The crucial home fleet would not be impaired.

The Turks were not thought to be formidable, but Churchill was wary. 'Germany is the foe, and it is bad war to seek cheaper victories and easier antagonists.' But it did seem a swift and efficient plan and the prizes were tempting. The War Cabinet was perhaps a little more preoccupied with how it would divide 'the carcase of the Turk' than with the practical details of the plan. Kitchener was in favour of it, Fisher opposed: 'I just abominate the Dardanelles operation,' he said. Churchill was in favour, although he hankered after a decisive naval action in the Baltic. But once it was decided upon by the Cabinet he flung himself into it. Things went wrong; the mines in the Dardanelles were much deadlier than had been anticipated. There were delays; the Greeks failed to co-operate. So it was decided to bring in the troops. They were the War Office's responsibility and the general direction of the operation passed from Churchill to Kitchener. But there were further delays and, over the landings, enormous valour was coupled with massive incompetence. General Monro in particular roused Churchill's scorn: 'He came, he saw, he capitulated'. Fisher liked it less and less: 'D—n the Dardanelles!' he

OPPOSITE In a *Punch* cartoon of 1914 by Bernard Partridge, Churchill, First Lord of the Admiralty, is shown summoning air power to the assistance of the navy.

Sir John Lavery's paintings
of Winston and Clementine
Churchill during the war
years. It was Lady Lavery
who first encouraged
Churchill to paint.

exclaimed. 'They will be our grave!' He threatened to resign, but Churchill urged him to remain. He was, said Churchill, committed to the enterprise: he argued that he could not forsake 'a great army hanging on by its eyelids to a rocky beach . . .'. But on 15 May Fisher resigned. 'In the King's name, I order you at once to return to your post,' Asquith commanded.

But he did not. The Government wobbled. Asquith was obliged to bring in the Conservatives and form a National Government. There was no longer any place for Churchill at the Admiralty. It was thought by many of his colleagues that he had conducted the war for his own personal glory and that his impetuosity was highly dangerous. He was considered reckless and irresponsible. Clemmie pleaded with Asquith: 'Winston may in your eyes, and in those with whom he has to work, have faults but he has the supreme quality which I venture to say very few of your present or future Cabinet possess; the power, the imagination, the deadliness to fight Germany'. But Asquith was cold and implacable, and made him Chancellor of the Duchy of Lancaster – a paltry job by comparison.

His removal at this time was taken by the public to mean that he was to blame for the fiasco at the Dardanelles and, as the wrath over the operation grew, it was vented on Churchill. For security reasons he was unable to defend himself. He forever resented the fact that Asquith did not speak up on his behalf, that he did not declare how he had supported every one of Churchill's decisions, and that the allegations were allowed to spread, unrefuted. In Clemmie's words, 'the Dardanelles haunted him for the rest of his life'.

So in 1915 he was shattered and isolated. He had nothing, comparatively speaking, to do. The Duchy of Lancaster was 'a farce so far as work is concerned', said Edward Marsh. The family took a farm in Surrey where they lived simply: 'but with all the essentials of life well understood and well provided for', Churchill wrote to his brother Jack – 'hot baths, cold champagne, new peas, and old brandy'. He began to paint. The big white canvas was an intimidating enemy. He began his attacks. 'Very gingerly I mixed a little blue paint on the palette with a very small brush, and then with infinite precaution made a mark about as big as a bean upon the affronted snow-white shield. It was a challenge, a deliberate challenge.' Then he was stuck; the battle stalled. By chance, along came Lady Lavery: '"But what are you hesitating about? Let me have a brush – the big one." Splash into the turpentine, wallop into the blue and the white, frantic flourish on the palette – clean no longer – and then several large, fierce strokes and slashes of blue on the absolutely cowering canvas. Anyone could see that it could not hit back. No evil fate avenged the jaunty insolence. The canvas grinned in helplessness before me.' So began a pastime from which he derived comfort and pleasure for the rest of his life.

Increasingly frustrated by his inactivity and disillusioned by the Government's conduct of the war – 'the soldiers who are ordered to their deaths have a right to a plan, as well as a cause' – he decided to leave politics and turn to soldiering again. His service on the Western Front proved a timely distraction as well as a valuable experience. After a while he was given command of the 6th Battalion, Royal Scots Fusiliers. They were demoralised and had seen much suffering, having been halved in numbers at the Battle of Loos; they were not inspired by the arrival of the politician colonel (accompanied by a long bath and a boiler contraption). But soon they rallied under the zest and colour of his command. He instigated delousing, created a football team and ordered better food. Churchill himself, however, cannot have found the rations sufficient, for he sent many requests to Clemmie for food boxes – 'large slabs of corned beef: Stilton cheeses: cream: hams: sardines – dried fruits: you might also try a big beef steak pie but not tinned grouse or fancy tinned things'. For the trenches he wanted a periscope. With or without it he was most insouciant for his safety and would plunge about in no man's land 'like a baby elephant'.

But Winston missed politics. At his request Clemmie kept in touch with useful people and kept him well informed, as well as giving him wise advice. On leave in March 1916 he spoke in a navy debate in the House of Commons. It was a good speech, until the end when quite unexpectedly he called for the return of Lord Fisher. It was a mad idea and one which confirmed many in their view that he lacked all judgment. He did not realise how little support he had in Parliament or the country. But his wife and friends did and he was persuaded by them to go back to his battalion for a while. When the 6th and 7th Battalions of the Royal Scots Fusiliers were amalgamated two months later he felt he could return to the House of Commons honourably, and resume the career on which his heart was set.

8
The Lion's Roar

Churchill joined the Coalition Government under Lloyd George as Minister of Munitions in 1917. He was efficient, energetic and a little subdued. Not only had his personal experience been hard, but the war sapped everyone's morale. Many friends had been killed. 'As the war lengthens and intensifies, and the extending lists appear,' wrote Churchill, 'it seems as if one watched at night a well-loved city whose lights which burn so bright, which burn so true, are extinguished in the distance one by one.' Although he was not a member of the Cabinet the Prime Minister often asked his advice. After the war Lloyd George made him, ironically, Secretary of State for War and for Air. This latter post was particularly suitable, for Churchill had been an early air enthusiast. Before the war he had taken flying lessons, but had never flown solo for, just as he was ready to take his pilot's licence he had given up flying. It was a sacrifice for him to do so and as such he offered it to his wife as 'a gift – so stupidly am I made – wh costs me more than anything wh could be bought with money. So I am vy glad to lay it at your feet, because I know it will rejoice and relieve your heart'. He turned his enthusiasm to the formation of the Royal Naval Air Service, which on the eve of war had more than ninety aeroplanes and seaplanes. The great pains that he took with the details of this small force were in keeping with his strong belief in the potential of air power. His understanding of its value was clearer than that of many of his contemporaries. As Secretary of State for Air after the war, he saw his fledgling air service grow into the Royal Air Force – and promptly pruned it drastically. His 154 squadrons were reduced to twenty-four on the assumption that there would not be a European

"FRESHENING UP YOUR CIVVIES, SIR"

A cartoon by David Low
from the *Evening Standard*,
28 May 1942.

war for ten years. The bulky problem of demobilisation he handled
with dexterity. As it was, men from key industries were demobbed
first; but since they were often the last to have joined up this system
caused much resentment. Churchill changed it so that those who had
served longest had priority.

He dealt less deftly with the problem of armed intervention in
Russia. He did not like the Bolsheviks at all. Bolshevism he considered 'a disease', 'a pestilence', and Lenin 'the plague bacillus'.
'The theories of Lenin and Trotsky have driven man from the civilisation of the twentieth century into a condition of barbarism worse
than the Stone Age.' The possibility of rescuing the Russians from
their unfortunate condition was tempting. When Churchill took
over the War Office many Czech and other troops were still stranded
in northern Russia. Since the war they had been given vague orders
to take nebulous anti-Bolshevik action – quite what had never been
decided. Churchill advocated further British commitment. Lloyd
George was not in favour of it and the Cabinet dithered. Churchill
had a meeting with President Wilson in Paris in the hope of eliciting
from him a positive plan for allied troops in northern Russia; but
Wilson, like Lloyd George, was disinclined to interfere. Churchill
then asked British soldiers if they were prepared to be drafted to
Russia: 'No,' they answered. So he sent money and equipment
instead to support Admiral Kolchak's anti-Bolshevik forces. A little
later it was asked whether Britain were at war with the Bolsheviks or
not. There was no categoric answer. Finally, a mutiny in General
Ironside's troops in Siberia and the advance of the Red Army
rendered further intervention in the north impracticable, and the
British garrison returned home. Churchill was disappointed and
pinned his hopes on General Denikin's force in southern Russia.
But the Red Army was too powerful for Denikin and drove him
back to the Crimea. Churchill had spent £100 million or so, and had
nothing to show for it except, in the eyes of the public, another failure
– a successor to Antwerp and the Dardanelles. Once again he had
displayed, they believed, a blatant taste for war.

His attitude had not endeared him to the labour movement. Labour leaders had formed a National Hands Off Russia Committee.
Churchill distrusted socialism. As early as 1909 he had explained how
it differed from liberalism in his view:

Socialism seeks to pull down wealth, Liberalism seeks to raise up
poverty. Socialism would destroy private interests; Liberalism would
preserve private interests in the only way in which they can be safely and
justly preserved, namely by reconciling them with public right. Socialism
would destroy enterprise; Liberalism would rescue enterprise from the

Churchill campaigning as a
Unionist and Anti-Socialist
candidate at Epping before
the election of 1924. He was
elected by a majority of
10,000. The next year he
formally rejoined the
Tory party.

trammels of privilege and preference . . . socialism exalts the rule; liberalism exalts the man. Socialism attacks capital; liberalism attacks monopoly. But in the following ten years his attacks on socialism had become much more strident.

Churchill, who was at first, like his father, opposed to Home Rule in Ireland, was now in favour of a settlement there – from a position of strength. He became Colonial Secretary in February 1921 and as such helped draw up, and indeed added his signature to, the Irish Treaty. He was proud of his contribution to it. The Irish delegates were hustled into signing the Treaty in December 1921. In the civil war that followed Churchill was prepared to support, militarily, the Irish Free State Government if it looked endangered; and in the event he did send arms and equipment. But his actions were considered and statesmanlike and slowly the system agreed on in the Treaty began to function.

When the Kemalists threatened the British garrison of Chanak in the neutral zone on the Gallipoli peninsula, Churchill was determined to stand up to them, for this invasion of the peninsula would be a violation of the Treaty of Sèvres of 1920. He was keen that the fleet should oppose them, that there would be a show of force and that an ultimatum should be delivered to Mustapha Kemal, which it was. Only through the tact and diplomacy of General Sir Charles Harington, the senior British officer on the spot, was confrontation avoided. The idea of British military action in that ill-starred area was, understandably, abhorrent to the British public. Churchill had again seemed to them to be dangerously trigger-happy. Conservative resignations from the Coalition Government on the issue precipitated its collapse. Lloyd George resigned on 19 October 1922 and within a month there was a general election.

Churchill had appendicitis and was unable to campaign for his seat in Dundee. But anyway the voters did not want to hear his fiery speeches, his doom-laden warnings about the perils of socialism. He was defeated – by more than 10,000 votes. 'In the twinkling of an eye,' he said, 'I found myself without an office, without a seat, without a party, and even without an appendix.'

Without a party: Churchill was drawing away from the Liberals. *The Times* had already noticed: 'Apart from some intellectual gristle,' it had said in 1920, 'his only connections with liberalism are personal.' He stood once more for Parliament as a Liberal, at Leicester, but was defeated again. While the Liberal Party was courting Labour he left them and, in March 1924, stood as an 'Independent and anti-Socialist' for the Abbey Division of Westminster. His invective against socialism was as vitriolic as ever and antagonised many people. He lost, however, by only forty-three votes. Nothing daunted

John Sargent's drawing of
Churchill as Chancellor of
the Exchequer, 1925, in
Lord Randolph's robes.

he was accepted by Epping six months later and returned as a
Unionist and Anti-Socialist member to the Parliament he so loved.
So ended two of the three years that were all that he spent out of
Parliament in this century; the third was the last of his life. On his
return he was immediately given a job by the Prime Minister, Stanley
Baldwin: he became Chancellor of the Exchequer.

'Everybody said I was the worst Chancellor of the Exchequer that
ever was,' he said later, 'and now I'm inclined to agree with them.'
It was not his metier. High finance did not interest him. He was
guided by his advisers and they misled him. His decision to return
to the gold standard was later judged disastrous, though at the time
Maynard Keynes was almost the only critic. It was an effort to revive

pre-war conditions, to return to a time when 'the pound could look the dollar in the face again', but those conditions, Keynes saw, were way past resuscitation. A new strategy was needed to deal with an entirely altered state of affairs. Churchill pruned the services – much to their irritation – on that same supposition that there would be no European war for ten years.

Predictably he took a firm line in the General Strike of 1926. Baldwin saw perhaps the glint in his eye at the possibility of an adventure and thought it prudent to keep him occupied. He was detailed to be editor-in-chief of the emergency newspaper, the *British Gazette*. The paper printed inflammatory material implying that the strikers were the enemy and, as such, must be crushed. 'No flinching', it urged. Its circulation rose from 230,000 on 5 May to more than two million a week later. Churchill's attitude had been in keeping with his principle of magnanimity in victory – that is quell the strike and then redress the grievances of the strikers.

A Labour administration was formed after the election of 1929 and Churchill found himself in Opposition. His six volumes of the First World War, *The World Crisis*, in which he tried to give a true picture of his part in it, were being published. They earned him about £40,000. He had written the work at Chartwell, the house he had bought in Kent in 1922. As a child he had been taught to be fond of Kent. 'It was, Mrs Everest said, "the garden of England". She had been born at Chatham, and was immensely proud of Kent. No county could compare with Kent, any more than any country could compare with England . . . Kent was the place. Its capital was Maidstone, and all around Maidstone there grew strawberries, cherries, raspberries and plums. Lovely!'

For Churchill England's glory was her Empire. He was able to visualise with the utmost clarity the history of that Empire and firmly resisted any fragmentation of it. His attitude was not possessive or avaricious, it was more romantic. He sincerely believed that the Empire was an excellent thing, that it was on the side of right. 'The rescue of India,' he said, 'from ages of barbarism, intestine war and tyranny, and its slow and ceaseless forward march to civilisation constitutes upon the whole the finest achievement of our history.' The forward march towards dominion status was, to him, undesirable. He could not understand Gandhi or see his point. He called him, rather unfortunately, 'a seditious Middle Temple lawyer, now posing as a fakir of a type well known in the East, striding half-naked up the steps of the Viceregal Palace, while he is still organising and conducting a defiant campaign of civil disobedience, to parley on equal terms with the representative of the King-Emperor'.

When the India Act was passed in 1935 Churchill was still hostile to it. He had broken with the Conservative leadership over India and moved to the backbenches, where he said what he felt. He always found it difficult to contain himself within party limits. 'At heart he cared little about parties as such,' Harold Macmillan has written. In 1934 Churchill was sixty; he was more in the political wilderness than ever. He neither had any party strut under him, nor did he represent the interests of any significant part of the country – although Epping cherished him. It looked as if his political life was coming to a rather unsuccessful end. He was respected by his colleagues, for he was, after thirty years, a formidable political creature. His talents were applauded, but they were not trusted. There was no niche for the powerful but unpredictable and highly individual old man. Harold Nicolson wrote perceptively in 1931:

He is more than interesting; he is a phenomenon, an enigma. How can a man so versatile and so brilliant avoid being considered volatile and unsound? . . . His dominant qualities are imagination, courage and loyalty; his dominant defect, impatience.

Nicolson also said: 'He is a man who leads forlorn hopes, and when the hopes of England become forlorn, he will once again be summoned to leadership.'

Churchill's literary output in the 1930s was enormous. He wrote *My Early Life*, which with its charm, its humour, its gaiety and its gentle style may, of all his books, last longest. *Thoughts and Adventures* was a collection of what its title suggests, and *Great Contemporaries* contained some fine portraits. He also completed his four volume biography of his ancestor, the first Duke of Marlborough. It was a large work in every sense and included brilliant descriptions of the battles. The main theme – that of England awaking to resist the tyranny of France, to check the rapid spread of her influence throughout Europe – was one to which Churchill was enormously sympathetic. Marlborough's Grand Alliance too was a noble thing; it had fought for liberty.

He began the work in 1933, the year that he made his first warning about the menace from Germany. 'The great dominant fact is,' he said, 'that Germany has already begun to re-arm.' He had always regretted the treatment of Germany after the First World War. It had not accorded with his belief in a fair and benevolent hand after victory. Now he observed with alarm the German reaction to the Treaty of Versailles. He urged that German grievances be promptly redressed 'before this peril of armament reaches a point which may endanger the peace of the world'. Although he had in the 1920s, first as Secretary of State for War and Air and then as Chancellor of the Exchequer, sponsored reductions in the services, he now thought differently. In particular he called for a strong Air Force. He foresaw

Friends of the Churchills
commissioned William
Nicholson to paint them
having breakfast at
Chartwell as a present for
their Silver Wedding in
1933.

in 1934 how 'the crash of bombs exploding in London and cataracts of masonry and fire and smoke will apprise us of any inadequacy which has been permitted in our aerial defences'. 'We are as vulnerable as we have never been before', he said. 'I cannot conceive how, in the present state of Europe, we can delay in the principle of having our Air Force at least as strong as that of any power that can get at us.' London he saw as 'the greatest target in the world, a kind of tremendous, fat, valuable cow tied up to attract beasts of prey'.

Re-armament became a central issue in the general election of 1935. The Conservatives, on that platform, won. But Baldwin did not invite Churchill to join his administration. Churchill swallowed his disappointment and went abroad with his paintbox. He returned on the death of George v in January 1936. By that time Italy had invaded Abyssinia, but Churchill failed to realise the significance of this event, for he considered Mussolini a good fellow – 'a really great man' he said. Although his judgment was faulty on this issue, as it was on various technical matters (for instance, he overestimated the role of the Air Force and underestimated that of the army, and thought both the tank and the submarine obsolescent), his main instinct about the danger of Germany was early and true. Slowly he gained an audience. The 'Arms and the Covenant' (of the League of Nations) movement emerged and attracted followers from all political parties. Churchill was one of its leading lights. It held its first big meeting in the Albert Hall on 3 December 1936. That was also the day that the delicate constitutional crisis over Edward viii and Mrs Simpson was revealed to the nation. Generally speaking the public thought the King should abdicate; Churchill did not. 'I realised that what had (as I thought) misled him,' wrote Violet Bonham Carter about his position on this matter, 'were in part his noble qualities – his romantic and protective loyalty to his young King – and in part his inability to gauge or guess at the reaction of the ordinary man and woman.' Suddenly the footing he had secured in the estimation of the public slipped from under him. 'All the effect of the Albert Hall meeting was destroyed – first by the Abdication and secondly by the catastrophic fall in Churchill's prestige,' wrote Harold Macmillan.

However he continued to give warnings to the House of Commons of the impending disaster. To the other members his 'sabre-rattling' became familiar, almost monotonous. He did not think war was inevitable, but should it come he was prepared to meet it. More so than his colleagues. A. P. Herbert, a great admirer of Churchill's, said: 'But I did think that he rather enjoyed a war: and, after three years in the infantry in Gallipoli and France, I did not'. It was a feeling that was widely shared.

When in 1938 Neville Chamberlain returned from his meeting
with Hitler at Munich to proclaim 'Peace in our Time', Churchill was
furious. 'The Government had to choose between war and shame,'
he is reported to have said. 'They chose shame and they will get war
too.' To him it seemed that 'the German dictator, instead of snatch-
ing the victuals from the table, has been content to have them served
to him, course by course . . .'. With the invasion of Czechoslovakia
in March 1939 the British appeasement was seen to be bereft of all
honour. England bustled into activity to prepare for war. A Ministry
of Supply was created and Churchill must have hoped to be made
responsible for it. But Chamberlain did not appoint him. The press
at last began to suggest Churchill's inclusion in the government: not
only had he been proved right about Germany but he also had the
obvious qualities for a wartime post. Not until 2 September 1939,
the day after the German invasion of Poland and the day before war
was declared, was Churchill given office. It was the first he had held
for ten years and the same that he had held at the outbreak of the
First World War. For the second time he became First Lord of the
Admiralty. The cable was transmitted to His Majesty's ships and
Naval Establishments: 'Winston is back'.

'So it was that I came again to the room I had quitted in pain and
sorrow almost exactly a quarter of a century before,' he wrote. He
pinned up his old First World War map and set to work with an ur-
gent energy that whirled his subordinates into activity. He examined
all papers, documents, relevant information with almost extravagant
thoroughness. He inspected the ships at Scapa Flow, the naval
establishments at Portsmouth. Little escaped his eye. He searched
for an alternative policy to that of convoy and blockade which the
Navy was having to follow; it was too passive a method of warfare
to appeal to Churchill. He welcomed and promoted the Norwegian
plan, an operation that he thought ingenious and enterprising and
with a good chance of success. But for various reasons, it was
delayed until April 1940 by which time the Germans were on the
spot, and the plan failed. Its failure provoked the loud call for
Chamberlain's removal and, on 10 May 1940, he resigned.

The King had to choose between Churchill and Lord Halifax to
succeed Chamberlain as Prime Minister. Churchill was by no means
the obvious choice. The King would have preferred Halifax, but he
was tainted with Munich and also did not want the post. So the
appointment went to Churchill, to be greeted by many with despair.
It was seen as a gamble at a very critical moment. Churchill himself
was far from desperate. For the very first time in his life he had supreme control over the affairs of the country. He most willingly
accepted the massive responsibility. Indeed he was 'conscious of a

profound sense of relief' he said. 'At last, I had the authority to give directions over the whole scene. I felt as if I were walking with destiny, and that all my past life had been but a preparation for this hour and this trial.'

The trial was the toughest imaginable. The liberty of the British Isles was more gravely in peril than it had been for several centuries. 'I have nothing to offer but blood, toil, tears and sweat,' he told the House of Commons three days after his appointment. His policy: 'To wage war against a monstrous tyranny never surpassed in the dark, lamentable catalogue of human crime'. His aim: 'Victory – Victory at all costs, victory in spite of all terror, victory, however hard and long the road may be; for without victory there is no survival. Let that be realised; no survival for the British Empire; no survival for all that the British Empire has stood for, no survival for the urge and impulse of the ages, that mankind will move forward towards its goal.' They were magnificent words for a very bleak moment. The Parliamentary support that in forty years he had never known was immediately behind him. He, and for the first time everybody else as well, felt that he alone was able to tackle the situation. They saw a statesman of tremendous courage and enormous confidence.

But the situation worsened. The German army marched on and with an 'armoured scythe-stroke almost reached Dunkirk – almost, but not quite'. The remarkable deliverance of the British Expeditionary Force from Dunkirk was greeted with joy and thankfulness. But Churchill cautioned: 'Wars are not won by evacuations'. And after revealing the full horror of the position and the very real danger of imminent invasion, went on:

Even though large tracts of Europe and many old and famous States have fallen or may fall into the grip of the Gestapo and all the odious apparatus of Nazi rule, we shall not flag or fail, we shall go on to the end, we shall fight in France, and we shall fight on the seas and oceans, we shall fight with growing confidence and growing strength in the air, we shall defend our island whatever the cost may be, we shall fight on the beaches, we shall fight on the landing-grounds, we shall fight in the fields and in the streets, we shall fight in the hills; we shall never surrender.

 Those legendary words betrayed, as Isaiah Berlin has called it, 'a bright heroic vision'. Churchill's oratory, which had so often in the past been too grandiose for the occasion, too heavy for the issue, now matched the moment superbly. Through the dark summer and autumn he cheered the British people and bolstered their morale. No one else could have done it. Simply and vividly he rendered noble the cause they found themselves fighting for; there was glory in the

ABOVE Churchill's notes for his famous speech to the Commons on 28 May 1940 during the evacuation from Dunkirk.
RIGHT A war poster.

struggle. Only he was able to express the concept of glory without dimming it. His confidence was contagious. 'In 1940 he assumed an indomitable stoutness,' wrote Berlin.

'I have only one aim in life,' said Churchill, 'the defeat of Hitler and that makes things very simple for me.' But in order to defeat Hitler Britain had to survive; it looked less and less likely that she would be able to as, throughout June, France's resistance to Nazism crumbled. Churchill said:

I expect that the Battle of Britain is about to begin . . . The whole fury and might of the enemy must very soon be turned on us. Hitler knows that he will have to break us in this island or lose the war.

If we can stand up to him, all Europe may be free and the life of the world may move forward into broad, sunlit uplands. But if we fail, then the whole world, including the United States, including all that we have known and cared for, will sink into the Abyss of a new Dark Age made more sinister, and perhaps more protracted, by the lights of perverse science. Let us therefore brace ourselves to our duties and so bear ourselves that, if the British Empire and its Commonwealth last for a thousand years, men will say 'This was their finest hour'.

Four days later France signed an armistice with Germany and the pilots of the Royal Air Force braced themselves. Churchill was not responsible for the direction of the Battle of Britain; he was responsible for invaluable encouragement and for that apt and evocative name, which (like the Home Guard) was inspiring in itself. He ordered his colleagues to set an example of courage and cheer. His memorandum, marked *Strictly Confidential*, ran thus: 'In these dark days the Prime Minister would be grateful if all his colleagues in the Government, as well as high officials, would maintain a high morale in their circles; not minimising the gravity of events, but showing confidence in our ability and inflexible resolve to continue the war till we have broken the will of the enemy to bring all Europe under his domination.' The Battle of Britain began on 8 August and ended on 15 September. On 17 September Hitler postponed his plans for invasion and in October scrapped them. The first step towards VE Day had been taken.

Churchill exercised a kind of presidential control over the Government, but he always respected Parliament, which gave him two votes of confidence during the war years. His affection for Parliament was such that he was moved to tears when he inspected the damage done to the Chamber of the House of Commons by a bomb. Through Sir Hastings Ismay he set up an effective chain of command between himself and the service chiefs. The structure lasted the war and helped to prevent the muddles between politicians and generals

OPPOSITE Churchill stands among the ruins of the House of Commons, after it had been bombed in May 1941. Such was his attachment to the chamber, that he was moved to tears to see it in rubble.

195

ACTION THIS DAY

373

10, Downing Street,
Whitehall.

PRIME MINISTER'S
PERSONAL MINUTE

SIR EDWARD BRIDGES.
GENERAL ISMAY.

SERIAL No. C.24.

Please look at this mass of stuff which reaches
me in a single morning, most of it having already appeared
in the Service and F.O. telegrams.   More and more people
must be banking up behind these different papers, the bulk
of which defeats their purpose.   Try now and simplify,
shorten and reduce.

Make me proposals.

12.11.40

A minute from Churchill on
the excess of paperwork
involved in the
administration of the war.

that had weakened the direction of the First World War. At his meetings with the chiefs he liked discussion – of a sort. He talked a lot and
listened sporadically. As he saw it: 'All I wanted was compliance
with my wishes after reasonable discussion'. The discussion was for
him a way of thinking, for, as Asquith had said: 'Winston thinks
with his mouth'. But he came to listen to Sir Alan Brooke. Brooke
replaced Ironside as Commander-in-Chief, and later Dill as CIGS.
With a cool temperament in work, a shrewd understanding of
Churchill's character, as well as sound judgment, he was able to
harness Churchill's exuberance and complement his administration.
    Many of the people who worked closely with Churchill during the

war have attested to the fact that he was a demanding taskmaster. Appallingly inconsiderate and maddeningly capable of not noticing other people, his eccentricities were exasperating; he was impossible, outrageous. Yet few would have changed their positions willingly. He had that capacity to inspire devotion and to ask the most impossible things of people without offending them. All remember him with the greatest affection and all agree that to work for him was 'Great Fun'. The sixty six year old Prime Minister had lost none of that sheer joy in life that had been so marked in the 4th Hussar. Because of those high spirits much could be forgiven. The 'boyish grin' soothed many cross or sour subordinates. He was deadly earnest, but he was not sombre. He did not lose his excellent sense of humour, and a stylish mot or a witty phrase would often relax the tension. He liked courage and spirit in others. If someone had those qualities he might well be blind to their faults. He did not like dim, grey, mousy people. People, like his paintings, should be brightly coloured. His friends – Lord Beaverbrook, Brendan Bracken, the 'Prof' Lindemann – had vivid, fearless personalities. Franklin Roosevelt said: 'It's fun to be in the same decade with you.'

Roosevelt had the spirit and gaiety that Churchill so admired. A similar appetite for life helped foster their friendship. Churchill began a correspondence with Roosevelt at the very beginning of the

In this war-time cartoon by David Low, Earl Winterton (a noted critic of all governments) has a dream in which Churchill assumes every responsible role in the running of the war.

197

war, signing his letters 'Former Naval Person'. He knew that America must come into the war before long. He trusted Roosevelt and Roosevelt supported him. The valuable lend-lease arrangement, which passed through Congress in March 1941, was the first present of one friend to another. As Isaiah Berlin said: 'They were royal cousins and felt pride in this relationship, tempered by a sharp and sometimes amused, but never ironical, perception of the other's peculiar qualities'. When the Americans came into the war, after the Japanese attack on Pearl Harbour on 7 December 1941, the supreme direction passed from Churchill to Roosevelt and their relationship was less close. Roosevelt became more secretive, which helped to make the situation frustrating for Churchill, but in the interests of his Grand Alliance he bowed to the American will. He succeeded in staving off a premature Operation Overlord, or invasion of Normandy, but he was unable to obtain full American support for his thrust at the 'soft under-belly of the crocodile' – those Central and Southern European countries whose liberation, he thought, would bring greater political advantages after the war. Perhaps his memories of the front in France in the previous war made him wary of Overlord and anxious to prove that a Balkan strategy was essentially sound. A successful enterprise in that theatre might, to some degree, have vindicated the Dardanelles. But once the Normandy landings were decided upon he gave his unequivocal support to the operation; the imaginative Mulberry Harbours were, for instance, Churchill's brainchild.

America entered the war in December 1941. In June of that year Hitler had invaded Russia. Churchill had always seen Russia as a potential ally against the Nazis. He now pledged his support to Stalin, welcoming an alliance with 'that foul baboonery', for he saw, he said, in explaining his attitude, 'the Russian soldiers standing on the threshold of their native land, guarding the fields which their fathers have tilled from time immemorial.' He saw 'advancing upon all this in hideous onslaught the Nazi war machine, with its clanking, heel-clicking, dandified Prussian officers.' He saw 'the dull, drilled, docile, brutish masses of the Hun soldiery plodding on like a swarm of crawling locusts . . . Any man or State who marches with Hitler is our foe. Any man or State who fights on against Nazidom will have our aid. It follows, therefore, that we shall give whatever help we can to Russia and the Russian people'. He had said earlier to his private secretary, John Colville: 'If Hitler invaded Hell I would at least make a favourable reference to the Devil in the House of Commons.' Stalin treated his overtures with circumspection, which was hardly surprising considering the extent of Churchill's former offensiveness towards the Soviet Union. But slowly and with

BRITISH EMBASSY,
CAIRO.

Directive to General Alexander

Commander in Chief in the Middle East

————————

1. Yr prime & main duty will be to take
or destroy at the earliest opportunity the German-
Italian Army commanded by Field Marshal
Rommel together with all its supplies &
establishments in Egypt & Libya.

2. You will discharge or cause to be discharged
such other duties as pertain to yr command
without prejudice to the task described in
paragraph 1. wh must be considered paramount
in His Majesty's interests.

WSC.
10. Aug. 42.

10.8.42

The Daily Telegraph

and Morning Post

4 A.M.

No. 27,943. LONDON, WEDNESDAY, MAY 9, 1945. Printed in LONDON and MANCHESTER. PRICE 1½d.

NATION'S VE OUTBURST OF JOY: ALL-NIGHT CELEBRATIONS

ROYAL FAMILY 8 TIMES OUT ON PALACE BALCONY

Mr. CHURCHILL: 'NO GREATER DAY IN OUR HISTORY'

A GREAT NATIONAL OUTBURST OF RELIEF AND THANKSGIVING AT THE END OF NEARLY SIX YEARS OF WAR IN EUROPE WAS EPITOMISED YESTERDAY, VE-DAY, BY TREMENDOUS SCENES OF REJOICING IN LONDON, WHICH BEGAN IN THE AFTERNOON WITH THE PRIME MINISTER'S ANNOUNCEMENT OF THE END OF HOSTILITIES AND CONTINUED ALL NIGHT.

Eight times within 10 hours, in response to the enthusiasm of huge crowds, the King and Queen, Princess Elizabeth and Princess Margaret stepped out on to the balcony of Buckingham Palace. On one occasion they were accompanied by Mr. Churchill, who later, addressing a throng of 50,000 people in Whitehall, declared: "In all our long history we have never seen a greater day."

Of the vast numbers of people who set out from home in the morning, tens of thousands made their way towards Buckingham Palace.

They cheered at every opportunity—the changing of the Guard, arrivals for an 11 a.m. Investiture, Mr. Churchill's appearance on his way to lunch at the Palace.

"ADVANCE, BRITANNIA"

Outside the Palace at 3 p.m. a great silence fell on the multitude, and through amplifiers came the opening words of the Prime Minister's broadcast.

Announcing the signing of the act of surrender at Rheims at 2.41 a.m. on Monday, and that the signature in Berlin would take place during yesterday, he said that hostilities would officially end at one minute past midnight—00·01 hours this morning.

Japan remained to be subdued, Mr. Churchill concluded. "Advance, Britannia." Long live the cause of freedom. "God save the King."

"God bless him!" came the echo from the great throng; and then their pent-up feelings broke loose.

They paraded in rejoicing, vociferous columns along the road, and in the parks; they waved flags, blew whistles, pulled one another's paper caps, and they persistently roared their desire to see the King.

From the dim interior of the Palace the Queen, the King, Princess Elizabeth and Princess Margaret waved and acknowledged the balcony and stood hand-in-hand.

PICCADILLY CIRCUS JAMMED

Crowds pouring towards Piccadilly Circus, time-honoured centre of public revelry, packed all the approaches. Before 3 p.m. no traffic could get through.

Meanwhile at Westminster, the Prime Minister had made in the House of Commons a statement in almost the same terms as his broadcast, and at Buckingham Palace, again answering the people's loyal call, the Royal family once more appeared on the balcony at 4.15.

Then, to the Bow Room of the Palace, his Majesty exchanged congratulations with the Prime Minister and the War Cabinet. About 5.30 the Royal family, together with Mr. Churchill, again went out on the balcony.

After leaving the Palace the Prime Minister, at 5.35 addressed a tremendous crowd in Whitehall—estimated to number 50,000—from the balcony of the Ministry of Health. It was then that he referred to "no greater day" in our history. He appeared a second time about 10 o'clock and addressed the throng.

Outside Buckingham Palace the crowd again saw the Royal family on the balcony at about 9 o'clock and two hours later Britain and the whole Empire heard his Majesty's voice on the radio.

At 9.45, when the King and Queen and the Princesses appeared on the balcony for the fifth time, the police estimated that the crowd numbered 100,000.

After dark the Princesses, escorted by Guards officers, walked among the people. They again appeared on the Palace balcony with the King and Queen at 10.45 and shortly before midnight. Finally, just before the floodlights were switched off about 12.30 a.m. their Majesties went out on to the balcony for the eighth time.

King's Broadcast—P1. Scenes in London—P5

BUCKINGHAM PALACE WAS FLOODLIT

PRINCESSES OUT IN NIGHT CROWD

The floodlighting of prominent London buildings and public places last night, including Buckingham Palace, St. Paul's, the Houses of Parliament, Trafalgar Square and Piccadilly Circus, aroused great enthusiasm among the crowds still celebrating VE-Day.

British family interest centred tens of thousands of men and women to go to the London home of their King and Queen, to VE-Day to share with them the joy of peace in Europe.

A vast crowd was massed outside Buckingham Palace throughout the day and until a late hour, a joyous and colourful crowd whose enthusiasm rose to a crescendo of patriotic fervour at the coincident appearances on the balcony of the smiling King and Queen and the Princesses.

Each time their Majesties came to the balcony in response to the insistent roar of the crowd, the scene of sheer devotion they were spontaneously joined in Princess Elizabeth and Princess Margaret.

On their third appearance the large flood-light played on the Royal party while crowds round the Victoria Memorial. He stood between the King and Queen as the Queen waved a greeting in response to the cheers. The crowd saw in the soft light of the Victoria Memorial.

100,000 CROWD. Greatest Ovation

It was evident a crowd of 100,000 arrived along the Mall. Then they clustered below the memorial and when he came out on the balcony he was met by the greatest ovation of the day.

They also after 10 o'clock came the crowd just below the memorial. As the night wore on the crowds thinned but there were thousands who made up to go in the view of the floodlighting, there thronged the band in the Mall until after midnight.

Refuse shelter branches were deep down could pause more than was quietly as they went in the adjoining time and no dead could be seen.

LEADERS MAY MEET SOON

URGENT PROBLEMS

By Our Diplomatic Correspondent
An early meeting of Mr. Churchill, President Stalin and President Truman was foreseen in the sphere of the San Francisco Conference yesterday.

There is no official confirmation, but there is every likelihood that a meeting will be arranged. Nothing less than personal contact will suffice to settle the European problems which now confront the major Allies.

Most pressing among these are problems of the release of refugees and matter for millions of refugees who will demand deliberation of the future of Germany.

PREMIER SANG WITH CROWD IN WHITEHALL

At noon last night Mr. Churchill appeared for the second time that day on the balcony of the Ministry of Health building in Whitehall waving his famous grey suit with his black hat. He waited to the thousands of Londoners below.

The Guards band which had been playing in the crowd sudden struck up "For he's a jolly good fellow" and Mr. Churchill sang it out, too.

CONDUCTED BAND

Then, as if to recapture the bond forged in fire of old days, the great singer led the crowd in the old song "Land of Hope and Glory." The Prime Minister conducted the band and conducted it, Mr. Churchill took several for the band, and then, before the crowd could sing on, announced:

Someone the crowd singing. "My friends, this is your victory. It is the victory of the cause of freedom in every land. In all our long history we have never seen a greater day than this. Everyone, man or woman, has done their best. Everyone has tried. Neither the long years, nor the dangers, nor the fierce attacks of the enemy, have in any way weakened the independent resolve of the British nation. God bless you all."

"GOD BLESS YOU ALL"

When the crowd called for a speech, Mr. Churchill was again in special mood and only could be heard. He announced: "Were was no surrender to any power in the world until we had nothing of freedom. We were the first, in this ancient island, to draw the sword against tyranny. After a while we were left alone against the most tremendous military power that has been seen. We were all alone for a whole year."

"EXTRA TRAINS FOR LONDON"

From a country the thousands of railway at the Railway Company was an assured steady flow of people to London to join in the celebrations. Provision for the Railway and the excursions were going to.

GERMAN FLEET TO GO TO ALLIED PORTS

ADMIRALTY ORDER

Two Admiralty announcements yesterday that the following orders have been issued for the U-boats:

All German and German warships and auxiliary merchant ships and other craft at sea are being ordered to report their position in plain language to the nearest Allied wireless telegraph station, and are being given orders to proceed to a port to which they are directed. They will remain in these ports until further directions are forwarded.

All warships, auxiliaries, merchant ships and other craft in harbour are being ordered to remain in harbour.

U-boats at sea are being ordered on surface, to fly black flag, and to report their position and to proceed to port when they are directed.

All warships, auxiliaries and other ships that have been fitted for demolition should be prepared for demolition and surface shipping, should not effect any damage, to scrap same. Demolition charges and completed demolition of all naval parts and harbours are to be rendered safe.

All personnel not to be required are to remain in their ports until the need for their abandonment orders offering movement or salvage service is directed.

Instructions will be given to base officers at ports and harbours as to port movement, and all demolition arrangements, from local Allied port authorities.

"Hitler's Remains"

So persistently are unnamed figures of Hitler found in the Berlin Chancellery by the troops that it is not only just his bones found round Russia's own remains, but it is not known yet where his own body finally lies.

Moscow also reported yesterday that the body of Dr. Goebbels, his wife and six children was found near the body of Hitler. They found the bodies of Goebbels and six of his children and also one of Goebbels' own children.

GERMANS SIGN CAPITULATION IN BERLIN

MOSCOW STATEMENT

Moscow radio announced the unconditional surrender of Germany shortly after one a.m. (B.S.T.) this morning. It said:—

The unconditional surrender of all German armed forces was ratified.

The German High Command 9.45 immediately been taken by all Allies to put into and get under the German High Command's unconditional military operations after 00·01 p.m. Moscow time.

The announcement stating the capitulation was signed by Field Marshal Keitel, representing the German High Command and the German armed forces; Admiral Friedeburg, representing the German Navy, and Colonel-General Stumpff, of the German Air Force. Marshal Zhukov, Commander of the Red Army, and Air Chief Marshal Tedder, Allied Deputy Supreme Commander, signed for the Allies.

A Special Order of the Day was broadcast announcing the victory to the Russian people.

Wherever possible, joint Christmas out to the United States forces and to the Turkish and Czech forces.

SEYSS-INQUART ARRESTED

WAR CRIME CHARGES

Seyss-Inquart, German Commissar in Holland has been arrested and Amsterdam and the Hague is told from Leyden. He will be tried as a war criminal.

Mussert and Rauter, another Quisling who were long names for arrest in Holland, are also on the list. Rauter they seek to know. Both are held prisoners.

Mussert had been the head of the Dutch National Socialist Party. He was the self-appointed "Leader" of the Fascist regime. Rauter was head of police and leader of the SS men in Holland.

KING LEOPOLD'S LIBERATION

SENATE'S MESSAGE

From Our Special Correspondent
BRUSSELS, Tuesday.
Troops of Gen. Patch's Seventh Army have liberated King Leopold, his wife, the Princess de Rethy and their three children. They were at Struth yesterday.

In consequence of news given to refugees a special declaration from the Belgian Government is now engaged in considering a message which the Royal family has been sent agreement, said a congress had not only decided to do it in.

The Belgian Government at last made for the King's return but also may be kept for. In the Senate today the President of the Senate, M. Robert Gillon, announced that the return of the King and also his cousin of welcome he has sent to King.

Earlier the Senate had cheered the announcement of the Liberation broadcast.

THE DAILY TELEGRAPH
In accordance with orders posting newspapers, The Daily Telegraph will not be published tomorrow.

2.40 a.m. SURRENDER SCENE AT ALLIED H.Q.

DRAMATIC 15 MINUTES THAT ENDED WAR

HUMBLED GERMANS

From DOUGLAS WILLIAMS,
Daily Telegraph Special Correspondent
RHEIMS, Tuesday.

This is how the war in Europe was ended.

At 2.41 a.m. yesterday, in the war room of Gen. Eisenhower's battle headquarters in this ancient city, two German delegates, acting jointly on behalf of Doenitz as head of the Reich, unconditionally surrendered all German land, sea and air forces to the Allied armies in the West, and simultaneously to the Russian armies in the East.

The German delegates were Adml. Hans Georg von Friedeburg, C.-in-C. of the German Navy in succession to Doenitz, and Col.-Gen. Gustav Jodl, Chief of Staff of the Wehrmacht.

All forces, both Allied and German, cease operations as from one minute after midnight on Wednesday morning.

The end of the war took place amid austere simplicity and with the least possible ceremonial in a classroom 36ft square of the Ecole Professionelle, a French commercial school facing a busy shunting yard, from which Gen. Eisenhower for the past three months has directed the operations of his vast armies.

Against a background of brilliantly lit battle maps 15 feet sat round a well old deal table chipped and scarred by the knives of a thousand scholars. Dilapidated yellow pine chairs were ranged around, and each place was marked with a name-card and furnished with a writing tablet and pencil and common china ashtray.

MAPS SHOW WAR'S LAST MOVES

The walls were covered with large-scale battle maps on which were still to be seen the front-line positions of the war's final hours marked in coloured chalks.

Searing Klieg lights installed for the benefit of film and Press photographers, threw the faces of the participants in the solemn ceremony into harsh relief. A sketch marked the date, May 7, 1945.

The Germans, three in number—Maj. Wilhelm Oxenius, being also present as an A.D.C. to Jodl—sat along one side of the table.

Facing them, reading from left to right, were Lt.-Gen. Sir Frederick Morgan, Maj.-Gen. Sevez, representing the French Army; Lt.-Gen. Bedell Smith, Gen. Eisenhower's Chief of Staff; Maj.-Gen. Ivan Susloparov, Russian representative, aided by a junior officer as interpreter; Gen. Carl Spaatz, of the American Air Force; Air-Marshal Sir J. M. Robb.

At the foot of the table sat another Russian delegate, Col. Ivan Zenkovitch and Maj.-Gen. H. R. Bull, an American officer on Shaef staff. Maj.-Gen. Strong, of the British Army, circulated around the room as Master of Ceremonies, and also acted when required as German interpreter.

(Continued on P. 6, Col. 3.)

RUSSIANS IN LAST FIGHT

The Russians, whose agreement was due to stand even after the reporting of the surrender, was yesterday fighting, in Czecho-Slovakia, where they were holding on the road between Prague and the Red Army.

A later order issued in London last night began to flow the line for the operation, when the full surrender also gave them details of German men, and it was announced that Marshal Malinovsky's troops had taken over all Czecho-Slovakia.

Each house earlier an Order gave her news that Marshal Koniev's troops had captured Dresden, the capital of Saxony. It was the cultural centre of Germany. The Czech fighting lay just south of the city.

WEATHER NEWS AGAIN

For the first time since the war began a weather forecast has been issued to the British public. With the cessation of hostilities in Europe the restriction of weather news has been removed by the Censor.

A 6 a.m. yesterday a chart of temperatures raised over Europe showing northern parts had been chilly. A 9 a.m. forecast was issued by the Meteorological Office.

LATE NEWS

QUISLING POLICE CHIEF FOUND

OSLO, 8.57 a.m.

BATTLE-SHIPS TO LEAVE OKINAWA

EXTRA TRAINS FOR LONDON

This Morning's News

VE-Day

Britain's VE-celebrations of joy with eight outstanding floodlit buildings. Crowds eight times out at Palace balcony (p. 1).

Mr. Churchill—"No greater day in history" (p. 1).

King's broadcast (p. 1) and scenes in London—Buckingham Palace (p. 1, 5).

Large crowds outside the balcony of Buckingham Palace (p. 1, 5).

Europe

German surrender scene at Rheims H.Q. (p. 1).

German Fleet to go to Allied ports (p. 1).

Germans capitulation in Berlin (p. 1).

3 Years Ago To-day

Japanese defeated in naval battle of Coral Sea, lasting two days, with carriers and heavy ships involved.

1 Year Ago

Sevastopol fell, whole of Crimea free of Germans.

perseverance Churchill formed his own twentieth-century Grand
Alliance.

To make plans, to co-ordinate strategy, the heads of the allied
countries had to meet. Churchill made fourteen or more wartime
journeys abroad. He went to Newfoundland, Washington (three
times), Cairo, Moscow (twice), Casablanca, Quebec (twice), Teheran;
to Yalta and Potsdam, for conferences, and also to various military
headquarters. After the first Washington conference he made a rash
but characteristic decision to return not by ship, but in a Boeing
flying-boat. Transatlantic flying was not the sophisticated hop it is
now. The aeroplane trundled across the Atlantic, lost its bearings,
narrowly missed the hostile defences at Brest, and just avoided being
shot down by six Hurricanes near Dover. No doubt Churchill enjoyed the trip.

The journeys, on top of all the work, were a strain and Churchill
suffered a mild heart attack in Cairo in December 1943. His doctor,
Lord Moran, was alarmed and Clemmie flew out to be with her husband. But he recovered quickly and, on Christmas Day, which he
spent in Tunis, was able to enjoy 'a magnificent Christmas dinner,
with soup, turkey, plum pudding – and champagne'. He was dressed
for the occasion in a padded silk dressing-gown, decorated with
blue and gold dragons. He rallied and returned to England and, if a
little slower in the final stages of the war, he never quailed under the
responsibility. Unlike Roosevelt, unlike Hitler, Churchill lived to see
the end of the war. 'I have no special statement to make about the war
position in Europe,' he told Parliament on 1 May 1945, 'except that
it is definitely more satisfactory than it was this time five years ago'.
The next day Berlin surrendered to the Russians and the following
day Hitler committed suicide. On 7 May the German forces surrendered unconditionally. Churchill broadcast the news. He added
that Japan was still to be defeated, and ended: 'Advance Britannia!
Long live the cause of freedom! God save the King!' He had
always thought constitutional monarchy an excellent system, for
as he said: 'A battle is won and crowds cheer the King. A battle is
lost: the Government falls'. But most Englishmen this time cheered
the Prime Minister. His part in the war was colossal: six volumes of
memoirs and seven of speeches bear witness to the magnitude of it.
Many details are still being evaluated: his direction was variable; he
harassed his generals for quick results. But two contributions in
particular stand out above all others: his courage, confidence and
defiance in 1940 that he communicated so effectively to the British
nation; and his welding of the Grand Alliance. His leadership and
statesmanship in both these achievements were faultless.

In *My Early Life* Churchill had written: 'Those who can win a war well can rarely make a good peace, and those who could make a good peace would never have won the war. It would perhaps be pressing the argument too far to suggest that I could do both.' Whether he could or not, the fact was that the electorate did not want him as its peacetime leader and, in the rather precipitate election of 1945, although the battle was won, the Government fell. His own election campaign, in which he had delivered thunderous speeches about the perils of socialism, had been insensitive. Now the Labour Party was in power and he was out. Clemmie said to him: 'It may well be a blessing in disguise'. Churchill replied morosely: 'At the moment it seems quite effectively disguised'. He picked up his pen again, or rather his secretaries picked up theirs, for Churchill dictated his books – although he preferred to write his speeches. His six volumes on the Second World War were published between 1948 and 1959. He also finished his *History of the English Speaking Peoples*, which he had begun before the war. Like the first Sir Winston Churchill, the cavalier, he wanted to record his view of British history. Throughout his life he never ceased studying in detail 'the present and the future in the light of the past'. He was awarded the Nobel prize for literature in 1953.

Churchill had the time to attend the House of Commons and still enjoyed a good Parliamentary row, but his speeches seemed old-fashioned; they were too long. Prime Minister Attlee's ordinary low-key style was in contrast more appropriate. Nevertheless Churchill was the dominant figure at home and almost more so abroad. International affairs were what interested him. At Fulton, Missouri, in 1946 he gave the famous speech in which he said that 'from Stettin in the Baltic to Trieste in the Adriatic an iron curtain has descended across the continent'. The revelation shocked most Americans and jolted opinion throughout the world. Many people had not realised the extent of Soviet influence until Churchill painted that clear picture for them.

During the war he had said that he hoped afterwards 'to see the economy of Europe studied as a whole. I look forward to a United States of Europe.' In Zurich in 1947 he made a broad appeal for the unity of European countries. 'Unite!' he urged them. That same year he founded the United Europe movement. 'Are the states of Europe,' he asked, 'to continue for ever to squander the first fruits of their toil upon the erection of new barriers, military fortifications, tarriff-walls and passport networks against one another?' Later, when he was once more Prime Minister, Europe expected his lead in the matter, but he did not give it.

At the outbreak of the First World War Churchill had told his wife how he was willing to give his 'period of existence to keep this country great and famous and prosperous and free'. By the end of the next war Britain was arguably great; famous – yes; free – certainly; but prosperous – no. The Second World War had made America rich: it had given Russia much new territory; but all England had got out of it was debts. She was no longer the imperial power that Churchill had always been so proud of. He said in 1947: 'It is with deep grief I watch the clattering down of the British Empire, with all its glories and all the services it has rendered to mankind.' England's imperial possessions were flaking away. Great Britain was slipping down the league of world powers. It was not the destiny – 'the broad sunlit uplands' – that Churchill wished for his country. He had warned in 1933 what would happen if England did not save herself; that 'stripped of her Empire in the Orient, deprived of the sovereignty of the seas, loaded with debt and taxation, her commerce and carrying trade shut out for foreign tarriffs and quotas, England would sink to the level of a fifth-rate power, and nothing would remain of all her glories except a population much larger than this island can support.' But despite her valiant effort in the war, that was more or less what had happened.

In 1951, at the age of nearly seventy-seven he was delighted to become Britain's Prime Minister again. He was thrilled with the new Queen, who came to the throne the following year, and took the greatest interest in the plans for her coronation. It was from her that he received the one title that he could not resist. In April 1953 he became a Knight of the Garter and so received the decoration coveted and won by so many of his forebears. He never accepted a peerage; he never left the House of Commons.

The Queen leaves No. 10 Downing Street after dinner with Churchill before his retirement in 1955.

His main policies as Prime Minister were 'Work, Homes and Food'. He was determined to rid the country of the food-rationing that was still in operation from the war. Meat was in poor supply. Pig-farming, he decided, was the answer, for the pig was 'an easy animal to rear, naturally gay, gratifyingly prolific.' He worked twelve hours a day, was able to cope with a massive volume of work and imbibe a quantity of details while younger, sprightlier colleagues flagged. Sometimes he seemed inattentive in Parliament. One MP was annoyed, while giving a long speech, to see the Prime Minister drowsing. 'Must you fall asleep when I am speaking?' he shouted. 'No,' replied Churchill with his eyes shut, 'it is purely voluntary.'

He did, however, have a stroke in 1953 but, true to his principle of defiance in defeat, he made a remarkable recovery. The press murmured about his age and his capability, hinted at his infirmity: 'Too old and too tired', said the *Daily Mirror*. But Cassandra in the *Daily Mail* wrote: 'There are those who urge the retirement of Sir Winston Churchill. *I am not among them*. The campaign is too much like stubbing your toe on history – and a pretty large and unyielding hunk of history at that . . .'.

Churchill's eightieth birthday was a splendid occasion. A red-coated orchestra played *Pomp and Circumstance* in Westminster Hall, while he was presented with a volume bound in green levant morocco with the signatures of the members of the House of Commons inside, a rather tasteless portrait of himself by Graham Sutherland which has since disappeared, and a cheque for £150,000 for a charitable trust in his honour. Tributes were given. Churchill was always able to respond directly to a sense of occasion 'with something of the unawareness of a child', and this was no exception. 'I have never accepted what many people have kindly said, that I inspired the nation,' he said in his speech of thanks. 'Their will was resolute and remorseless and it proved inconquerable. It fell to me to express it and if I found the right word you must remember that I have always earned my living by my pen, and by my tongue.' He went on: 'It was the nation and the race dwelling all round the globe that had the lion's heart. I had the luck to be called upon to give the roar.'

Everyone felt that it was a kind of farewell. 'I am now nearing the end of my journey,' he said. Lord Salisbury, the leader of the House of Lords, recalling Churchill's long experience, said: 'These last eighty years have crammed into them more revolutionary changes in the life of man than all the centuries that went before.' Churchill had lived through many of those changes. He had written in 1930: 'Scarcely anything material or established which I was brought up to believe was permanent and vital, has lasted. Everything I was sure

or taught to be sure was impossible has happened.' That was but a foretaste. How much more had happened since then. Trained on a cavalry charge, he had lived to see the effects of the atom bomb. Born thirty years before the Wright brothers made their historic flight, he lived into the age of space travel. Reared on Victorian values, he lived to see them utterly disparaged. He had been able to absorb all the changes and most of the upheavals in opinion. That was because his great conviction – his belief in England's greatness, in her championship of freedom, in her noble destiny, her nobler heritage – remained unaltered from the time when it was first fashioned in Bangalore or before. Perhaps for the first time at the end of his life that conviction looked a little less rock-like; things were essentially different. The future to him was a rosy glow. He had no clear vision of it. He never had had. His imagination looked to the past and in a sense he had fulfilled it.

He resigned in April 1955. Before he left the prime ministership he gave a dinner party for the Queen. 'I have the honour,' he addressed her, 'of proposing a toast which I used to enjoy drinking when I was a cavalry subaltern in the reign of your Majesty's great-great-grand-mother, Queen Victoria.' The Queen, in her turn, proposed a toast to her elderly Prime Minister. After his resignation he occasionally hobbled in to the House of Commons, supporting himself with the gold-topped cane that Edward VII had given him as a wedding present. He went until he could no longer do so. Then he announced that he would not stand for Parliament again. So at the next election, in 1964, he officially left the House of Commons. He soon became ill and on 24 January 1965 – seventy years to the day after Lord Randolph – he died.

His funeral was of course magnificent. It was said that he had planned it in detail. His body lay in state in Westminster Hall for three days; more than a quarter of a million people passed by to pay homage. Then his coffin was taken by train from Waterloo Station to Woodstock. Trains to Woodstock usually run from Paddington Station. Churchill had insisted on Waterloo, because he said he would like to remind President de Gaulle, who would attend the funeral, of that famous battle when England triumphed over the French. There was a bit of fun, a reminder of history and a touch of glory in the arrangement. It was very typical.

'At Blenheim,' he had said, 'I took two very important decisions: to be born and to marry. I am happily content with the decisions I took on both those occasions', and there, in the churchyard of Bladon, he was buried: 'The largest human being of our time'.

9
Sons and Cousins

C HURCHILL RECOMMENDED his friends to have four children:
'One to reproduce your wife, one to reproduce yourself, one for
the increase in population, and one in case of accident'. He and
Clemmie had five in fact, but Marigold died in 1921 at the age of
three. Diana, Randolph, Sarah and Mary were the four who grew up,
though Diana died before her father and Randolph shortly after.

Throughout a long and very public life Clementine had guarded
her privacy with an effortless dignity. Randolph, her son, did not.
He was always conspicuous and seldom gracious. He was too loud,
too brash and much too rude. Outrageous, impossible, insensitive,
boorish, quarrelsome, ridiculous are all adjectives ascribed to him.
Nine times out of ten, he cut an absurd figure. The tenth time – all
was forgiven; then he would be charming, funny and affectionate
and his exuberant company would for once be exhilarating, not
embarrassing. He was also courageous, frank and honest. Too often
these qualities were obscured by his tactlessness. ('It is not as if I'm
accusing you of *personal* cowardice,' he was heard saying to Montgomery during a wartime meeting of the chiefs of staff.) He was
articulate and always interesting; but he was intolerable, 'a slave to
his strange pride'. Of course, everyone explained, Randolph was like
that because he was overshadowed by his father. He took the words
out of their mouths: 'I wanted a show of my own,' he said, 'so
struggling to establish my own individuality and personality, I often
said and wrote rather reckless things, which I suppose if I hadn't felt
this frustration I would have tempered down.' There were, he
agreed, 'difficulties naturally inherent in the situation.'

He liked to say that he came from 'poor but honest parents', and

Randolph Churchill and
Pamela Digby leave
St John's, Smith Square,
after their wedding in 1939.
The bride was the daughter
of Lord Digby of Minterne
in Dorset (the first Sir
Winston's estate). The
marriage ended in divorce.

while he was growing up his father's career, if spectacular, looked
unpromising to say the least. Randolph, throughout, was intensely
loyal to his father and would always spring to his defence. He wanted
to follow him into politics. He stood for Parliament seven times.
Only once, when unopposed in 1940, did he get in. Constituencies
distrusted him: he was too undisciplined and too unpredictable. So
he was a journalist most of his life – and was indeed a good, occasionally brilliant, reporter. If all was too quiet at the trouble-spot from
which he was reporting he was quite capable of conjuring up, not a
story, but action itself. Corker in *Scoop* gives some flavour of what
Randolph was like.

In the war Randolph, like Winston in Queen Victoria's reign,
wanted some excitement. He joined the Special Air Service for a raid
on Benghazi. Brigadier Fitzroy Maclean then recruited him to join
the partisans in Yugoslavia. 'His parachute deposited him in a sitting
position in a puddle of melting snow in the highlands of Bosnia.' He

proceeded to show courage and curiosity and the Balkan people liked his temperament and his style. He was later awarded an MBE.

Country Bumpkins Ltd was the name of the small publishing company he set up at his country house in Suffolk, where he had moved after the war. That was where he spent most of his last years. He kept in touch with friends and political developments by telephone. He loved the telephone and would make six or more calls an hour. Sir John Betjeman has testified to his life on the wires, how he was always 'on the telephone or about to telephone'. Others noticed his essential loneliness. His two marriages ended in divorce. His first wife, Pamela Digby, the mother of his son, Winston, had been brought up at Minterne, the house in Dorset which had belonged to the first Sir Winston Churchill. That Winston, the last Winston in this story, was therefore a descendant of Minterne twice over. His second wife, June Osborne, was the mother of his daughter, Arabella.

After the death of his father Randolph wrote, with the help of his team of 'Young Gentlemen', the first two volumes of the life of his father. They were much better than many thought they would be – sober, honest and stylish. They were widely praised. With work he enjoyed and which was successful, a house and garden he loved, he seemed at last more content, less obstreperous. He had found his metier in his family history. Robert Kennedy suggested that he might write the life of John Kennedy. He was very excited about that and talked with enthusiasm of 'Project K.'. But he was no longer at all well, and in the summer of 1968, within hours of Robert Kennedy's assassination, he died at East Bergholt.

He was buried at Bladon near his father. His obituaries spoke of failure, but his friends lost someone who was too life-enhancing to be aptly denoted a failure. They missed his 'glorious buoyant company'.

Randolph was only second cousin to the tenth Duke of Marlborough – not a very close relation. To return briefly to the other Spencer-Churchills – the Blenheim ones – Lord Randolph's brother, the eighth Duke, had been found dead in his bed in 1892. It was most unexpected and his wife, on hearing the news, fell ill, 'being prostrated by the calamity'. He had dabbled in politics, but the scandals in his private life (his own and the Aylesburys' divorce actions) had prevented him achieving much in the public service. He was notorious for what he sold. The *Ansidei Madonna* and Vandyck's equestrian portrait of Charles I were disposed of; the Paris Rothschilds bought three Rubens; and much fine china went to the sale rooms. He was, however, interested in art and wrote lively articles attacking the prevailing schools.

His son, the ninth Duke – Winston's friend, Sunny – married an eighteen-year-old American heiress, Consuelo Vanderbilt. Both were in love with someone else at the time and, as Consuelo said of his proposal to her in the Gothic room of the Vanderbilt residence: 'There was no need for sentiment'. The nuptials, at which Consuelo was in tears, bore closer resemblance to a business merger than to a wedding ceremony; for afterwards, 'in a small room in the church itself, the bridegroom and the bride's father signed an agreement giving Marlborough a dowry of $1·6 million in cash and the income from $2 million in gilt-edge stocks; other subventions later given to the Duke and Duchess and their sons brought the total close to $20 million'.

Marlborough had 'a small aristocratic face with a large nose and rather prominent blue eyes'. His young wife was beautiful with dark hair and a very long neck; she was taller than her husband. From the start she was out of sympathy with the English aristocratic way of life and described her husband's reading and categorising of congratulatory telegrams after their wedding as her 'first lesson in class consciousness'.

He took her to meet his grandmother, the Dowager Duchess. 'Dressed in mourning with a little lace cap on her head and an ear trumpet in her hand, she bestowed a welcoming kiss in the manner of a deposed sovereign greeting her successor.' Then they went back to Blenheim. The Mayor of Woodstock greeted the special train that brought them from Oxford to Woodstock and said to her: 'Your Grace will no doubt be interested to know that Woodstock had a mayor and Corporation before America was discovered' – to her intense displeasure.

She found the Blenheim household organisation, with its defined hierarchy of butlers, footmen, housekeeper and housemaids, restrictive and the ambiance unsympathetic. The Rysbrack chapel in which family prayers were held every morning was creepy. Dinner alone with her husband would be spent in silence. Marlborough twiddled a ring on his finger and ate very slowly. She 'took to knitting and the butler read detective stories in the hall'. She paints a picture of Marlborough as a cold and callous man: others have said he was popular and amiable. They were ill-suited, and separated in 1906. After their divorce in 1920 she remarried a Frenchman, Jacques Balsan, and Marlborough married a friend of hers, Gladys Deacon.

The Duke was a good landlord at Blenheim and he made many improvements both to the estate and to the house. He enlisted Duchêne to redesign the gardens on the east front. Together they created an uninterrupted view from the house of the terraces and fountains leading down to the lake.

As a Conservative he held one or two minor parliamentary posts.
For a time in the South African war he was assistant military secretary to Lord Roberts, but Lord Roberts found that he had too many
dukes on his staff, so Sunny left him and joined up with Winston.
Together they marched to Pretoria and released Winston's former
fellow prisoners. Like the first, fourth, fifth and seventh Dukes
before him, he was given the Garter.

During the latter half of the First World War, after he returned
from serving in France, he 'substituted sheep for mowers in the
Blenheim Palace Gardens and grew cabbages in the flower beds'.
He died of cancer in 1934.

MI5 were given the use of Blenheim in the Second World War by
his son, the tenth Duke. Schoolchildren were also evacuated there
and its ornate rooms were turned into dormitories. Afterwards in
1950 the Duke opened the house to the public. Ten years later the
Government gave him a grant of £50,000 for its restoration and he
contributed a similar amount.

His son, who succeeded to the dukedom in 1972, welcomes thousands of visitors each year to look at his house and his park and, if
he is away, his private apartments (for people are curious to see the
habitat of a modern duke). The place has not changed much; the
house with its faded ochre stone walls has a dignity that the ugly
trappings of parking signs and public notices cannot dispel, and the
park with its elderly trees and beautiful lake retains an old tranquility that is not disturbed by its many visitors. Marlborough, who
nearly fell off his column a few years ago, has been propped up, and
continues to watch serenely over it all.

Winston Churchill, the third cousin of the eleventh Duke, is
Conservative Member of Parliament for Stretford. As the Duke tries,
as many of his ancestors have done, to raise money to keep Blenheim
going, and as Winston Churchill, in the tradition of his side of the
family, pursues his political ambitions on the floor of the House of
Commons, so continues still the story of the Churchills.

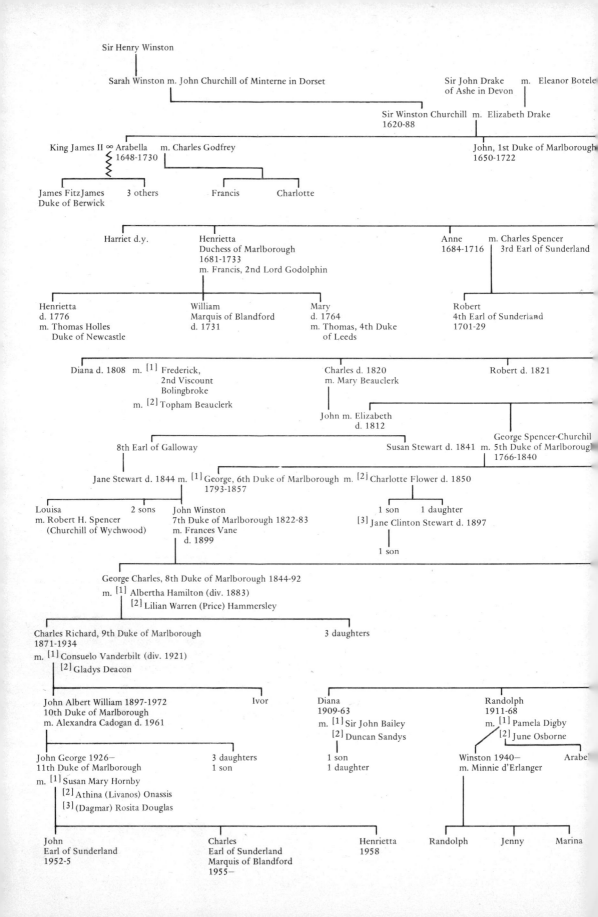

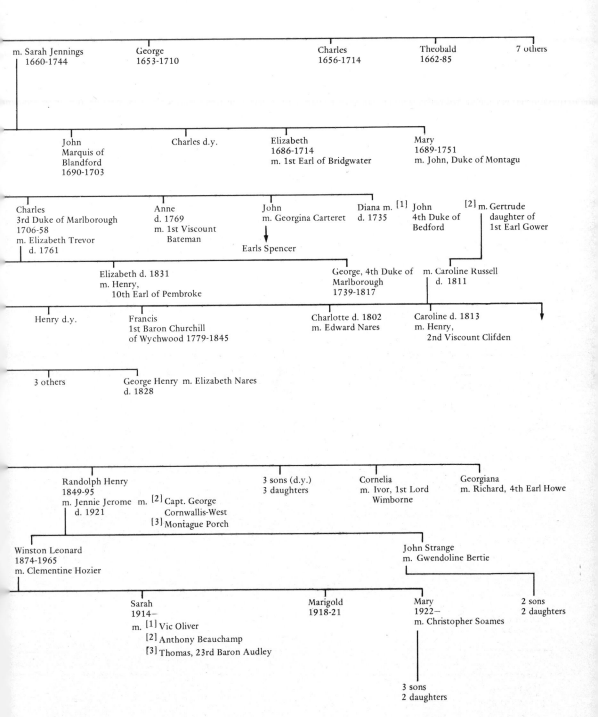

m. Sarah Jennings
1660-1744

George
1653-1710

Charles
1656-1714

Theobald
1662-85

7 others

John
Marquis of
Blandford
1690-1703

Charles d.y.

Elizabeth
1686-1714
m. 1st Earl of Bridgwater

Mary
1689-1751
m. John, Duke of Montagu

Charles
3rd Duke of Marlborough
1706-58
m. Elizabeth Trevor
d. 1761

Anne
d. 1769
m. 1st Viscount
Bateman

John
m. Georgina Carteret

Diana m. [1] John
d. 1735   4th Duke of
             Bedford

[2] m. Gertrude
daughter of
1st Earl Gower

Earls Spencer

Elizabeth d. 1831
m. Henry,
10th Earl of Pembroke

George, 4th Duke of
Marlborough
1739-1817

m. Caroline Russell
d. 1811

Henry d.y.

Francis
1st Baron Churchill
of Wychwood 1779-1845

Charlotte d. 1802
m. Edward Nares

Caroline d. 1813
m. Henry,
2nd Viscount Clifden

3 others

George Henry m. Elizabeth Nares
d. 1828

Randolph Henry
1849-95
m. Jennie Jerome m. [2] Capt. George
d. 1921   Cornwallis-West
              [3] Montague Porch

3 sons (d.y.)
3 daughters

Cornelia
m. Ivor, 1st Lord
Wimborne

Georgiana
m. Richard, 4th Earl Howe

Winston Leonard
1874-1965
m. Clementine Hozier

John Strange
m. Gwendoline Bertie

Sarah
1914—
m. [1] Vic Oliver
   [2] Anthony Beauchamp
   [3] Thomas, 23rd Baron Audley

Marigold
1918-21

Mary
1922—
m. Christopher Soames

2 sons
2 daughters

3 sons
2 daughters

Select Bibliography

Addison, Joseph	*The Campaign*	Jacob Tonson 1705
Ashley, Maurice P.	*Marlborough*	Duckworth 1939
Balsan, Consuelo Vanderbilt	*The Glitter and the Gold*	Heinemann 1953
Bardens, Dennis	*Churchill in Parliament*	Hale 1967
Baxter, Stephen B.	*William* III	Longmans 1966
Berlin, Sir Isaiah	*Mr Churchill in 1940*	John Murray 1964
Bonham-Carter, Violet	*Winston Churchill as I knew him*	Eyre & Spottiswood 1965
Burnet, Gilbert	*History of his own Time*	Thomas Ward 1724
Cecil, Lord David	*The Cecils*	Constable 1973
Chandler, David	*Marlborough as Military Commander*	Batsford 1973
Churchill, Randolph S.	*Twenty-One Years*	Weidenfeld & Nicolson 1965
	Winston S. Churchill (Vol. I*)*	Heinemann 1966
	Winston S. Churchill (Vol. II*)*	Heinemann 1967
Churchill, Sir Winston	*Divi Britannici*	Tho. Roycroft 1675
Churchill, Winston L. S.	*Arms and the Covenant*	G. G. Harrap & Co. 1938
	Into Battle	Cassell & Co. 1941
	Great Contemporaries	T. Butterworth 1937
	Lord Randolph Churchill	Odhams Press 1952
	Marlborough: his life and times	G. G. Harrap & Co. 1933–8
	My African Journey	Hodder & Stoughton 1908
	My Early Life	T. Butterworth 1930
	Savrola: a tale of the revolution in Laurania	Longmans & Co. 1900
	Thoughts and Adventures	T. Butterworth 1932
	The World Crisis	T. Butterworth 1922–31
	The Second World War	Cassell & Co. 1948–54
La Colonie, J. M. de	*The Chronicles of an Old Campaigner*	John Murray 1904
Colville, Olivia	*Duchess Sarah*	Longman, Green 1904
Cornwallis-West, Mrs George	*The Reminiscences of Lady Randolph Churchill*	Edward Arnold 1908
Coxe, William	*Memoirs of John, Duke of Marlborough*	Longmans, Hurst, Rees, Orme & Brown 1818
Eade Charles (ed.)	*Churchill: by his contemporaries*	Hutchinson 1953
Erskine, Mrs Steuart	*Lady Diana Beauclerk*	T. Fisher Unwin 1903
Gilbert, Martin	*Winston S. Churchill (Vol.* III*)*	Heinemann 1971
Green, David B.	*Blenheim Palace*	Country Life 1951
	Sarah, Duchess of Marlborough	Collins 1967
Green, V. H. H.	*Oxford Common Room*	Edward Arnold 1957
Hallé, Kay	*Randolph Churchill*	Heinemann 1971
Hodges, John C. (ed.)	*William Congreve: the Man*	New York 1941
	Letters and Documents of William Congreve	Macmillan 1964
Lediard, Thomas	*The Life of John, Duke of Marlborough*	J. Wilcox 1736

Leslie, Anita	*The Fabulous Leonard Jerome*	Hutchinson 1954
	Jennie: The Life of Lady Randolph Churchill	Hutchinson 1969
Lewin, G. Ronald	*Churchill as Warlord*	Batsford 1973
Macmillan, Harold	*Tides of Fortune 1945–55*	Macmillan 1969
	The Blast of War 1939–45	Macmillan 1967
Marlborough, S. C.	*Private Correspondence of Sarah,*	
	Duchess of Marlborough	Henry Colburn 1838
	Letters of a Grandmother 1732–5	Jonathan Cape 1943
	An Account of the Conduct of	
	the Dowager Duchess of Marlborough	G. Hawkins 1742
Martin, Ralph G.	*Lady Randolph Churchill*	Cassell 1969, 1972
Rhodes James, Robert	*Lord Randolph Churchill*	Weidenfeld & Nicolson 1959
	Churchill: A Study in Failure	Weidenfeld & Nicolson 1970
Roberts, Brian	*Churchills in Africa*	Hamilton 1970
Robson, R. J.	*The Oxfordshire Election of 1754*	Oxford University Press 1949
Rosebery, Lord	*Lord Randolph Churchill*	Arthur L. Humphreys 1906
Rowse, A. L.	*The Early Churchills*	Macmillans 1956
	The Later Churchills	Macmillans 1958
Sedgwick, Romney (ed.)	*Lord Hervey's Memoirs*	W. Kimber 1952
Sitwell, Osbert	*The Winstonburg Line*	Hendersons 1919
Taylor, A. J. P. & others	*Churchill: Four Faces and the Man*	Allen Lane 1969
Toynbee, Mrs Paget (ed.)	*Letters of Horace Walpole*	Clarendon Press 1970
Wheeler-Bennet,		
Sir J. and others	*Action This Day*	Macmillan 1968

Index